Haunted
Places
of Scotland

Haunted
Places
of Scotland

by
Martin Coventry

GOBLINSHEAD

MUSSELBURGH

Haunted Places *of* Scotland

First Published 1999
Reprinted 2000
© Martin Coventry 1999

Published by GOBLINSHEAD
130B Inveresk Road
Musselburgh
EH21 7AY
Scotland
Tel: 0131 665 2894
Fax: 0131 653 6566
Email: goblinshead@sol.co.uk

British Library Cataloguing in Publication Data
A catalogue record for this book is available from the British Library.

ISBN 1 899874 04 6

Typeset by GOBLINSHEAD using Desktop Publishing
Typeset in Galliard

Other related titles from Goblinshead
Wee Guide to Haunted Castles of Scotland £3.95
Wee Guide to Haunted Hotels of Scotland £3.95
Castles of Scotland 3E (pbk) £15.95
Castles of Scotland 3E (hbk) £25.00
Castles of Glasgow and the Clyde £9.95
Wee Guide to Old Churches and Abbeys of Scotland £3.95
Wee Guide to the Castles and Mansions of Scotland £3.95

Contents

List of illustrations
Acknowledgements
How to use the book
Preface
Introduction
Warning

Maps
HAUNTED PLACES – NORTHERN SCOTLAND   2-3
HAUNTED PLACES – SOUTHERN SCOTLAND   4-5

Haunted Places of Scotland   7
330 places associated with ghosts

Ghost Tours   169

Selected further reading   173
Index by place   178
Index by haunting   180
Index by area   184
General index   187

List *of* illustrations

Elcho Castle/monument,
 Rothesay   front cover
Dunrobin, Newbattle   back cover
Gateway, Spynie Palace   front
St Mary's Haddington   title page

Neidpath Castle   1

HAUNTED PLACES –
 NORTHERN SCOTLAND   2-3
HAUNTED PLACES –
 SOUTHERN SCOTLAND   4-5

Dunnottar Castle   7
Stair, Caroline Park   8
Abergeldie Castle   9
Airlie Castle   11
Airth Castle   12
Ardblair Castle   14
Ardrossan Castle   17
Ardvreck Castle   17
Ashintully Castle   18
Auchinvole House   19
Balgonie Castle   22
Ballindalloch Castle   23
Balvenie Castle   25
Barcaldine Castle   26
Barnbougle Castle   27
Bedlay Castle   28
Benholm Castle   29
Borthwick Castle   30
Braemar Castle   31
Brodick Castle   33
Buchanan Castle   35
Carleton Castle   38
Castle Cary   39
Castle Fraser   40
Castle Grant   41
Castle Levan   42
Castle Stuart   43
Cawdor Castle   46
Claypotts Castle   47
Comlongon Castle   50
Corgarff Castle   51

Cortachy Castle   53
Craigcrook Castle   55
Craighouse   56
Craignethan Castle   56
Crathes Castle   58
Crichton Castle   59
Culcreuch Castle   60
Dalhousie Castle   63
Dalkeith House   64
Dalzell House   66
Dean Castle   67
Delgatie Castle   68
Drumlanrig Castle   70
Dunnottar Castle   72
Dunrobin Castle   74
Dunskey Castle   75
Duntulm Castle   77
Dunvegan Castle   78
Earlshall   79
Edinample Castle   80
Edinburgh   80
Edzell Castle   82
Ethie Castle   83
Falkland Palace   84
Fernie Castle   86
Ferniehirst Castle   86
Fyvie Castle   91
Galdenoch Castle   92
Glamis Castle   94
Glencoe   96
Grange House   97
Hermitage Castle   99
Holyroodhouse   101
Huntingtower Castle   103
Invergarry Castle   105
Iona Abbey   106
Kellie Castle   108
Killiecrankie   109
Kinnaird Castle   111
Kinnaird Head Castle   111
Kinneil House   112
Liberton House   115
Linlithgow Palace   115
Lochleven Castle   117

Lordscairnie Castle   118
Luffness House   119
Macduff's Castle   120
Meggernie Castle   122
Melgund Castle   124
Melrose Abbey   125
Moy Castle   128
Muchalls Castle   129
Neidpath Castle   129
Newark Castle   131
Newbattle Abbey   132
Newton Castle   132
Noltland Castle   133
Penkaet Castle   136
Pinkie House   137
Rait Castle   139
Rosslyn Castle   142
Rosslyn Chapel   142
Rothesay Castle   143
Roxburghe House   144
Royal Lyceum Theatre   145
Ruthven Castle   146
Saddell Castle   147
Sanquhar Castle   148
Spedlins Tower   152
Spynie Palace   152
St Andrews Castle   153
St Mary's Church, Haddington   154
Stirling Castle   157
Thirlestane Castle   161
Tibbie Shiel's Inn   162
Traquair House   163
Vayne Castle   164
West Bow, Edinburgh   165
Wrychtishousis   167

Drawings are taken from MacGibbon, David and Ross, Thomas, The Castellated and Domestic Architecture of Scotland, *Edinburgh, 1887.*

Acknowledgements

Many thanks to everyone who has helped in compiling this book. A big hullo and particular thanks to Joyce Miller (as ever), Hilary Horrocks at The National Trust for Scotland, Donna Laidlaw at Historic Scotland, Gordon Mason, George Montgomery, Graham Coe, Norman Adams, Duncan Jones, Caroline Boyd, Grace Ellis, Bob Schott, Hamish at Altered Images, Edinburgh, Stephen at Mitchell Graphics, Glasgow, and Charlie at Bath Press, Blantyre.

Thank you also to the staff at various Tourist Information Centres, particularly those at Lanark, Dumfries, Abingdon, Oban, Glasgow, Aberdeen, Edinburgh, St Andrews, Kirkcaldy, Inverness and Fort William. Many thanks also go to the staff and proprietors of all the many hotels and visitor attractions who have helped with numerous ghost inquiries. And particular thanks to the following for permission to use photographs or illustrations: Joan Johnston at Delgatie; Jim MacDonald at Neidpath; Clare Simpson at the Royal Lyceum; Peter McKenzie at Dunnottar; Dalkeith House; Tibbie Shiel's Inn, St Mary's Loch and Susan Robinson at The Roxburghe Hotel (formally Sunlaws). Also to Melanie Newman at Dunvegan Castle; Meryl Duncan, Castle of Park, Cornhill; David Littlefair at Culcreuch Castle; Scott Trainer, Fasque; Jessie Fraser at Ferniehirst; Cathy Fyfe at Ravenswood Hotel, Ballater; Gordon Stewart at Mercat Tours; Shirley Young, the original St Andrews Witches Tour, Bon Accord Tours, Aberdeen for their time and help.

We are also grateful to the following for help given with our inquiries: Abbotsford House; Ackergill Tower; Arbigland House; Ardblair Castle; Ardoe House Hotel, Blairs; Atholl Palace Hotel, Pitlochry; Barcaldine Castle; Stuart Morris of Balgonie; Wilma at Borthwick Castle; Broadford Hotel, Skye; Braemar Castle; Buccleuch Heritage Trust, Bowhill (Newark); Busta House Hotel, Shetland; Tom Gardner, Byre Theatre, St Andrews; Cartland Bridge Hotel; Castle Stuart; Cawdor Castle; Jennie Gardner, Citizens' Theatre, Glasgow; Clydesdale Hotel, Lanark; Stephen Levy, The Cobbler Hotel, Arrochar; Comlongon Castle; Coylet Inn, Loch Eck; Dalhousie Castle; Audrey at Dalmahoy; Dalmeny House; Dean Castle; Discovery Point, Dundee; Claire Fisher, Drumlanrig Castle; Dryburgh Abbey Hotel; Dunrobin Castle; Eden Court Theatre, Inverness; Edinburgh Festival Theatre; Eilean Donan Castle; Neil Blackburn at Fernie Castle; Floors Castle; Gairnshiel Lodge, Ballater; Glamis Castle; Glengarry Hotel (Invergarry Castle); His Majesty's Theatre, Aberdeen; Holyroodhouse; Valerie McDougal, Hopetoun House; Jedburgh Castle Jail; Lauriston Castle; Joyce Cleave, Loch Ness Youth Hostel; Loudon Castle; Megginch Castle; Meldrum House; Graham McIntosh, Montrose Air Station Museum; New Lanark Mills; Norwood Hall; Perth Theatre; Salutation Hotel, Perth; Scone Palace; Shieldhill Hotel, Biggar; Skaill House, Orkney; St Michael's Parish Church, Linlithgow; St Nicholas Church, Aberdeen; Peter Jarvis at Thirlestane Castle; Traquair House; Lorna at Witchery Tours.

Thanks also to all the other individuals, staff and custodians at various sites throughout the country who contributed to the research for this book. In some cases, information had to be edited because of limited space.

How to use the book

The introduction gives a brief summary about areas of ghostly activity and discussion about alleged supernatural phenomena.

The main section begins with maps covering the whole of Scotland over four pages. The north part of Scotland is covered on pages 2-3, while the southern part is on pages 4-5. The map is divided into grid squares, with number for north to south, and letters for west to east, which are referred to in the entries in the main text. Places within in towns are listed under the name of the town. Maps are only for guidance: locations may be approximate.

From page 7, Each entry begins with the name of the site, then the location, whether the site is owned by Historic Scotland (His Scot), The National Trust for Scotland (NTS), Private or local authority (Pri/LA) and ruin or site. This does not mean that all ruins have open access as many are still on private land. The map reference should be used in conjunction with the maps on pages 2-5.

The description and ghost story(s) follows, then information on opening times and hours: it should be assumed unless stated explicitly otherwise that manned visitor attractions are normally closed at Christmas and New Year. Many hotels are unofficially closed during quiet periods so always check accommodation availability before setting off.

Features of the site then follow. These should be self explanatory except for price and tariff. Price of entry: £ = up to £3.50; ££ = £3.50-£5.00; ££ = £5.00+ – concessions for children, students, OAPs and groups normally apply. Tariff for accommodation: $ = up to £50.00 per night; $$ = £50-£100; $$$ = £100-£150; $$$$ = £150-£200; $$$$+ = more than £200, sometimes a lot more. Tariff ranges may include special features such as four-poster beds and jacuzzi.

The telephone, fax, email and web addresses then follow – where available.

Ghost tours follow the main section (page 169), then Selected further reading (page 173), then indexes by place (page 178), haunting (page 180), area (page 184) and General index (page 187)

Preface

In a book about ghosts it is probably important to establish the viewpoint of the author: what exactly are my beliefs about ghosts and bogles. Like much else in life, they are muddled.

My own interest in the this area stems from a very young age: my favourite story was that of the haunting of Burton Agnes Hall by the spirit of Anne Griffith, who died in 1620, read over and over (along with the nameless horror of Berkley Square) to frighten myself and my wee sister. The story goes that Anne was murdered by robbers, but before she died she asked that part of her – her severed head – be kept at Burton Agnes, as she had loved the building. Her family, perhaps not surprisingly had all her remains buried, but then fearful disturbances plagued the building until eventually her coffin was opened, her head removed, and brought to the hall. All was peace, but on several occasions her skull was removed from Burton Agnes, and each time the terrible disturbances also returned.

It was years later that I discovered Burton Agnes Hall was a real place, the events do appear to have happened as described, and there was even a portrait of Anne. And, of course, her skull is said to have been sealed up in the great hall so that she would finally rest in peace. This is the kind of story I liked, with internal consistency and a historical basis. The Canterville Ghost and Water Ghost of Harrowby Hall were pale and factually insubstantial phantoms in comparison.

Despite the thrill of a really good ghost story, and visiting a supposedly haunted site, I do retain a scepticism about the whole area of the paranormal. Besides which, hunting bogles is a perilous pastime, not least from the spooks lurking in the dark recesses of our own imaginations.

I have had some unusual experiences, along with my family, but these do not fall into the area of terrifying, and there may be 'rational' explanations for them all. These are some of them.

When we were children, my three sisters and I remember visiting a house in Newbattle Terrace, Edinburgh, when my parents were looking to purchase a new property. Although my wee sister can only have been six or seven at the time, we all clearly remember that this house, particularly the area around the stairs, had a strong unpleasant

– even evil – feel. Apparently a murder had been committed there.

While staying by myself in a modern council house at Greater Sankey, near Warrington, there were a series of unexplained thumps on the ceiling above the lounge coming from one of the bedrooms. This was prolonged, and has no explanation.

My younger sister had a frightening dream about a man dressed in an RAF uniform around the time my grandfather died – he had been in the RAF during the war. This happened before my parents were phoned and told that my grandfather had died – he had not previously been ill.

Joyce and I, on separate occasions, saw a man going up to the terraced house we were renting in Helmsley – but on approaching the door we found there was nobody there. We did not tell each other about our independent sightings until we were on our way home.

A few days before my aunt died after a long illness, I had a dream about my mother coming into my bedroom and telling me that my aunt was dead. I told my parents about the dream and they went to visit my aunt, and a few days later my mother came into my bedroom to tell me my aunt was dead – just as in the dream.

While visiting the toilets at Craignethan Castle I had an urgent feeling that I should leave and was being watched. I am not prone to these feelings: it was a fantastic summer day and I did not know of the supposed haunting. I have also, with Joyce, visited many castles and sites in the dead and dark of winter, stood in many rooms which were supposedly haunted, just the two of us, and never given it a second thought.

I relate these simply as experiences from my life, and have no idea of their significance or validity as events of a supernatural nature – nor do I care. They are simply events that happened, which cannot easily be explained away.

Introduction

Do ghosts exist? And if they do what exactly are they? Many stories have been gathered together in this book to try to gain an understanding, although the emphasis has been on the tales which have stood the test of time, and on historic sites. These are, however, only a small proportion of ghostly activity – most disturbances are now said to happen in council houses. Despite the assertion that this is a sceptical and materialistic age, belief in the supernatural and in ghosts appears to be stronger than ever. Many custodians, owners and managers have been delighted to help in providing information, and while few endorse or confirm the ghost stories, a bogle can attract visitors and guests. Others, however, are extremely hostile to the whole idea – which is interesting in itself. So far, this book has drawn more interest and stirred up more protest – in the form of brusque letters and abrupt phone calls ('not the right thing to do') – than anything published so far by Goblinshead.

  Many of the reported ghosts are believed to be those of real people, most of whom died in horrific or tragic circumstances. Yet there is a general mixing up of witchcraft and hauntings into a general brew of the 'supernatural'. Most ghost stories make no reference to sorcery, black witchcraft, or the diabolic arts, and usually the people described are just ordinary folk. While ghosts of the dead may be frightening – and challenge beliefs regarding life and death – it is the living who are far more dangerous.

Hauntings themselves are not of one type, and there are several different areas of activity, although no attempt is made at a clear distinction here – apparitions are often accompanied by poltergeist activity, while poltergeists can occasionally be accompanied by apparitions; some harbingers of doom are also ghosts in the true sense, while others appear to be 'real' creatures.

- **Apparitions**.
  Although these are mostly reported, particularly 'Green Ladies' in Scotland, they are rarely witnessed. Far more common are the sounds of feet or rustle of clothing, unexplained raps and bangs,

the opening and closing of doors, and interference with electrical equipment. All this activity is often associated with a violent event, such as a murder, killing or suicide, and if apparitions are experienced it tends to be in the same place or repeating the same – often mundane – task, such as walking from one area to another and then vanishing. Other causes seem to be when the person has some unfinished business, such as searching for a baby or loved one, repaying a loan, or making sure a hotel is kept in good order.

Other reported apparitions, or disturbances, are associated with folk simply too wicked to rest or who have dabbled in witchcraft or had dealings with the devil. Many of these stories originate in the Covenanting times of the late 17th century, although they share details with older tales. These dark characters include Alexander Stewart, the Wolf of Badenoch; Earl Beardie, the Earl of Crawford; Tam Dalziel of The Binns; the lairds of Pringle and Buckholm, Skene and Kinnaird; and Bruce of Earlshall.

- **Crises apparitions**
  These tend to be witnessed when the person is in a great crisis, often facing death, as the name suggests. The apparition appears to a relative, loved one or even an acquaintance during some catastrophe. The apparition, however, is not how the person appears at the time – which is probably just as well if they are suffering a violent death – but a vision of how the person has appeared sometime in the past. Perhaps it is a reflection of how the person saw themselves.

- **Poltergeist activity**
  This involves the movement of objects, often violently, as well as noises, cries, footsteps and the rest without an apparent apparition. This activity is often associated with teenage girls and boys, or old people nearing death, and may have a telepathic rather than ghostly cause. These are sometimes reported after a violent event, sometimes the activity is centred around one individual. Often the haunting stops suddenly, or when the individual leaves the place. Poltergeists have – if anything – become more restrained compared to their ancient counterparts.

- **Premonition spirits or activity**
  A spectre or corporeal creature exhibits a specific behaviour as a portent of coming disaster or – less often – good fortune. These are particularly numerous in Scotland, and a wide range of phenomena and creatures are involved, from robins, red-breasted swans and white deer to ghostly drummers, 'Green Ladies' and headless horsemen. These are not always accurate: the laird of Cameron House was predicted to die when Loch Lomond froze over. While there may be excellent reasons why someone might perish in a year of extreme cold, it has been shown that the freezing over of the Loch had nothing to do with the life expectancy of the laird. People also fit the facts to suit the witnessing of the phenomena. In the case of the Cortachy drummer, on one occasion he was supposedly heard six months before one of the family died – this seems just a little far in advance.

- **Brownies and guardian ghosts**
  There are numerous tales of brownies, household spirits who would carry out repetitive tasks, such as threshing corn, cleaning, clearing stones from roads, but who would need to be rewarded with presents, food or drink – often milk or cream – otherwise the spirit would leave or calamity would occur. These creatures seem to have inhabited a world between the corporeal and the supernatural, and to have much in common with fairies. Descriptions of them vary between small and hairy to golden-haired and green clad.
  Gruagach, often the spirits of former mistresses who had died in child birth or been enchanted, were said to share in the fortunes of their house, although not necessarily the occupants – they were bound to the site. When they would weep, there was ill news to follow, when they were happy, good tidings were to come. They also reputedly looked after young children and babies.
  Glaistig, an amphibious sprite, was another supernatural being akin to the brownie, who would tend cattle and the like.
  Guardian spirits, ghosts or creatures are also recorded, mostly in Highland areas.

Many suggestions have been put forward as to the cause of hauntings, but none are satisfactory.

In a Christian cosmology, apparitions could be explained in terms of the immortal soul, that a part of the person survives after death. This part, the soul, could be 'trapped' on earth, unable to travel on to whatever lies beyond, as a punishment, or desiring to complete business on earth. Stories often relate that manifestations cease when the mortal remains are buried in consecrated ground or when the task is completed, such as the repaying of a loan or a grave being moved because it is waterlogged.

One explanation for crises apparitions is that they are experienced through telepathy between the person suffering the crisis and the 'viewer', that an enormous amount of stress seems to open a telepathic 'door'.

Another suggests that a psychic record is imprinted on a building or location when a violent act is committed – that the apparition is simply like a video recording of the event and is not the result of a 'sentient' spirit. Corpses exude nucleic acids which remain in the atmosphere. Those sufficiently sensitive to this telepathic message can then pick it up and 'view' it.

Ghosts are also said to exist in a spirit world where the temperature is 3 Kelvin, which is as cold as outer space. This is thought to explain why rooms become cold when ghostly activity is present or imminent, and ghosts are said to have failed to achieve sufficient energy to cross to the other world.

Some believe that ghosts 'fade' over time, that colour slowly drains away – a 'Green Lady' gradually becomes 'White'. Eventually the apparition itself becomes less strong and defined, often described as being like a mist, and finally all that is left is a 'presence', a feeling in an area or that someone is pushing past.

All these theories have deficiencies when compared to the many stories.

If ghosts are the souls of dead people, but only humans have souls, what are the manifestations of animals or objects? Some ghosts just have no unpleasant reason to haunt an area, and appear to have been happy in life. Indeed ghosts are sometimes believed to 'hang about' because they particularly liked a place. Ghostly activity has also been reported to increase when remains are give a Christian burial.

Activity does often not relate to the committing of a violent crime –

indeed apparitions wander about doing the mundane, even when carrying their head under their arm. Ghosts seem interested in modern machinery and activities, suggesting a more 'sentient' spirit, and spend much of their time interfering with electrical apparatus.

Parts of the ghost can be missing, such as their head, hands and whole torso. It must be assumed that the person was dead before being dismembered, and it seems unlikely that the apparition could include information conducted by telepathy when the person was already dead. Whole groups of people are also reported to witness paranormal disturbances at the same time, so other factors must also come into play apart from the sensitivity of a particular individual.

It should be emphasised that the stories in this book are usually no more than that. Virtually all female ghosts are beautiful – which may be a comfort to ugly folk in that only good-looking people come back as ghosts – but it is more probable that the extra attractiveness of the apparition is a later artistic embellishment. There is also little evidence that ghosts float or glide about, but it sounds more eerie than simply walking.

Investigations undertaken in Victorian times and before – and even in this century – can be untrustworthy, and reports have been deliberately misleading: it tends to be believers or those with a preexisting agenda who did and are doing the investigations. The Meggernie ghost story, when two friends shared adjoining rooms and were kissed by the resident phantom, sounds fabricated and doubts were raised at the time. Other investigations at Ballechin and Penkaet seem similarly exaggerated. It should be remembered that was a huge growth of interest in spiritualism from late Victorian times, but virtually all spiritualists were later shown to be frauds. There were, however, some interesting findings when Hermitage Castle was recently investigated using state-of-the-art equipment.

The lengths some will go to fool or trick others can not be underestimated. Nor how easy it is for the viewer, particularly the believer, to fool themselves or to ignore inconsistencies or trickery. The falling in temperature during ghostly activity can be due to the adrenaline response, provoked by fear, rather than by bogles. One belief is that during the incidents associated with restless spirits the temperature drops, while activity attached to evil or black witchcraft involves a rise in temperature. It many instances, however, the witness is unaware – until later – that anything unusual has happened: often apparitions are thought to be real people.

Noises sound much louder at night than during the day – a dripping tap can go ignored during the day but can drive the sleeper demented at night. During sleep paralysis – a period of limbo between sleep and being awake when a person can believe they are awake, but are unable to move – may also be responsible for many stories, such as waking up being strangled or feeling a large weight loaded on their chest. The waker can have auditory and visual hallucinations, such as voices and apparent phantoms, as they believe they are awake.

Besides which, it is a myth that all ghostly activity is reported during the night. Incidents are as likely to happen on a beautiful sunny afternoon as in the dead of the night.

Having said all this, there does seem a good case for belief in the phenomena of ghosts – there are simply too many stories reported by sensible people for the whole body of evidence to be dismissed as superstition, fabrication or just plain foolishness. On the pages that follow are many of these stories, some detailed, some fragmentary, some derivative, some unique, some famous, some less well known.

Readers will have to make up their own minds.

Warning

The contact numbers listed in the book are provided in order to check opening times, the availability of accommodation and facilities. Many owners, members of staff and custodians are happy to discuss hauntings and other stories, but others have businesses to run and should be left in peace. The inclusion of a site in the text is not a recommendation that it should be visited. Many are private homes, offices or businesses and are not open unless specifically indicated. All opening information and facilities have been checked as far as possible, but information is subject to change and should be confirmed with the site. The publisher and author take no responsibility for omissions or inaccuracies.

Lastly – and most importantly – many of the sites are ruins in inaccessible or dangerous locations. Great care must be taken when visiting.

The
Maps

Neidpath Castle

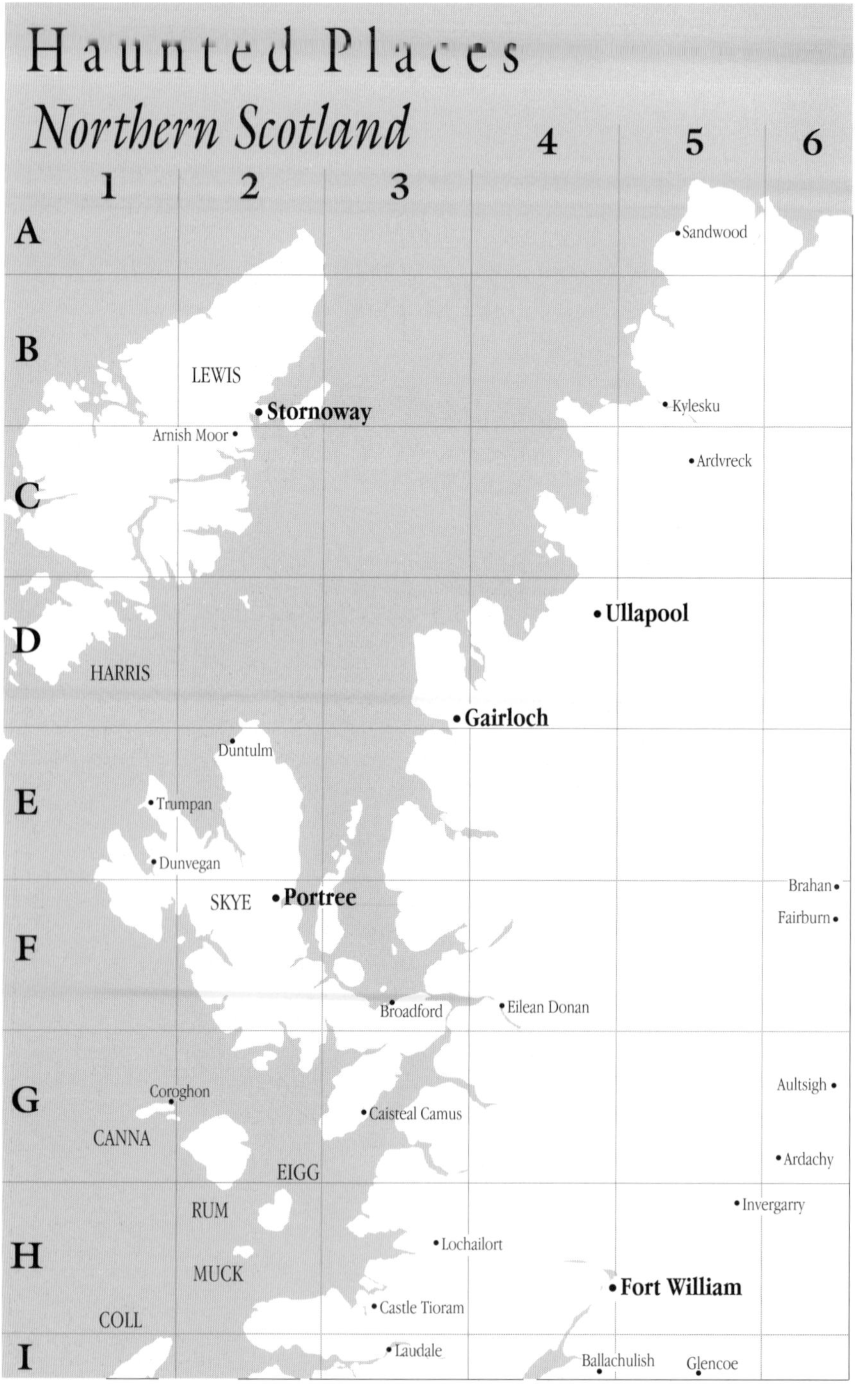

Haunted Places
Northern Scotland

	1	2	3	4	5	6

A

• Sandwood

B

LEWIS

• **Stornoway**

Arnish Moor •

• Kylesku

• Ardvreck

C

D

• **Ullapool**

HARRIS

• **Gairloch**

Duntulm

E

• Trumpan

• Dunvegan

Brahan •

Fairburn •

SKYE • **Portree**

F

• Broadford

• Eilean Donan

Aultsigh •

G

Coroghon
•

• Caisteal Camus

CANNA

• Ardachy

EIGG

RUM

• Invergarry

H

MUCK

• Lochailort

• **Fort William**

COLL

• Castle Tioram

I

• Laudale

Ballachulish   Glencoe

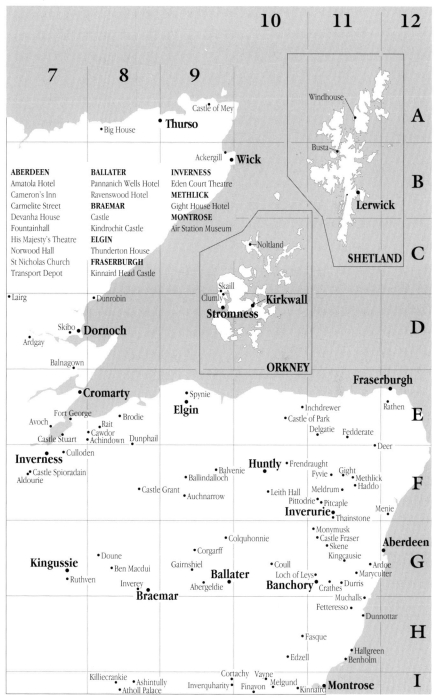

10   **11**   **12**

7   **8**   **9**

Castle of Mey
• Big House   **Thurso**   **A**

Windhouse

Busta

Ackergill •   **Wick**

ABERDEEN   **BALLATER**   **INVERNESS**   **B**
Amatola Hotel   Pannanich Wells Hotel Eden Court Theatre
Cameron's Inn   Ravenswood Hotel   **METHLICK**
Carmelite Street **BRAEMAR**   Gight House Hotel
Devanha House   Castle   **MONTROSE**
Fountainhall   Kindrochit Castle   Air Station Museum   **Lerwick**
His Majesty's Theatre **ELGIN**
Norwood Hall   Thunderton House   • Noltland   **SHETLAND** **C**
St Nicholas Church **FRASERBURGH**
Transport Depot Kinnaird Head Castle

• Lairg   • Dunrobin   Skaill   Clumly   **Kirkwall**
                                            Stromness   **D**
Skibo • **Dornoch**
Ardgay

Balnagown   **ORKNEY**

                                            Fraserburgh
• **Cromarty**   • Spynie
Fort George   • Brodie   **Elgin**   • Inchdrewer   Rathen   **E**
Avoch •   • Rait   • Castle of Park
Castle Stuart • Cawdor   Delgatie Fedderate
               • Achindown Dunphail
                                            • Deer
• Culloden
Inverness   • Balvenie   **Huntly** • Frendraught
• Castle Spioradain • Ballindalloch   Fyvie • Gight • • Methlick   **F**
Aldourie   • Haddo
               • Castle Grant   • Leith Hall Meldrum •
               • Auchnarrow   Pittodrie •• Pitcaple   Menie
                                            Inverurie• • Thainstone

                                            • Monymusk
               • Colquhonnie   • Castle Fraser   **Aberdeen** **G**
               • Corgarff   • Skene
• Doune   Kingcausie
Kingussie   • Ben Macdui Gairnshiel   • Coull   • Ardoe
• Ruthven   Inverey   **Ballater** Loch of Leys• • Maryculter
            Braemar Abergeldie •   **Banchory**• Crathes • Durris
                                            Muchalls •
                                            Fetteresso •
                                            • Dunnottar   **H**

                                            • Fasque
                                            • Hallgreen
                        • Edzell   • Benholm

            Killiecrankie Cortachy Vayne
            • Ashintully Inverquharity • Finavon • Melgund **Montrose** **I**
            • Atholl Palace   • Kinnaird

3

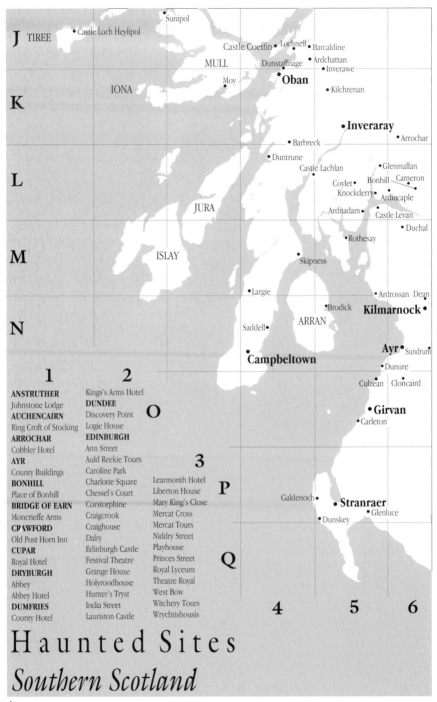

J TIREE • Castle Loch Heylipol

Sunipol

Castle Coeffin • Lochnell • Barcaldine
MULL   Dunstaffnage • Ardchattan
                                      • Inverawe
                    Moy •   **•Oban**

K   IONA   • Kilchrenan

                                    •Inveraray
                                            • Arrochar
                    • Barbreck

                • Duntrune
            Castle Lachlan   •Glenmallan
L   Coylet• Bonhill ⌐Cameron
                    Knockderry• Ardincaple
            JURA   Ardnadam • Castle Levan
                                    • Duchal
                            •Rothesay

M   ISLAY   Skipness

                • Largie
                                    • Ardrossan Dean
                        •Brodick **Kilmarnock •**
N   Saddell• ARRAN

                                    Ayr• Sundrum
                Campbeltown   •Dunure

1   **2**   Culzean | Cloncaird

ANSTRUTHER   Kings's Arms Hotel
Johnstone Lodge **DUNDEE**   **•Girvan**
AUCHENCAIRN Discovery Point **O**   •Carleton
Ring Croft of Stocking Logie House
ARROCHAR   **EDINBURGH**
Cobbler Hotel   Ann Street
AYR   Auld Reekie Tours   **3**
County Buildings Caroline Park
BONHILL   Charlotte Square Learmonth Hotel
Place of Bonhill Chessel's Court Liberton House **P**
BRIDGE OF EARN Corstorphine   Mary King's Close   Galdenoch• **•Stranraer**
Moncrieffe Arms Craigcrook   Mercat Cross   •Glenluce
CRAWFORD   Craighouse   Mercat Tours   •Dunskey
Old Post Horn Inn Dalry   Niddry Street
CUPAR   Edinburgh Castle Playhouse
Royal Hotel   Festival Theatre Princes Street **Q**
DRYBURGH   Grange House   Royal Lyceum
Abbey   Holyroodhouse   Theatre Royal
Abbey Hotel   Hunter's Tryst West Bow
DUMFRIES   India Street   Witchery Tours
County Hotel   Lauriston Castle Wrychtishousis   **4**   **5**   **6**

Haunted Sites
Southern Scotland

Garth • • Tombuie
Fortingall • • Ballechin • Airlie
Taymouth / Grandtully • Newton • Glamis • Ethie
Ardblair

J

• **Arbroath**

• Claypotts

Meggernie • Huntingtower • Scone • **Dundee** •
Perth • Megginch
Lordscairnie • Earlshall

K

• Edinample
Bridge of Earn •
Fernie • **Cupar** **St Andrews**
• Balcomie
• Braco • Falkland • Kellie
• Anstruther

Lochleven
• Nivingston • Balgonie
• Macduff's
• Wemyss

Stirling
• Buchanan • Culcreuch
Culross • Balwearie
• **Dunfermline** • **Edinburgh**
Airth • Fordell
Kinneil • • Barnbougle
Castle Cary The Binns • Hopetoun • Luffness • Biel
Auchinvole •
• Bedlay • **Linlithgow** Dalmahoy • Pinkie • Garleton
Melville • Dalkeith Penkaet • **Haddington**
Glasgow Howlet's • • Newbattle • Saltoun
• Hawkhead • Blantyre Fulford • Dalhousie • Pathhead • Houndwood
Mains Greenlaw • Roslin • Crichton • Cranshaws
• **Motherwell** Borthwick
• Dalzell Old Woodhouselee • Allanbank
• Broomhill • Medwyn • **Duns** • Berwick
• Thirlstane

L

M

Craignethan • • Cartland Bridge
• **Lanark** **Peebles** Buckholm • **Melrose**
• Loudon Auchlochan • New Lanark Neidpath Abbotsford • • Littledean
• Cessnock Shieldhill • • Floors
• Windgate Traquair Newark • Dryburgh Roxburgh
• Marlfield

N

• Wellwood
• Crawford • Tibbie Shiel's **Jedburgh** •
• Ferniehirst
• Dolphinston

• **Sanquhar**
• Dalpeddar

ENGLAND

O

• Drumlanrig
• Closeburn • Hermitage
Langholm
• Glenlee • Tarras

• Spedlins
Dumfries Rockhall • Rammerscales
• Comlongon

P

• Arbigland

• Baldoon • Auchencairn

Q

7   **8**   **9**   **10**   **11**   **12**

GLASGOW	HADDINGTON	MOTHERWELL	PERTH	ROXBURGH(E)	Cathedral
Cathedral House	St Mary's Church	New Century Th.	Salutation Hotel	Castle	Orig. Witches Tour
Citizens's Theatre	**LANARK**	**PATHHEAD**	Theatre	House (Sunlaws)	
Gartloch Hospital	Clydesdale Hotel	Stair Arms	**ROSLIN**	**ST ANDREWS**	
Infirmary	**LINLITHGOW**	**PEEBLES**	Rosslyn Castle	Byre Theatre	
Theatre Royal	Palace	County Hotel	Rosslyn Chapel	Castle	
Western Infirmary	St Michael's Church	Cross Keys Hotel			

Haunted
Places
of Scotland

Dunnottar Castle

Site ownership:

His Scot   Historic Scotland
NTS   The National Trust for Scotland
Pri/LA   Private or local authority

Many ruins are on private land.

The map reference should be used with the maps on pages 2-5.

Manned visitor attractions are normally closed at Christmas and New Year.

Price of entry: £ = up to £3.50;
££ = £3.50-£5.00; £££ = £5.00+

Concessions for children, students, OAPs and groups normally apply.

Tariff for accommodation: $ = up to £50;
 $$ = £50-£100; $$$ = £100-£150;
$$$$ = £150-£200; $$$$+ = £200+.

Staircase, Caroline Park

Abbotsford

On B6360, 2 miles W of Melrose, Borders.
Pri/LA   (map ref: 10N)

The famous Scottish author and historian Sir Walter Scott built the large castellated mansion of Abbotsford, after purchasing the property in 1812. Scott wrote the famous Waverley novels, as well as *Ivanhoe*, the *Lay of the Last Minstrel*, *Marmion* and many others. He was one of the most popular authors of his day, both in Britain and abroad, and also a distinguished historian. Scott was responsible for the rediscovery of the Scottish crown jewels at Edinburgh Castle, and collected many historic artefacts: there is an impressive collection of armour and weapons at the house, including Rob Roy MacGregor's gun and the Marquis of Montrose's sword. His library of more than 9000 rare volumes is preserved at the house.

The ghost of Sir Walter Scott is said to haunt the dining room, where he died in 1832 after exhausting himself trying to pay off a huge debt. Sightings of his apparition have been reported in recent times.

Another ghost, said to have been witnessed here, is the spirit of George Bullock, who died in 1818 and was in charge of the rebuilding of Abbotsford. The sounds of furniture being dragged across the floor was reportedly heard.

Open 3rd Monday in Mar-Oct, Mon-Sat & Sun Jun-Sep only, 10.00-17.00; also Sun Mar-May & Oct 14.00-17.00; other dates by appt.

Guided tours. Gift shop. Tearoom. Extensive gardens and grounds. WC. Disabled access by private entrance and WC. Car and coach parking. Group concessions. ££.

Tel: 01896 752043   Fax: 01896 752916

Abergeldie Castle

Off B976, 5 miles W of Ballater, Kincardine.
Pri/LA   (map ref: 9G)

Abergeldie Castle, a simple rectangular tower house, has been a property of the Gordons from 1482. During a feud with the Forbes family, the seven sons of Gordon of Knock were murdered by Forbes of Strathgirnock. They had been cutting peats on disputed land, and their severed heads were spiked on their spades. Forbes was tracked down and executed by Gordon of Abergeldie.

Abergeldie was attacked and burnt by the Mackenzies in 1592, but was restored and saw action in the first Jacobite Rising of 1689-90. It was leased to Queen Victoria from 1848, and is again occupied by the Gordons.

The castle is reputedly haunted by the spirit of a French maid, Catherine Frankie, known as 'Kittie Rankie', who is said to have been accused of witchcraft at the end of the 16th century. The story goes that the unfortunate Catherine was asked by the wife of the house what her husband was doing delayed aboard ship. When Catherine told her that he was dallying with other women, the wife had Catherine imprisoned in the castle dungeon and accused of witchcraft – a similar story is told of the Brahan seer. Catherine was then burnt at the stake, and her ghost has reputedly been seen in the castle, most often in the tall clock tower. Other disturbances include mysterious noises, and the ringing of a bell when misfortune is about to strike the family.

Achindown

Off B9090, 1 mile S of Cawdor, Highland.
Pri/LA   (map ref: 8E)
Part of the Cawdor estate and set in fine gardens, Achindown, a square mansion of about 1700, was occupied by a Hamish Munroe in 1746. He gave shelter to Jacobites fleeing from the slaughter at the Battle of Culloden, and hid them in the basement. A band of Hanoverian troops, under the orders of Butcher Cumberland, searched the house and found the fugitives. They were taken from the house and then shot, along with Munroe himself. The shot marks can still be seen in a garden wall.

The house is allegedly haunted. The apparition of a girl, thought to be Elspeth, daughter of the Hamish Munroe who died in 1746, is said to have been seen collecting flowers. Her apparition is reported as wearing a blue dress and has brown hair. Elspeth is said to have eloped with a shepherd from the estate.

Ackergill Tower

Off A9, 2.5 miles N of Wick, Caithness.
Pri/LA   (map ref: 9B)
Ackergill Tower is a strong, impressive 15th-century castle, which was formerly surrounded by a 12-foot-wide moat. The castle was remodelled by the architect David Bryce in 1851, restored in 1987, and is still occupied. It is now used as a conference and hospitality centre.

The lands were a property of the Cheynes, but passed by marriage to the Keith Earls Marischal in about 1350, who built the present castle.

The family had a long and bitter feud with a local family, the Gunns, and caught up in the murder and mayhem was Helen Gunn, the 'Beauty of Braemore'. Although she was already betrothed to a man she loved, she was seized and carried off to Ackergill by Dugald Keith, who desired her for himself.

The poor girl was imprisoned in an upstairs chamber, but rather than yield to Dugald, threw herself from the tower and was killed – a stone is said to mark the spot where she hit the ground. Her ghost, a 'Green Lady', is said to have been seen in the castle, and a rowan tree 'Fair Ellen's Tree' still grows at Braemore.

The property was sold by the Keiths in 1612.

Open all year.
Offers totally exclusive use. Accommodation: 25 bedrooms, including 17 in castle, all with private facilities. Fine Scottish kitchen. Conferences and meetings. Opera house. Angling and golf. Garden. Parking. $$$$+.
Tel: 01955 603556   Fax: 01955 602140
Email: www.ackergill-tower.co.uk   Web: AckergillTower@compuserve.com

Airlie Castle

Off A926, 4 miles NE of Alyth, Angus.
Pri/LA   (map ref: 9J)

Standing on a commanding position between two rivers, Airlie Castle was built in 1432 by the Ogilvies, later Earls of Airlie, and was once a place of great strength. The family were much involved in the troubles of 17th and 18th centuries. James Ogilvie, 1st Earl of Airlie, escaped from Scotland rather than sign the National Covenant, and in 1640 the castle was sacked by the Earl of Argyll. Ogilvie joined the Marquis of Montrose, but in 1645 was captured after defeat at the Battle of Philiphaugh; fortunately for him he managed to escape execution. The 4th Earl fought in the Jacobite Rising of 1745, but had to flee the country, although he was later pardoned. The castle was replaced by a mansion in 1793, which is still occupied by the Ogilvies.

A ram, the 'Doom of Airlie Castle', is said to circle the castle when one of the family is near death or bad fortune is about to strike.

11

Airth Castle

Off A905, 4 miles N of Falkirk.
Pri/LA   (map ref: 8L)
In acres of woodland, Airth Castle consists of a squat 14th-century keep, now known as Wallace's Tower, and many later extensions and additions. The castle was given a new castellated and towered front in the 19th century.

William Wallace rescued his uncle from the castle after imprisonment by the English. Airth was a property of the Bruces, but in 1488 was torched by James III before the Battle of Sauchieburn; it was restored using monies from James IV. Airth passed by marriage to other families, and since 1971 has been used as a hotel and country club.

One room of the castle is said to be haunted by the ghost of a 17th-century housekeeper. The story goes that she neglected two children in her care, and still searches the building for them after they were killed in a fire.

Hotel – open all year.
129 rooms, 23 in the old castle. Restaurants and cocktail bar. Country club, with health centre, gymnasium, sauna and swimming pool. Conference facilities. Parking. $$$.
Tel: 01324 831411   Fax: 01324 831419

Aldourie Castle

Off B862, 6 miles SW of Inverness, Highland.
Pri/LA   (map ref: 7F)
A 'Grey Lady' is said to haunt Aldourie Castle, and her apparition reputedly walks from a bedroom in the ancient part of the castle to the old hall. The mansion dates from the 17th-century, and was a property of the Frasers, the Grants, then the Mackintoshes.

Allanbank House

Off B6437, 4.5 miles east of Duns, Borders.
Ruin or site   (map ref: 11M)
Allanbank House, a small mansion designed by David Bryce in 1848, was demolished in 1969. The mansion replaced an earlier house, dating from the 17th century, which was a property of the Stewart family.

Robert Stewart of Allanbank, made a baronet of Nova Scotia in 1687, met a pretty Italian or French girl, Jean, in Paris and they became lovers. Stewart, however, seems to have tired of her or his parents disapproved: whatever, he planned to return to Allanbank. On the day of his departure, Jean tried to stop him leaving, but was thrown under Stewart's carriage and trampled to death under the horses' hooves.

The ghost, called 'Pearlin Jean' because of the lace she wore, is said to have followed Stewart back to Allanbank and started to haunt the grounds and house. Her apparition was seen, doors would open and close by themselves, and ghostly feet and the rustling of her gown were heard round the passages. The room in which the ghost was most commonly witnessed was abandoned. The old house was demolished in 1849, and a new mansion built, but the disturbances appear to have continued, occurrences being reported as late as the turn of the century.

Amatola Hotel, Aberdeen

Off A92, 448 Great Western Road, Aberdeen.
Pri/LA   (map ref: 12G)
The hotel is reputedly haunted. A lady, garbed in 19th-century dress, reportedly appears on the landing of the old part of the building. It is believed that she is the great-great-grandmother of the house owners, as she is dressed in a similar outfit to that seen in a portrait hanging in the hotel.

Hotel – open all year and to non-residents.
53 bedrooms. Restaurant and bar. Parking.
Tel: 01224 318724   Fax: 01224 312716

Ann Street, Edinburgh

Off A90, 0.5 miles NW of Edinburgh Castle, Edinburgh.
Pri/LA   (map ref: 9L)
A house here is said to be haunted by the ghost of Mr Swan, a former occupant. Although he died abroad, his apparition – a small man dressed in black – was reportedly seen in the house. An exorcism was performed, but when the house changed hands in 1936, the apparition apparently reappeared, and was witnessed most often in one of the bedrooms. His ghost seems to have been friendly, and to have said good night to children sleeping in the room.

Arbigland House

Off A710, 2 miles E of Kirkbean, Dumfries & Galloway.
Pri/LA   (map ref: 8P)
Arbigland House is a fine classical mansion, with a main block and pavilions, built by William Craik in 1755 to replace an older house. The property was held in turn by the MacCullochs, Murrays, and Carnegie Earls of Southesk, but was sold to the Craik family in 1679, then the Blacketts in 1852, who still own the house. John Paul Jones, father of the American Navy, was born at

13

nearby Kirkbean and worked on the estate as a gardener. The 15-acre garden, dating from 1750, includes formal woodland and water gardens.

The grounds around the house are reputedly haunted by the daughter of one of the Craik owners, the 'Ghost of the Three Crossroads'. She is said to have fallen in love with a groom called Dunn, but her parents thought the lad was beneath her station and forbad them to marry. Dunn disappeared: he may have been murdered by the girl's brothers, and she reportedly fled the house, and was not seen again. Whatever end she came to, her apparition is said to have been seen in the grounds, and occasionally in the house. Dunn's ghost, on a phantom horse, has also been reported near the main gates.

House open only 22-31 May, plus by appt; gardens open May-Sep, Tue-Sun & Bank Holiday Mon 14.00-18.00.
Gift shop. Tearoom. Picnic area. WC. Disabled access to grounds & WC. Gardens and grounds. Car and coach parking. 400 yards from John Paul Jones birthplace museum. £.
Tel: 01387 880283   Fax: 01387 880344

Ardachy

Off A82, 1 mile S of Fort Augustus, Highland.
Pri/LA   (map ref: 6G)
Ardachy, a modern mansion, stood on lands which were held by the Frasers of Lovat from the 15th century. The property was sold to the MacEwans in 1952, and is said to have been haunted by the apparition of a previous owner, Mrs Brewin.

Ardblair Castle

Off A923, 0.75 miles W of Blairgowrie, Perthshire.
Pri/LA   (map ref: 9J)
Ardblair Castle is a fine 16th-century tower house, designed on the L-plan, with later wings and a wall enclosing a courtyard. The lands were held by the Blairs of Balthayock from 1399, and the family feuded with the Drummonds. In 1554 Patrick Blair of Ardblair was beheaded after being found guilty of the murder of a George Drummond.

More trouble was to come when Lady Jean Drummond, of nearby Newton, fell in love with one of the Blairs of Ardblair. Her love was doomed, and she appears to have died of a broken heart,

drowned in a local marsh. Her ghost, a 'Green Lady', dressed in green silk, is said to have been witnessed at Ardblair. She is reportedly seen in the late afternoon and early evening on sunny afternoons, sitting in the gallery staring out of a window, or searching for her love through the chambers of the castle.

Ardblair passed by marriage in 1792 to the Oliphants of Gask, and the Blair Oliphant family now own the castle. Laurence Oliphant was an aide-de-camp to Bonnie Prince Charlie; and Caroline Oliphant, using the pen-name Mrs Bogan of Bogan, wrote many ballads, including 'Charlie is my Darling' and 'Will ye no come back again?'

Open by appointment only.
Tel: 01250 873155   Fax: 01250 873155

Ardchattan Priory

Off A828, 6.5 miles NE of Oban, Argyll.
His Scot   (map ref: 4J)

Set in a peaceful location, Ardchattan Priory, a Valliscaulian establishment dedicated to St Modan, was founded in 1231 by Duncan MacDougall. Robert the Bruce held a parliament here in 1309, but the lands passed to the Campbells of Cawdor in 1602. The buildings were burnt in 1644 by Alasdair Colkitto MacDonald, and again in 1654 by Cromwell's forces. Colin Campbell of Glenure, murdered in 1752, is buried here – the events surrounding his death feature in the novel *Kidnapped* by Robert Louis Stevenson.

Part of the church, used by the parish until 1731 but now ruinous, is in the care of Historic Scotland and houses 16th-century carved grave slabs and an early Christian carved wheel cross. Other priory buildings were incorporated into a mansion, which was altered and enlarged in the 1840s, and is still occupied by the Campbells. A fine four-acre garden features herbaceous borders, roses, sorbus and many varieties of hebe.

Ardchattan is said to be haunted by the ghost of a nun. The story goes that she was the lover of one of the monks, and during a nocturnal visit suffocated in her hiding place.

Ruins of church open all reasonable times; house NOT open; gardens open Apr-Oct daily 9.00-18.00, tearoom 11.00-18.00.
Facilities as gardens. Explanatory displays. Tearoom. WC. Disabled access. Car and limited coach parking. £.
Tel: 01631 750274/750204

Ardgay

In Ardgay, 1 mile SW of Bonar Bridge, Highland.
Pri/LA   (map ref: 7D)
An old house in Ardgay was thought to be haunted at one time. Reported disturbances included items being thrown about and footsteps from unoccupied areas were also heard. The occupant called in the local priest, and he stayed in the bedroom where the activity was centred. Here he is said to have witnessed the apparition of a woman clothed in black, and to have exorcised the ghost. It was believed that a servant at the house had become pregnant, and when the baby was born, she had suffocated it and hid its body in a chest of drawers in the room.

Ardincaple Castle

Off A814, W of Helensburgh, Dunbartonshire.
Pri/LA   (map ref: 6L)
Ardincaple Castle, a sprawling mansion which incorporated part of an ancient stronghold, was mostly demolished in 1957. It was a property of the MacAulays from the 13th century until 1767, when it was acquired by the Campbells, then the Colquhouns of Luss.
   Ardincaple reputedly had a brownie.

Ardnadam

On A815, 1.5 miles N of Dunoon, Argyll.
Pri/LA   (map ref: 5L)
A house at Ardnadam was allegedly haunted by the apparition of an old man, dressed in white trousers and shirt, and a red turban. There were also reports of the sounds of heavy objects being pulled over the floor of the attic when it was empty. The story goes that the house had been occupied by an old soldier, who served for many years in India and often wore a turban. He is said to have shot himself in the attic after piling furniture up against the door.

Ardoe House Hotel

Off B9077, Banchory Devenick, Aberdeenshire.
Pri/LA   (map ref: 11G)
Commanding a magnificent view of the River Dee and open country, Ardoe House Hotel is a castellated mansion dating from 1879 and now used as a luxury hotel.
   It is reputedly haunted by a 'White Lady', said to be the apparition of Katherine Ogston. She was the wife of Alexander Milne Ogston, who bought the property in 1839 – he was involved in the manufacture of soap. A portrait of Katherine

hangs above the main stair of the building, and it was here that in 1990 the apparition was reported before vanishing at the main entrance.

An alternative version of the story is that ghost is that of a daughter of a previous owner, who was raped and became pregnant. She despaired and killed the child and herself.

Hotel – open all year.
71 rooms. Restaurant and bar. Conferences and banquets. Parking. $$-$$$$.
Tel: 01224 867355   Fax: 01224 861283

Ardrossan Castle

Off A78, in Ardrossan, Ayrshire.
Ruin or site   (map ref: 5M)

Standing on a hill overlooking the town, Ardrossan Castle is a ruinous ancient stronghold of the Barclay family. William Wallace captured the castle from the English during the Wars of Independence, slew the garrison and piled their bodies into the basement: the episode afterwards known as 'Wallace's Larder'. Wallace's ghost is still reputedly seen here on stormy nights.

The castle was acquired then rebuilt by Sir John Montgomery, who fought at the Battle of Otterburn in 1388, capturing Harry 'Hotspur' Percy. The family later became Earls of Eglinton, and sheltered here in 1528 when their castle at Eglinton was burnt by the Cunninghams. Ardrossan was then abandoned and became ruinous, and may be in a dangerous condition – not the least from all the empty drink cans and bottles.

Open all year – view from exterior.
Parking Nearby.

Ardvreck Castle

Off A837, 1.5 miles NW of Inchnadamph, Highland.
Ruin or site   (map ref: 5C)

In a lonely and picturesque situation, Ardvreck Castle consists of a ruined square keep, with a distinctive round stair-turret which is corbelled out to square at the top. The lands were a property of the MacLeods of Assynt from the 13th century, and they built the present castle about 1490. It was here that in 1650 the Marquis of Montrose took refuge, but he was turned over to the Covenanters, and executed in Edinburgh. The castle was sacked in 1672, and replaced by nearby Calda House, itself burnt out in 1760 and never restored.

Ardvreck is reputed to be haunted by the daughter of a MacLeod chief, who threw herself out of one of the windows. The story goes that the chief wanted a grander castle than he could afford, and the devil offered to build him one, but the price was his soul. MacLeod offered the hand of his daughter in marriage instead, which the devil accepted, and the wedding took place. When the poor girl found out who her bridegroom was, she climbed to the top of the castle and in despair threw herself to her death. Her weeping apparition has reportedly been witnessed.

Another ghost is said to be a tall grey-clothed man, who is thought to be friendly but only speaks Gaelic.

Access at all reasonable times.
Parking Nearby.

Arnish Moor, Lewis

Off A859, 2.5 miles SE of Stornoway, Lewis.
Ruin or site   (map ref: 2C)
The main road between Stornoway and Harris, where it crossed bleak moorland at Arnish, was long believed to be haunted. The apparition of a man, wearing a coat and woollen stockings in the manner of the 18th century, was reputedly often seen on the road, even as late as the 1960s. It was thought that a young man had been murdered here by a friend sometime in the 18th century, and his remains buried on the moor to conceal the crime. The remains of a man were found in 1964, near where the hauntings took place, dressed in a similar fashion to the reported apparition.

Ashintully Castle

Off B950, 2 miles NE of Kirkmichael, Perthshire.
Pri/LA   (map ref: 8I)
Ashintully Castle was built by the Spalding family in the 16th-century, and is a tall L-plan tower house, later extended and remodelled.

During the ownership of the Spaldings, the property is said to have been held by Jean, a daughter of the house, in her own right. Her ruthless uncle, however,

wanted Ashintully for himself. He visited Jean, and in one of the castle chambers slew her by slitting her throat; he also murdered her servant, whose body he hid up the large chimney. Jean's ghost, dressed in a green gown, then began to haunt the castle. She is said to have been seen at the family burial ground, beside her memorial, and her footsteps have also been reported in the castle.

Two other ghosts are recorded as haunting the vicinity. One was Crooked Davie, a messenger killed when it was thought he had not delivered a message – which in fact he had; the other a tinker, hanged for trespassing, who cursed the family.

The property passed to the Rutherfords in 1750, and the castle is still occupied.

Atholl Palace Hotel, Pitlochry
Off A9, SE of Pitlochry, Perthshire.
Pri/LA   (map ref: 8I)
Standing in 48 acres of wooded parkland with magnificent views over the Perthshire countryside, the Atholl Palace is a sprawling castellated hotel, built in 1875 as a hydropathic establishment. It is said to be haunted by a 'Green Lady', and her apparition has – reputedly – often been seen by staff and guests in one of the rooms.

Hotel – open all year.
78 rooms with ensuite facilities. Restaurant. Outdoor heated pool, and other sports facilities. Conferences and meetings. Parking. $$.
Tel: 01796 472400   Fax: 01796 473036

Auchinvole House
Off B802 or B8023, 0.5 miles S of Kilsyth, Lanarkshire.
Pri/LA   (map ref: 7L)
Auchinvole House was thought to be haunted by a ghost at one time, and the apparition of a lady was said to have been seen at an upstairs window. The story goes that her lover had been treacherously murdered, and she gazed out to where he was buried. The house incorporated an L-plan tower house, later altered and extended, and dated from the 16th century.

Auchlochan House

Off B7078, 1.5 miles S of Lesmahagow, Lanarkshire.
Pri/LA   (map ref: 8N)
The house was said to be haunted by a 'Black Lady', the beautiful black wife of one of the Browns of Auchlochan.

Auchnarrow

Off B9008, 2 miles S of Tomnavoulin, Moray.
Pri/LA   (map ref: 9F)
The farm of Auchnarrow reportedly had a brownie called Maggie Moloch, or 'Hairy Meg'.

Aultsigh

On A82, Loch Ness, 10 miles NW of Fort Augustus, Highland.
Pri/LA   (map ref: 6G)
Standing on a picturesque spot on the shore of Loch Ness, the former Aultsigh Hotel, now the Loch Ness Youth Hostel, is reputedly haunted.

It is recorded that two brothers, Malcolm and Alasdair Macdonnell, desired the same attractive lass Annie Fraser. Annie and Alasdair were together on the hill behind the building when they were surprised by Malcolm, who was furious about the couple's meeting. He attacked and killed his brother, then strangled or stabbed the unfortunate Annie and hid her body under the floor in a then abandoned room of what is now the Youth Hostel. He gathered together his belongings and fled, but drowned crossing the loch.

The room in which Annie's remains were concealed is reputedly plagued by ghostly footsteps, crossing and recrossing the floor – although the present building was only completed in 1930. Her apparition has also reportedly been witnessed, both at the hostel and in the neighbouring countryside.

Youth Hostel – closed Nov–mid Mar.
Tel: 01320 351274   Fax: 01320 351274

Avoch

In Avoch, on A832, Highland.
Pri/LA   (map ref: 7E)
The phantom of a young boy was reported in an old house in the village of Avoch. The apparition was allegedly witnessed in one of the bedrooms, and toys and other items were moved around when nobody had been present in the room. The ghost is said to be a previous owner's son, who fell to his death from the bedroom window while sleepwalking.

Balcomie Castle

Off A917, 1.5 miles NE of Crail, Fife.
Pri/LA   (map ref: 10K)
The ghost of a young man is said to haunt Balcomie. No apparition has been reported, but manifestations reportedly consist of the sound of whistling. The ghost is said to be of a lad starved to death here because he would not stop whistling.

The lands of Balcomie belonged in 1375 to a John de Balcomie, although the castle dates from the 16th century, by which time the property had passed to the Learmonths of Clatto. Mary of Guise stayed here on her way to marry James V.

The building is now used as a farmhouse.

Baldoon Castle

Off A746, 1.5 miles SE of Wigtown, Dumfries & Galloway.
Ruin or site   (map ref: 7Q)
Little remains of Baldoon Castle, a stronghold of the Dunbars, but the ruins are said to be haunted by the apparition of a woman in a blood-stained wedding dress. The ghost is said to date from events in 1669.

Janet Dalrymple of Carscreugh was in love with Archibald Rutherford, son of Lord Rutherford, but he was poor and her parents were against their marriage. They chose Sir David Dunbar of Baldoon, and persuaded Janet to marry him. All was not well, however, although there are different versions of what happened next. Janet was either murdered on her wedding night, after having tried to slay her new husband, or died insane soon afterwards. Her ghost is said to be seen here on the anniversary of her death, 12 September. Sir Walter Scott's *Bride of Lammermoor* includes events based here.

Dunbar recovered sufficiently to marry a daughter of the Montgomery Earl of Eglinton.

Balgonie Castle

Off A911, 3.5 miles E of Glenrothes, Fife.
Pri/LA   (map ref: 9L)
Balgonie Castle is haunted by several ghosts. The fine building consists of a 14th-century keep within a courtyard enclosing ranges of buildings.

The original castle was built by the Sibbalds, but passed to the Lundies, then the Leslies; and famous visitors include James IV, Mary Queen of Scots and Rob Roy MacGregor.

One owner was Alexander Leslie, who died here in 1661. Leslie was captured at Alyth in Angus after the Battle of Dunbar in 1650, while on the losing side against Cromwell, and was imprisoned in the Tower of London – only the

intervention of the Queen of Sweden saved his life. An apparition seen here has been identified as his ghost.

The most haunted part of the castle is the grand hall, where ghostly voices and apparitions have been witnessed. A 'Green Lady', Green Jeanie, thought to be the spirit of one of the Lundies, has been seen in one of the ranges in recent times, and was recorded in 1842 as being a 'well-known ghost'.

The apparition of a 17th-century soldier has been witnessed in the courtyard, said to have one arm outstretched as if opening a door. An outhouse once stood on the spot where this ghost appears. This apparition is also recorded as being seen walking through the gateway of the castle.

The sounds of a spectral dog have also been reported, as well as other phantoms, including a hooded figure and a medieval apparition.

Open daily 10.00-17.00 daily all year, unless hired for a private function, including Christmas &
New Year.
Guided tours. Picnic area. Disabled access to ground floor. Car and coach parking.
Weddings. £.
Tel: 01592 750119   Fax: 01592 753103

Ballachulish House

Off A82, Ballachulish, Highlands.
Pri/LA   (map ref: 4I)
Ballachulish House, dating from the 18th century, replaced an earlier building which was torched in 1746. It was a property of the Stewarts of Appin, and it was from here that Campbell of Glenorchy ordered the start of the infamous Massacre of Glencoe in 1692. The town was a centre of slate mining in the 19th century, which at one time employed over 600 people.

The house is believed, by some, to be haunted by several ghosts. One is thought to be the apparition of one of the Stewarts of Appin, who rides up to the door and then vanishes; the sounds of his horse have also reportedly been heard on the drive to the house. Other ghosts are said to be of a tinker; and an apparition which walked through a wall.

Ballechin

Off A827, 4 miles E of Aberfeldy, Perthshire.
Pri/LA (map ref: 8J)

Ballechin, a mansion of 1806, was partly demolished because of dry rot in 1963. Much is now ruinous, although a wing of 1884 survives and is still occupied. It was a property of the Stewarts until sold to the Honeyman family in 1932.

The reports of a ghost here caused much controversy. The mansion was said to be haunted by the spirit of Major Robert Stewart, who died in 1876. After his death the inexplicable sounds of voices, footsteps, banging, rapping, groans and shrieks and other noises were heard; and are said to have continued for decades. In the 1890s one family renting the house for a year reputedly left early because of the hauntings, as had a governess; and the house was psychically investigated a few years later, when noises and apparitions were recorded. This investigation caused a furore, as the then owner had not been told, and the reports of activity were refuted. Later occurrences of noises were reported, however.

Another phantom is alleged to be a 'Grey Lady', the apparition of a nun, which has reportedly been seen on the drive near the mansion and in a nearby cottage.

Ballindalloch Castle

Off A95, 7.5 miles SW of Charlestown of Aberlour, Moray.
Pri/LA (map ref: 9F)

Set in fine gardens and grounds, Ballindalloch Castle is an impressive 16th-century Z-plan tower house, altered and extended in later centuries to form a fine sprawling mansion. Several ghosts have been recorded in the castle and in the vicinity.

A 'Green Lady' has reputedly been seen in the dining room, and reports of a 'Pink Lady' are also recorded. Another ghost is said to be that of General James Grant, who died in 1806. Grant was very proud of the improvements he had made to the estate, and his phantom is said to ride around the lands every night to survey his achievement. He is then said to go into the wine cellar.

Another ghost, reportedly seen at the nearby Bridge of Avon, is a that of a girl believed to have been unlucky in love.

The lands had passed to the Grants by 1499, and the castle was looted and burned by the Marquis of Montrose in 1645 after the Battle of Inverlochy. The castle was rebuilt, and now houses a good collection of 17th-century Spanish paintings.

Open Easter–Sep 10.00-17.00.
Explanatory panels. Gift shop. Tearoom. Famous breed of Aberdeen Angus cattle. Disabled access to ground floor and grounds; WC. Garden and grounds. Car and coach parking. £.
Tel: 01807 500206   Fax: 01807 500210
Email: ballindalloch@great-houses-scotland.co.uk   Web: www.great-houses-scotland

Balnagown Castle

Off A9, 8 miles NE of Alness, Highland.
Pri/LA   (map ref: 7D)
Balnagown Castle, a much-altered tower house, dates from the 14th century. It was a property the Ross family until 1978, who were an unruly lot in medieval times.

Alexander, 8th laird, terrorised the neighbouring properties until imprisonment in Tantallon Castle curtailed his activities. George, his son, was accused of murder and with helping Francis Stewart, 5th Earl of Bothwell, who – among other things – was accused of trying to sink James VI's ship by witchcraft. Ross's sister, Katherine – wife of Robert Munro of Foulis – was actually tried for witchcraft, incantation, sorcery and poisoning. Some of her friends were found guilty and executed, but at her own trial she packed the jury with her own people, the accusations were judged unproven, and she was freed.

It is not, however, one of the Ross family who haunts Balnagown. 'Black' Andrew Munro was a man believed guilty of many dastardly deeds. He was finally brought to account in 1522, and hanged from one of the windows off the Red Corridor of the castle. His ghost is said to haunt Balnagown, and to manifest itself to women, who he had liked to abuse in life: his female servants were made to thresh corn naked. Sounds of footsteps from unoccupied areas have also been recorded.

The castle is also thought to be haunted by a 'Grey Lady', the ghost of a young woman, clad in a grey dress with auburn hair and green eyes: a murdered 'Scottish princess'. Her apparition is said to have appeared in the dining room, then walked to the drawing room, and there vanished.

Both ghosts are recorded as having been witnessed in the 20th century.

Balvenie Castle

Off A941, N of town of Dufftown, Moray.
His Scot   (map ref: 10F)

In a pleasant peaceful location, Balvenie Castle is a large ruinous courtyard castle, dating from the 13th to 17th centuries. The Comyns has a stronghold here, which was taken by the forces of Robert the Bruce in 1308. Balvenie was later held by the Douglases, the Stewarts, the Innes family, then the Duffs.

Mary, Queen of Scots, visited in 1562. The castle was garrisoned during Covenanting times and the Jacobite Risings.

The apparition of a woman, a 'White Lady', has reportedly been seen here. The phantom of a groom and two horses, with other disturbances, was apparently witnessed by a visitor in 1994.

Open Apr-Sep daily 9.30-18.30, last ticket sold 18.00.
Gift shop. Picnic area. Group concessions. Car parking. £.
Tel: 01340 820121

Balwearie Castle

Off B925, 2.5 miles SW of Kirkcaldy, Fife.
Ruin or site   (map ref: 9L)

Balwearie Castle is a ruinous castle, dating from the 15th century, which may stand on the site of an earlier stronghold. It was a property of the Scotts until the 1690s, and may have been home to Sir Michael Scott. Scott is said to have been born at Aikwood in the Borders; and to have studied at Oxford, Toledo and Padua, after which he became known as 'the Wizard' because of his alleged supernatural powers. He died about 1250, and is associated with Glenluce and Melrose Abbeys: Melrose is where he is said to be buried.

The ghost story relates to a later owner. Thomas Scott of Balwearie, justice clerk, died in 1539, and on the night of his death his apparition – with a company of devils – is said to have appeared to James V in his bed chamber at Linlithgow Palace. Scott apparently told the king that he was damned to everlasting hell for serving him.

Banchory

Off A93, Banchory, Aberdeenshire.
Pri/LA   (map ref: 11G)
The old part of the town is believed by some to be haunted by the apparition of a monk, which is said to have been seen in recent times. The spectre may be associated with the old monastery founded by St Ternan about 430. The town had long associations with the saint – he is reputedly buried at Banchory – and his head, bound books of gospels and *Ronnecht*, a bell gifted by the Pope, were preserved here, although they have now been lost.

Barbreck House

Off A816, 4 miles N of Kilmartin, Argyll.
Pri/LA   (map ref: 4K)
The vicinity of Barbreck House, an 18th-century mansion of the Campbells, is said to be haunted by an apparition of a young woman dressed and hooded in plaid and tartan, sitting on a rock. The apparition reputedly fades away and then disappears should anyone attempt to approach.

Barcaldine Castle

Off A828, 4 miles N of Connel, Argyll.
Pri/LA   (map ref: 4J)
Set in a magnificent situation near the sea, Barcaldine Castle is a restored L-plan tower house, which dates from the 16th century. It was – and is – a property of the Campbells. The building was ruinous at one time, but has been completely restored.

In December 1691, MacIan, chief of the MacDonalds of Glencoe, was held at Barcaldine for 24 hours by government troops. MacIan was on his way to Inveraray, after having wrongly gone to Fort William, to swear an oath of allegiance to William and Mary. The delay contributed to his late arrival at Inveraray – the oath had to be taken before the end of the year – and the subsequent massacre of Glencoe, which took place on 13 February 1692.

John Campbell of Barcaldine tried James Stewart for the murder of Sir Colin Campbell of Glenure in 1752, and had him hanged – most of the jury was made up of Campbells. The episode is the background to Robert Louis Stevenson's novel *Kidnapped*.

A 'Blue Lady', an apparition of Harriet Campbell who died around the turn of the century, has reputedly been seen in the castle, and it is said that a phantom piano can be heard on windy nights.

Open May-Sep, daily 11.00-17.30; other times by appt. Accommodation available.
Explanatory displays. Gift shop. Tearoom. Garden. Car parking. £.
Tel: 01631 720598   Fax: 01631 720529

Barnbougle Castle

Off B924, 2.5 miles E of South Queensferry, Edinburgh.
Pri/LA   (map ref: 9L)
Standing in the picturesque grounds of Dalmeny House, Barnbougle Castle dates from the 16th and 17th centuries, although there was an ancient stronghold on the site.

Barnbougle was held by the Mowbrays from the 12th century until 1615, and the story dates from their ownership. A ghostly hound is said to haunt the grounds of Barnbougle, and appears howling shortly before the Laird of Barnbougle is to die. The story dates from the time of the Crusades and Sir Roger Mowbray: this is reputedly the origin of 'Hound Point', just to the north-west of Barnbougle, and now a tanker berth.

In 1662 Barnbougle was acquired by the Primrose family, and in 1815 they built the far more comfortable and impressive Dalmeny House. Barnbougle was allowed to fall into ruin, but was restored around 1880 by Archibald Philip Primrose, 5th Earl of Rosebery, who was Prime Minister from 1894-5.

Dalmeny House: Open Jul-Aug, Sun-Tue 14.00-17.00.
[Dalmeny House] Guided tours. Tearoom. Disabled access and WC. Car and coach parking. Group concessions by special arrangement. ££. Party rate over 20 (£).
Tel: 0131 331 1888   Fax: 0131 331 1788   Email: events@dalmeny.co.uk

Bedlay Castle

Off A80, 3 miles SE of Kirkintilloch, Lanarkshire.
Pri/LA   (map ref: 7L)

Bedlay Castle is said to be haunted by the ghost of Bishop Cameron, who died in suspicious circumstances about 1350, having been found face down in a nearby loch.

Hauntings in the house, including mysterious footsteps and the apparition of a large bearded man, were recorded in the 1970s. In the 1880s a priest had been called in to exorcise the ghost, during a period of increased activity, but his attempts do not appear to have been successful.

The castle, an L-plan tower house, was built by the Boyds of Kilmarnock in the 16th century on the site of an older stronghold, and the property later passed to the Campbells. The Campbells built a mausoleum in the garden, and subsequently there were reports of apparitions around the castle. The mausoleum was relocated to Lambhill, and the ghosts are said to have followed.

Ben Macdui

Off A9, 10 miles SE of Aviemore, Cairngorm Mountains, Highland.
Ruin or site   (map ref: 8G)

The mountain and surrounding area are reputedly haunted by the 'Grey Man of Ben Macdui'. The mountain, one of the highest in Britain, is situated in the Cairngorms and rises to a height of well over 4000 feet (1309 metres). There are many reports of unexplained footsteps following climbers when the hill is swathed in mist. Other stories are of a huge grey apparition, said to be ten feet in height. Reports of both footsteps and the apparition have been recorded many times from 1890 until recent times.

Accessible weather permitting – long walk!

Benholm Castle

Off A92, 2 miles SW of Inchbervie, Aber-deenshire.
Ruin or site (map ref: 11H)

Standing above a deep ravine, Benholm Castle consists of a ruinous tower, dating from the 15th century, and a later mansion. The castle was built by the Lundies but later passed to the Ogilvies, then the Keith Earls Marischal and the Scotts.

The castle is believed to be haunted.

Berwick Castle

Off A1, Berwick-upon-Tweed, England (!).
Ruin or site (map ref: 12M)

Although now in England, Berwick was an important Scottish burgh by 1120, and had its own strong fortress. In 1296, at the onset of the Wars of Independence, it was seized by Edward I, and 16000 men, women and children were slaughtered by the English. The 'Ragman Roll' was signed here, the list of the many Scots, nobles and churchmen, who paid homage to Edward. Isabella Duff, Countess of Buchan, who had crowned Robert the Bruce – although she was married to the Comyn Earl of Buchan, an enemy of Bruce – and was imprisoned for four years in a cage hung from the castle walls. One story relates that the ruins are haunted by the ghost of Edward I.

The Scots recaptured the burgh and castle in 1318, and it was fought over for many years until in 1482 when taken by the English for the last time. Much of the old castle was destroyed when the railway was built, and the station stands on the site of the great hall.

Biel

Off B6370, 3.5 miles W of Dunbar, East Lothian.
Pri/LA (map ref: 10L)

Biel was a property of the Hamiltons, who were made Lords Belhaven in 1647. John Hamilton, 2nd Lord Belhaven, was imprisoned for opposing the succession of James VII, and strongly opposed to the Union of Parliaments. He died in 1708.

The mansion dates mostly from the 19th century, but incorporates the basement of a 14th century castle. The grounds are said to be haunted by the wife of the 3rd Lord Belhaven, who himself died in 1721. The ghost, the 'White Lady of Biel', is thought to be the apparition of Anne Bruce of Earlshall. The house is still occupied, but has passed from the Hamiltons.

Big House

Off A836, 14 miles W of Thurso, Sutherland.
Pri/LA   (map ref: 8A)
The large symmetrical mansion, dating from the 18th century with later additions, was a property of the MacKays of Big House from the 1750s. It is said to be haunted by a 'Green Lady', the spirit of a woman who hanged herself in one of the bedrooms at the end of the 19th century.

Blantyre Priory

Off B758, 1.5 miles N of Blantyre, Lanarkshire.
Pri/LA   (map ref: 7M)
Perched on a steep bank of the Clyde opposite Bothwell Castle, little remains of the Augustinian priory, founded around 1240 by Patrick, Earl of Dunbar. The property passed to Walter Stewart of Minto in 1599 after the Reformation, the family having been Commendators, lay administrators of the priory. The Stewarts were made Lords Blantyre in 1606.

One of the family was Frances Stewart, Duchess of Richmond and Lennox, who was the model for Britannia seen on British coins. She was responsible for changing the name of Lethington Castle to Lennoxlove.

The Stewarts lived in the priory, but by 1606 Lady Blantyre had left with her daughters, leaving Lord Blantyre in the building. The reason given was the ghostly activities and unexplained noises that plagued the household at night.

Borthwick Castle

Off A7, 2 miles SE of Gorebridge, Midlothian.
Pri/LA   (map ref: 10M)
One of the most impressive castles in Scotland, Borthwick Castle is a magnificent tall U-plan tower house, built by Sir William Borthwick in 1430. The tomb of Borthwick and his wife are in nearby Borthwick Church – which is open to the public.

Mary, Queen of Scots, and Bothwell stayed here in 1567, but Mary had to escape, disguised as a pageboy, when they were besieged in the castle. It is recorded that her apparition, garbed as a man, has been seen here.

The Red Room in the castle is said to be haunted by the ghost of Ann Grant, a local girl, who had been made pregnant by one of the Borthwick lords. He apparently murdered the unfortunate lass to hide his dallying. Her ghost has reputedly been seen in this room, and other manifestations include doors closing by themselves. Her ghost is believed to be somewhat hostile to men. One of the later castle occupants had the room exorcised, but seemingly with little success.

Hotel: open mid-March to January 2 and to non-residents. Borthwick Church open daily all year.
10 rooms with ensuite facilities. Castle may be booked for exclusive use. Conferences,
weddings, banquets and meetings. Not suitable for disabled. Garden. $$-$$$$+.
Tel: 01875 820514   Fax: 01875 821702
Email: No   Web: No

Braco Castle

Off B8033, 6 miles N of Dunblane, Stirlingshire.
Pri/LA   (map ref: 8K)
The old part of Braco Castle is said to be haunted, and doors to open by themselves. The castle dates from the 16th century, although there are later extensions and alterations, and was long a property of the Grahams.

Braemar Castle

On A93, 0.5 miles NE of Braemar, Kincardine & Deeside.
Pri/LA   (map ref: 8G)
Braemar Castle is an L-plan tower house, dating from the 17th century, with later artillery defences. It was built by the Erskine Earls of Mar, and saw action

in the Jacobite Risings. It was burnt in 1689 by John Farquharson of Inverey, the 'Black Colonel', who is said to haunt the tower. John, 11th Earl of Mar, led the 1715 Jacobite Rising. The castle has a massive iron yett, and an unlit and unventilated pit prison, which measures just 12 feet by 6 feet.

The property passed to the Farquharsons of Invercauld, and in 1748 the tower was turned into a barracks. The Farquharsons reoccupied and renovated the castle in the early 19th century.

Another ghost story dates from the 1880s. The tower is said to be haunted by the blonde-haired ghost of a pretty young woman. A newly wed bride – for reasons which are not clear – believed herself abandoned by her husband, although he had actually only gone hunting. The poor woman despaired and committed suicide in the building.

A sighting of the ghost was reported in 1987, and it is believed she only appears to recently married couples. Ghostly footsteps, the light tread of a woman, have also reputedly heard.

Open Easter-Oct daily 10.00-18.00 except closed Fri.
Many interesting rooms. Guided tours. Explanatory sheets. Gift shop. WC. Picnic area. Car and coach parking. Group concessions. £.
Tel: 01339 741219/741217   Fax: same as telephone
Email: invercauld@aol.com

Brahan Castle

Off A835, 3.5 miles SW of Dingwall, Highland.
Ruin or site   (map ref: 6F)

Once a splendid building, Brahan Castle was the seat of the Mackenzies of Brahan, Earls of Seaforth, but was demolished in the 1950s.

The Mackenzies lost everything as foretold by the Brahan Seer, Kenneth Mackenzie, so called because the Mackenzies of Brahan were his patrons. The episode dates back to about 1670. Isabella, 3rd Countess of Seaforth, wanted to know why her husband remained in Paris, and consulted Kenneth. She was furious when she was told that her husband had been dallying with a French woman, accused Kenneth of witchcraft, and ordered him to be burnt in a barrel of tar on Chanonry Point. A similarly ungrateful response to unwelcome news was suffered by Kitty Rankie at Abergeldie.

Before he died, presumably in some discomfort, Kenneth prophesied that the last Mackenzie chief would follow his sons to the grave, deaf and dumb, and that one of his daughters would kill the other. This all seems to have come true: the last chief did become deaf through illness and was finally too weak to speak after seeing his four sons predecease him. His eldest daughter succeeded him, but a carriage she was driving, near Brahan, overturned and killed her sister.

A ford of the Conon River was reputedly frequented by a kelpie or water sprite, who tried to drown the unwary.

Broadford Hotel

On A850, Broadford, Skye.
Pri/LA   (map ref: 3F)
The hotel is said to be haunted by the apparition of a housekeeper, and in some of the rooms a 'presence' has been reported. The apparition is recorded as being shadowy and ill-defined, like a mist. Other manifestations include the moving of objects, including ladders and lamps.

After the Battle of Culloden in 1746, Bonnie Prince Charlie was a fugitive from the forces of Butcher Cumberland for some months. He was sheltered on Skye after help from Flora MacDonald and aided by the chief of the Mackinnons. As a reward, Charlie gave the chief the recipe for Drambuie, a whisky liqueur, although the original recipe apparently should have been for cognac. This event is said to have taken place at the hotel.

Hotel – closed Nov-Mar. Open to non-residents.
Tel: 01471 822204   Fax: 01471 822414

Brodick Castle

Off A841, 2 miles N of Brodick, Arran (ferry enquiries 01475 650100).
NTS   (map ref: 5N)
Brodick Castle, an ancient stronghold but much extended and remodelled in later centuries, was long a property of the Hamiltons. It has a long and turbulent history, being sacked on several occasions, and was occupied by Cromwell's troops in the 1650s. In more peaceful times, extensive additions were made in 1844 by the architect James Gillespie Graham, when the 11th Duke married Princess Marie of Baden. In 1958 Brodick was taken over by The National Trust for Scotland.

A 'Grey Lady', clad in grey with a large white collar, is said to haunt the older part of the castle, her spirit possibly that of one of three women starved to death in the dungeons around 1700 because they had plague. Another version is that a servant lass committed suicide at the Old Quay below the castle after becoming pregnant to one of the Cromwellian garrison. Whatever the story, her apparition is said to have been seen many times.

The spectre of a man dressed in a green velvet coat and light-coloured breeches has allegedly been witnessed in the 17th-century library.

A white deer is said to be seen when members of the resident family are near death, and this occurrence has been recorded several times.

Castle open daily 1 Apr (or Good Friday if earlier)-Oct 11.00-16.30, last admission 16.00; Jul-Aug daily 11.00-17.00, last admission 16.30 restaurant 11.00-17.00; reception centre & shop 10.00-17.00; garden & country park open all year 9.30-sunset; Goatfell open all year.
Collections of furniture, porcelain, pictures and silver. Gift shop. Licensed restaurant. WC. Gardens and country park, ice house, summer house and adventure playground. Nature trail and access to Goatfell. Disabled WC and access. *££.*
Tel: 01770 302202   Fax: 01770 302312

Brodie Castle

Off A96, 4.5 miles W of Forres, Moray.
NTS   (map ref: 8E)
Brodie Castle, on land held by the Brodie family from 1160, consists of a large 16th-century Z-plan tower house, with extensive additions. The castle was renovated in 1980 after passing to The National Trust for Scotland, and the garden has a fine daffodil collection.

An apparition of a woman is said to have been witnessed in the nursery room in 1992.

Disturbances, including footsteps and other noises coming from a locked study, were also reported on the night that Hugh, 23rd Brodie of Brodie, died in 1889, but nothing has been recorded since then.

The skeleton of a small child was found when a turnpike stair, from one of the corner turrets, was being renovated. The bones are kept in a glass-fronted cabinet in the Charter Room.

Open daily 1 Apr (or Good Friday if earlier)-Sep, wknds in Oct, Mon-Fri 11.00-17.30, Sun 13.30-17.30, last admission 16.30. Tearoom closes 16.30. Grounds open all year 9.30-sunset.
Collection of paintings and furniture. Guided tours available. Explanatory displays. Gift shop. Tearoom. WC. Picnic area. Garden and adventure playground. Car and coach parking. Group concessions. Disabled facilities including Braille guides. *££.*
Tel: 01309 641371   Fax: 01309 641600

Broomhill

Off B7078, 0.5 miles west of Larkhall, Lanarkshire.
Ruin or site   (map ref: 8M)
Nothing remains of the mansion of Broomhill, a property of the Hamiltons from 1473. The house later passed to the McNeil-Hamiltons of Raploch, but was demolished after a fire in 1943.

Broomhill is reputedly haunted by a 'Black Lady', seen in both the house and in the area. The story goes that a beautiful Indian woman, either a servant or princess, disappeared about 1900, and may have been murdered. She was believed to be the mistress of Captain Henry McNeil-Hamilton, who died in 1924.

The house featured in a television programme 'Tonight', with Fyfe Robertson, in the 1960s, when an exorcism was performed. Her ghost, however, is also said to have been witnessed in nearby Applebank Inn, a public house, after a lintel from Broomhill was used in an extension. Items are reported to been mysteriously moved around the inn, while others have been hidden.

Other ghosts in the area include a phantom coach and horses, and the apparition of a young lad fishing.

Applebank Inn open all year round.

Buchanan Castle

Off B807, 0.5 miles W of Drymen, Stirlingshire.
Pri/LA   (map ref: 7L)
Standing by the golf course, Buchanan Castle, a huge castellated ruin, incorporates an old castle of the Buchanans, which passed to the Grahams in 1682.

Buchanan is reputed to be haunted. Manifestations are said to have consisted of an unexplained gasping sound, heard during summer nights.

Buckholm Tower

Off A7, 1 mile NW of Galashiels, Borders.
Ruin or site   (map ref: 10N)
Buckholm, a ruinous tower house built by the Pringles in the 16th century, and has a gruesome story associated with it.

During the Covenanting troubles of the late 17th century, the laird of the time was a cruel man and spent his time persecuting those attending illegal conventicles – the open-air services of Covenanters. Pringle captured several Covenanters, took them back to the dungeon at Buckholm, and there impaled them on hooks hanging from the ceiling – the hooks are still said to ooze ghostly blood.

Pringle, however, was cursed by the wife of one of his victims, and afterwards lived in great terror, as if pursued by ghostly hounds. Pringle's ghost has reputedly be seen running from a pack of dogs on the anniversary of his death, and screams and cries heard from the dungeon of the tower.

Busta House

Off A910, 10 miles NW of Lerwick, Shetland.
Pri/LA   (map ref: 11B)
With its own harbour in a quiet and picturesque location, Busta (pronounced 'Boosta') House is a tall harled mansion dating from 1588, then extended in 1714 and 1984. It was a property of the Giffords of Busta.

Thomas Gifford, laird in the 1700s, was a prosperous merchant. In 1748, however, his four sons were tragically drowned. The only heir, Gideon, was the son of a maid, Barbara Pitcairn, who had been secretly married to John, the eldest son. Although Gideon as heir was accepted, Barbara was not, and died at the early age of 35 in the house of a poor relation. It is said that her sad ghost haunts the building, searching for her son.

Other manifestations include the sound of footsteps coming from the 'Foula Room' when unoccupied, as well as lights and other electrical equipment turning themselves off and on.

Sightings in the 'Linga Room' of the apparition of a grey-haired woman, in a brown dress and lace cap, have also been reported by several guests.

Hotel – open all year.
Accommodation with ensuite facilities. Refreshments and fine food. Ideal location for touring, wildlife, archaeology and history and walking. Parking. $$.
Tel: 01806 522506   Fax: 01806 522588
Email: busta@mes.co.uk   Web: www.mes.co.uk/busta

Byre Theatre, St Andrews

Abbey Street, St Andrews, Fife.
Pri/LA   (map ref: 10K)
The theatre was converted from a byre in 1933, but demolished in 1970 and a new theatre was built. This newer building was itself closed in 1996 and will not open again until 2000.

The theatre was said to be haunted by a ghost known as 'Charlie'. Manifestations consisted of cold feelings on the stairs leading to the Green

Room, and the impression that a person was pushing past when nobody was apparently present.

Theatre.
174 seats. Bar and cafe. Parking.
Tel: 01334 476288

Caisteal Camus

Off A851, 3.5 miles N of Armadale, Skye.
Ruin or site   (map ref: 3G)
Standing in a picturesque location on a steep headland of the Sound of Sleat, Caisteal Camus is a very ruinous stronghold of the MacLeods, then the MacDonalds. It was abandoned about 1689.

The castle was said to be haunted by a 'Green Lady', a *gruagach*, a spirit who associated itself with the fortunes of their families. If good news was to come the *gruagach* would appear happy, but if there was bad news she would weep and look sad. The castle is also said to have had a *glaistig*, who was particularly concerned with looking after cattle.

Cameron House

Off A82, 2 miles NW of Alexandria, Dunbartonshire.
Pri/LA   (map ref: 6L)
Set in a picturesque position on the banks of Loch Lomond, Cameron House is a castellated mansion, dating mostly from 1830 and 1865, which may incorporate part of a 14th-century castle. The lands were originally held by the Lennox family, but were sold to the Smolletts in 1763. The house is now a luxury hotel and leisure centre.

One of the rooms is said to be haunted, and non-existent objects appear only to vanish when touched.

Hotel & leisure centre – open all year.
96 rooms with ensuite facilities. Restaurants. Conferences, weddings and banquets. Leisure facilities, including indoor pools. Marina. 9 hole golf course. $$$-$$$$.
Tel: 01389 755565   Fax: 01389 759522

Cameron's Inn, Aberdeen

Off 956, Little Belmont Street off Union Street, Aberdeen.
Pri/LA   (map ref: 12G)
Cameron's Inn, an old coaching inn and public house of considerable character, is believed to be haunted.

Public House – closed Sun.

Carleton Castle

Off A77, 6 miles S of Girvan,
Ayrshire.

Ruin or site (map ref: 5O)

The ruins of Carleton Castle are said to be haunted by the phantom of Sir John Cathcart. Cathcart was married several times – seven times in all – after each of his previous wives had mysteriously died or disappeared. Cathcart may have been killing them for their dowries, but finally he wed May Kennedy of Culzean, who may have been suspicious of him from the outset. When they were walking along cliffs, Cathcart tried to push May to her death, but she was ready for him, and it was only he who wound up dead on the rocks below.

Ghostly screams have been reported from the vicinity of the old castle.

Access at all reasonable times – care should be taken.

Carmelite Street, Aberdeen

Off A956, Carmelite Street, Aberdeen.

Pri/LA (map ref: 12G)

Carmelite Street runs along side the site of a Carmelite friary, founded about 1273 and dissolved in 1560 after being sacked by a mob. There are no remains, and only the street name survives. The site was being excavated before redevelopment, and human bones were found, said to date back 600 years. The publican of a nearby hostelry reported experiencing a 'strange presence' in his pub during the excavations. The apparition of a friar, an old man in a dark brown hooded robe, was reported in the adjoining shop by two witnesses

Caroline Park House, Edinburgh

Off A901, 3 miles N of Edinburgh Castle, Granton, Edinburgh.

Pri/LA (map ref: 9L)

Caroline Park, although much modified and extended in later centuries, incorporates a tower house built by Andrew Logan in 1585. The property was originally known as Royston, but passed to the Mackenzies, then the Campbell Duke of Argyll, then through Campbell's daughter – Caroline, hence the name – to the Scott Dukes of Buccleuch.

A 'Green Lady', the apparition of Lady Royston, wife of Sir James Mackenzie, younger son of Lord Tarbat, is said to haunt the house. On certain days, her phantom is reported to appear at midnight from an old well, and go to the entrance of the house, where she vanishes. She is said to then reappear in the small courtyard and ring an old bell.

A ghostly cannon ball is also said to have been witnessed several times smashing through the window of the Aurora Room. This is recorded as being a relatively common occurrence in the 1850s.

Cartland Bridge Hotel

Off A73, Glasgow Road, 1 mile NW of Lanark, Lanarkshire.
Pri/LA   (map ref: 8M)
Originally the private home of Captain James Farie of Farme, 'Baronald House' was converted into a hotel in 1962. The Farie family, who owned the house, had a seven-year-old daughter named Annie, who met with an untimely end while riding in the grounds of the house. Her ghosts has been witnessed at the hotel, and she is said to be particularly fond of the room which was once her 'Dolls Room'. Annie is buried in a private graveyard within the grounds overlooking the River Mouse. A large oil painting of Annie hangs in the Portrait Room Restaurant.

Hotel – open all year.
18 rooms with ensuite facilities. Restaurant, bars and conservatory. Weddings, conferences and meetings. Parking. $-$$.
Tel: 01555 664426   Fax: 01555 663773

Castle Cary

Off A80, 2 miles NE of Cumbernauld, Lanarkshire.
Pri/LA   (map ref: 8L)
Castle Cary consists of a 15th-century keep and 17th-century wing. It was held by the Baillies from the 17th century until 1730, and was burned in 1645.

The castle is said to have two ghosts. One is reputedly the Covenanter, General Baillie, who was defeated in 1645 by the Marquis of Montrose at Kilsyth.

His daughter, Lizzie Baillie, also reputedly haunts the building. She absconded with a poor farmer, but her apparition reputedly searches the castle chambers for her father: the manner of her departure is said to have killed him.

Bed and breakfast – open all year to residents.
2 ensuite guest rooms. Vaulted dining room. Beamed lounge. Walled garden. Parking. $$.
Tel: 01324 841330   Fax: 01324 841330
Email: bobhunter@easynet.co.uk

Castle Coeffin

Off B8045, 8.5 miles N of Oban, Lismore, Argyll.
Ruin or site   (map ref: 4J)
Perched on a steep rock on the island of Lismore, Castle Coeffin is a ruinous and overgrown castle of the MacDougalls of Lorn. It is said to be named after one of its ancient owners, Caifen, the son of a Norse king. An old story tells that Beothail, his sister, died heartbroken after the man she loved was slain fighting in Scandinavia. Beothail was buried on Lismore, but her ghost returned to haunt the castle. She did not rest until her remains were taken to Norway and buried beside her love.

Castle Fraser

Off B993 or B977, 6.5 miles SW of Inverurie, Aberdeenshire.
NTS   (map ref: 11G)
Impressive and well preserved, Castle Fraser is a tall massive Z-plan tower house, dating mostly from 1575-1636, long a property of the Fraser family. In 1976

the castle was donated to The National Trust for Scotland, and there is a walled garden.

One story associated with the castle is that a young woman was murdered in the Green Room of the castle's Round Tower – either in the 19th century or the distant past depending on the version of the tale – and that her body was dragged down stairs before being buried. It was said that blood from her corpse, which stained the stairs and the hearth of the chamber, could not be cleaned off, and the stairs were eventually boarded over to hide the stains. The stairs, on the other hand, may have been boarded over simply to provide greater comfort.

Other unexplained events include the sound of piano music and voices coming from the apparently empty hall; and the apparition of a woman in a long black gown, said to be Lady Blanche Drummond, who died in 1874.

Castle open Good Friday-Easter Monday; then May-Sep 13.30-17.30; Jul-Aug daily 11.00-17.30; wknds only in Oct 13.30-17.30 ; garden open all year 9.30-18.00; grounds all year daily 9.30-sunset.
Explanatory sheets. Gift shop. Tea room. Picnic area. Garden and grounds. Adventure playground. Car and coach parking. Group concessions. ££.
Tel: 01330 833463

Castle Grant

Off A939, 1.5 miles north of Grantown-on-Spey, Moray.
Pri/LA   (map ref: 8F)

Castle Grant is reputedly haunted by the ghost of Lady Barbara Grant, daughter of a 16th-century laird. She was imprisoned in a dark closet, off an upper bedroom in the old part of the castle, known as 'Barbie's Tower'. She had fallen in love with a man of low station, a suitor considered unsuitable by her father, who meanwhile chose another husband. Barbara died of a broken heart, choosing death rather than marriage to a man she did not love.

Her ghost is said to appear from behind tapestries concealing

the closet, and flit across the bedroom. She stops to wash her hands, then disappears through the doorway leading to the turnpike staircase.

Castle Grant is a Z-plan tower house, incorporating work from the 15th century, with lower wings enclosing a paved courtyard. It was chief seat of the Grants. The family were Hanoverians, and fought against the Jacobites in both the 1715 and 1745 Risings, although the castle was occupied by Jacobites.

Castle Lachlan

Off B8000, 7 miles SW of Strachur, Argyll.
Ruin or site   (map ref: 4L)
In a pleasant location by the sea, Castle Lachlan is an ancient ruinous stronghold of the MacLachlans. The clan were Jacobites and fought at Killiecrankie in 1689, and also took part in the 1715 and 1745 Risings: their chief was killed at Culloden. The castle became ruinous after the building of a new house nearby, which is also called Castle Lachlan.

The old castle was said to have had a brownie.

Castle Levan

Off A770, 1.5 miles SW of Gourock, Renfrewshire.
Pri/LA   (map ref: 5L)
Standing by the edge of a ravine, Castle Levan is reputed to be haunted by a 'White Lady', the ghost of a Lady Montgomery. The story goes she was starved to death by her husband for mistreating local tenants and farmers.

The strong castle was built by the Mortons in the 14th century, and extended and altered in later centuries.

Castle Loch Heylipol

Off B8068, 3 miles W of Scarinish, Tiree.
Ruin or site   (map ref: 1J)
On a former island in the loch is the site of castle, which was replaced by a factor's house, Island House, in 1748. The factor, called MacLaren, who had the house built, is said to have died before he could enter it. His ghost reputedly haunts the house, as does a 'Green Lady', a *gruagach*, said to be responsible for

unexplained noises in the 1970s. Mysterious lights have also reputedly been seen in the windows when the house is empty.

Castle Spioradain

Off B862, 6 miles SW of Inverness, at or near Bona Ferry, Highland.
Ruin or site   (map ref: 7F)
The castle, a property of the MacLeans, was said to be haunted, and its name 'Castle Spioradain' means fortress of ghosts. In the 15th century there was a long-running feud between the MacLeans and the Camerons of Lochiel. The fighting resulted in several Camerons being executed and their dead bodies hung from the battlements, but then many MacLeans were slain in reprisal. Their ghosts, united in death by revenge, haunted the castle and terrorised the neighbourhood. Or so it is said.

The old castle was demolished at the beginning of the 19th century, with the construction of the Caledonian Canal, and human bones were found.

Castle Stuart

Off B9039, 6 miles NE of Inverness, Highlands.
Pri/LA   (map ref: 7E)
Castle Stuart is an early 17th-century tower house, although it may incorporate work from the 14th century. The building is riddled with stairways and hidden doorways.

The property was held by the Mackintoshes, but passed to the Stewart Earls of Moray, who built the present building about 1625. The castle was seized by the Mackintoshes during a dispute over ownership and compensation. Bonnie Prince Charlie may have visited in 1746.

One of the turret rooms is reported to be haunted. It is said that the then Earl offered a reward to anyone who would spend a night in the haunted chamber. A local man, known as Big Angus, is recorded as having agreed. The next morning he was found dead in the courtyard, having fallen from the turret, a terrible look of terror on his face.

Guided tours by appointment. Overnight accommodation by appointment. Parking. ££/$$-$$$.
Tel: **01463 790745** Fax: **01463 792604**
Email: castlestuart@postservices.com Web: www.castlestuart.com

Castle Tioram

Off A861, 3 miles N of Acharcle, Moidart, Highland.
Pri/LA   (map ref: 3H)

A picturesque ruin in a wild and unspoilt location, Castle Tioram dates from the 14th-century and was the main seat of the MacDonalds of Clan Ranald. It was modified by Amy MacRuari, wife of John, Lord of the Isles, who was divorced by her husband so he could marry Margaret, daughter of Robert II. The Clan Ranald branch of the MacDonalds came through her.

During the Jacobite Rising of 1715, the castle was torched so that Hanoverian forces could not use it, and the chief of Clan Ranald was killed at the Battle of Sheriffmuir. The castle was never reoccupied. It must have been in a fair state of repair, however, as Lady Grange was imprisoned here for a few weeks in 1732 before being taken to the outer isles.

Clan Ranald had a set of magic bagpipes which, when played, were thought to ensure victory in battle. The clan is also said to have had a familiar spirit, a frog, which had the power to create storm or calm at sea.

Care needs to be taken with tides.

Castle of Mey

Off A836, 7 miles N of Castletown, Caithness.
Pri/LA   (map ref: 9A)

Castle of Mey is an extended and altered 16th-century Z-plan tower house, now owned by the Queen Mother. The lands originally belonged to the Bishops of Caithness, but in 1566 were acquired by the Sinclair Earls of Caithness, who built the castle. MacLeod of Assynt, who betrayed the Marquis of Montrose, was imprisoned here.

The castle is said to be haunted by the ghost of a daughter of the 5th Earl. She fell in love with a ploughman, and her father, who disapproved, had her imprisoned in one of the attic rooms, 'Lady Fanny's Room'. Here she pined, but got some comfort from seeing her lover from the window – but her father would have none of it, and had the window blocked. She then despaired, and threw herself from one of the windows on the other side, and was killed on the courtyard below. Her sad spectre, a 'Green Lady', reportedly haunts the castle. Her ghost is said to have been witnessed during the renovations of 1953.

The gardens are occasionally open in the summer.

Castle of Park

Off A9023, 4 miles NW of Aberchirder, Banff and Buchan.
Pri/LA   (map ref: 10E)
The oldest part of the Castle of Park, dating from 1292, was rebuilt into a Z-plan tower house in 1563. It was a property of the Gordons of Park, who were active Jacobites, and the house was extended and altered in later centuries. There are extensive grounds with ornamental walks, park and woodland.

A 'Green Lady' reputedly haunts Park: she is said to be a servant lass who killed herself after falling pregnant and being dismissed from service. Her ghost is said to have been seen in the grounds, as well as in the house, where the figure of a cloaked and hooded woman has been witnessed.

Other apparitions and occurrences include a monk, who was walled up in one of the castle chambers; and the sounds of a child's voice and music box, only heard in the upper quarters. Objects are also frequently moved. The owner's point out that the occurrences are never unpleasant but mostly playful or watchful.

All ghosts and occurrences have been experienced in recent times.

Open all year to residents by arrangement.
Castle offers by arrangement a choice of a serviced and self-catering accommodation, licensed restaurant with disabled access and gallery are situated on the ground floor.
Murder mystery evenings. Weddings and functions. Parking.
Tel: 01466 751667   Fax: 01466 751667
Email: Jamesd600@aol.com

Cathedral House, Glasgow

Off M8, Cathedral Square, Glasgow.
Pri/LA   (map ref: 7M)
The hotel here is said to be haunted by the ghosts of two children.

Hotel – open all year.
8 ensuite bedrooms. Refreshments and food. Parking. $.
Tel: 0141 552 3519   Fax: 0141 552 2444

Cawdor Castle

Off B9090, 5 miles SW of Nairn, Highlands.
Pri/LA   (map ref: 8E)
A magnificent and well-preserved stronghold, Cawdor Castle incorporates a tall 14th-century keep with later ranges around a courtyard. There are fine gardens.

The title 'Thane of Cawdor' is associated with Macbeth, but Duncan was not murdered here – the castle is not nearly old enough – as he was killed in battle near Spynie. The Campbells acquired Cawdor by abducting the infant heiress, Muriel Calder, in 1511 and marrying her to Sir John Campbell, son of the Earl of Argyll. The six sons of Campbell of Inverliver were slain during the abduction. The family still owns the castle.

An apparition of a lady in a blue velvet dress has reputedly been seen here, as has a phantom of John Campbell, 1st Lord Cawdor.

Open May-mid-Oct daily 10.00-17.30; last admission 17.00.
Fine collections of portraits, furnishings and tapestries. Explanatory displays. Three shops: gift shop, wool and book shop. Licensed restaurant and snack bar. Gardens, grounds and nature trails. Golf course and putting. Disabled access to grounds; some of castle. Car and coach parking. Group concessions. Conferences. £££.
Tel: 01667 404615   Fax: 01667 404674
Email: cawdor.castle@btinternet.com

Cessnock Castle

Off B7037, 1 mile SE of Galston, Ayrshire.
Pri/LA   (map ref: 7N)
Standing above a ravine, Cessnock Castle is a massive rectangular tower house, dating from the 15th century, and later mansion.

Cessnock was a property of the Campbells. Mary, Queen of Scots, came to Cessnock after her defeat at Langside in 1568. One of her ladies died here, and is believed to haunt the castle. John Knox also visited, and his ghost is also said to haunt the castle – quoting scriptures – although the two spirits may make uncomfortable companions.

Charlotte Square, Edinburgh

Off A1, Charlotte Square, Edinburgh.
Pri/LA   (map ref: 9L)
Standing in the elegant New Town of Edinburgh, Charlotte Square dates from between 1792 and 1820, and was designed by Robert Adam. The square is said to be haunted by several ghosts, including the insubstantial and shifting figure of a monk; a woman in 18th-century garb; an old man; and a phantom coach.

Accessible at all times.

Chessel's Court, Edinburgh

Off A1, top of Canongate on Royal Mile, Edinburgh.
Pri/LA (map ref: 9L)
Chessel's Court, a courtyard in the Old Town of Edinburgh surrounded by fine restored tenements, dates from about 1745. In the 1850s one of the upper flats was said to be haunted by the ghost of a woman who had hanged herself there. Breathing and other sounds were heard, and the apparition of a tall woman in a black silk dress with a black veil was also seen.

Citizens' Theatre, Glasgow

Off A74, 119 Gorbals Street, Glasgow.
Pri/LA (map ref: 7M)
The theatre, which was built in 1878, became the Citizens' in 1945. It is reputedly haunted by a 'Green Lady', the ghost of a woman, a former front of house manager, who committed suicide by jumping from the upper circle. Her apparition has reputedly been witnessed in the theatre.

Theatre.
Disabled access to most areas of theatre & WC. Induction loop, signed performances and audio-described performances available. Parking Nearby. *£-£££*.
Tel: 0141 429 0022 (Box office)   Fax: 0141 429 7374
Web: www.citz.co.uk

Claypotts Castle

Off A92, 3.5 miles E of Dundee.
His Scot (map ref: 10J)
An unusual and impressive building, Claypotts Castle is a Z-plan tower house with a rectangular main block and two large round towers at opposite corners. The castle is associated with John Graham of Claverhouse, Viscount Dundee, who was known as 'Bloody Clavers' for his cruel persecution of Covenanters and 'Bonnie Dundee'

after his death in 1689 at the Battle of Killiecrankie, when his Jacobite forces were victorious.

One ghost story dates from 150 years before his death. The building is said to be haunted by a 'White Lady', reputedly the ghost of Marion Ogilvie, mistress (and wife) of Cardinal David Beaton. Her apparition is reputed to have been seen at a castle window on 29 May each year: the date of Beaton's murder at St Andrews Castle in 1546. It seems more likely, however, that she lived at Melgund Castle, as there was apparently no castle here in 1546. There have, however, been many reports of sightings of the ghost.

Claypotts is also said to have had a brownie, which left when one of the servants refused to allow it to help.

Open Jul & Aug, Sat & Sun 9.30-18.30, last ticket 18.00.
Parking Nearby. £.
Tel: 01786 450000

Cloncaird Castle

Off B7045, 4 miles E of Maybole, Ayrshire.
Pri/LA (map ref: 6O)
The apparition of a man is said to have often been seen on the stairs of the castle, even in recent times, although his identity is not recorded. The building incorporates an old tower house of the Mure family, and was extended and remodelled in Victorian times.

Closeburn Castle

Off A702, 3 miles SE of Thornhill, Dumfries & Galloway.
Pri/LA (map ref: 7O)
One of the oldest continuously inhabited houses in Scotland, Closeburn Castle consists of a large rectangular 14th-century keep and a 19th-century mansion. The castle was held by the Kirkpatricks from 1232 until 1783, and the story dates from their ownership. A pair of swans, which nested by the nearby lake, returned year after year until the son of the house shot one with a bow and arrow. From then on only one swan returned, with red breast feathers, as a harbinger of death in the family. The swan has apparently not been seen since the family left Closeburn.

Clumly Farm

On A967, 4 miles N of Stromness, Orkney.
Pri/LA (map ref: 10D)
The area around the farm is said to be haunted by a ghostly horseman. The story relates that two brothers desired the same woman, and they argued and then fought. One killed the other by striking him with a flail, then disposed of

his rival's body by dumping it over cliffs into the sea. As he rode back, he was chased by the dead man's ghost – or perhaps by his own conscience – and during his mad ride home dislodged stones from a wall, which afterwards could not be repaired.

His apparition is said to have been witnessed several times.

Clydesdale Hotel, Lanark

Off A73, 15 Bloomgate, Lanark, Lanarkshire.
Pri/LA   (map ref: 8N)
The Clydesdale Hotel, formerly known as the New Inn, was built in 1792 on the site of the Franciscan friary of Lanark. The friary was founded around 1326 by Robert the Bruce, but was dissolved before 1566, and the property passed to the Lockharts of the Lee. The basement is said to incorporate part of the friary buildings, the dormitory. It is here that the apparition of a monk is reputed to have been seen, but the ghost – the 'Grey Friar' – is said to be friendly and concerned with the welfare of the hotel. Other manifestations include the sound of slamming doors and rattling glasses, as well the feeling of someone pushing past folk in the cellar.

The weeping of a child has also been reported from the upper floor of the building, when no children are staying in the hotel. In the 1800s a young child is said to have died in a fire in the attic.

Hotel – open all year. Open to non-residents.
Bedrooms with ensuite facilities. Restaurant and bar. Conferences, banquets, weddings and
meetings. Parking. $-$$.
Tel: 01555 663455   Fax: 01555 662153

Cobbler Hotel, Arrochar

Off A83, Arrochar, Dunbartonshire.
Ruin or site   (map ref: 6K)
The Cobbler Hotel is believed by some to be haunted. The events surrounding the haunting are that the Colquhoun laird came home unexpectedly early one morning and discovered his wife in a compromising position with one of his neighbours. In fury Colquhoun slew the neighbour, then mortally wounded his wife, who dragged herself along a passageway and died in one of the bedrooms. Colquhoun hanged himself in despair at what he had done. The spirit of his wife, a 'Green Lady', haunted the building, but was only experienced when one of the family was about to die.

The present hotel stands on the site of a house of the MacFarlanes, who held the property from the 13th century and fought against Mary, Queen of Scots, at Langside in 1568. The clan defeated the Colquhouns of Luss at Glen Fruin,

but they were forfeited and their lands seized. The property passed to the
Colquhouns of Luss in the 18th century, then into other hands.

Hotel – open all year and to non-residents.
109 rooms with ensuite facilities. Refreshments and dinners. Car and coach parking.
Themed tours. User friendly for less well-abled guests.
Tel: 01301 702238   Fax: 01301 702353

Colquhonnie Castle

On A964, 10.5 miles N of Ballater, Kincardine & Deeside.
Ruin or site   (map ref: 9G)
Not much survives of Colquhonnie Castle, a ruined 16th-century L-plan tower
of Forbes of Towie. It was apparently never completed as three of the lairds
were killed while supervising the building work.
   The nearby Colquhonnie Hotel is said to be haunted by a phantom piper, one
of the Forbeses, who fell from the top of the old castle in the 1600s.

Hotel.
Tel: 01975 651210   Fax: 01975 651210

Comlongon Castle

Off B724, 8 miles SE of Dumfries.
Pri/LA   (map ref: 8P)
Standing in 120 acres of secluded woodland and gardens, Comlongon Castle
consists of a massive keep to
which a mansion was added
in the 19th century.
Comlongon was held by the
Murrays from 1331 until
1984. The family became
Earls of Annandale, and
later of Mansfield. The
building is now a hotel.
   The castle is believed to be
haunted by a 'Green Lady',
the spirit of Marion
Carruthers of Mouswald.
She was the heir to her
father's lands because he did
not have a son. The poor
girl was forced into a
betrothal of marriage with
Sir James Douglas of

Drumlanrig – or to John MacMath his nephew, depending on the version of the story. Either way she was to marry a man she did not love, although the motive appears to have been to seize her lands rather than desire for Marion herself.

Marion fled to Comlongon after being imprisoned in Hermitage Castle to force her to wed – even the Privy Council seemed to be against her and ordered her into the wardenship of Borthwick Castle. Although she was sheltered in Comlongon by the then laird, Sir William Murray, her uncle, she was so distraught over the long dispute that she committed suicide by jumping from the lookout tower. An alternative version is that she was murdered by the Douglases. Because she had committed suicide, she was not given a Christian burial, and it is said no grass will grow where the poor girl died.

Her apparition is said to have been witnessed, both in the grounds and castle, as have the sounds of her weeping, and a ghostly presence, which has pushed past people, has also been recorded.

Hotel – open all year round.
11 bedrooms, most with four-poster beds. Weddings and banquets. Parking. $$-$$$$.
Tel: 01387 870283   Fax: 01387 870266

Corgarff Castle

Off A939, 10 miles NW of Ballater, Aberdeenshire.
His Scot   (map ref: 9G)
Corgarff Castle consists of a plain 16th-century tower house, altered in later centuries and surrounded by later pavilions and star-shaped outworks.

The castle was leased to the Forbes family. The Forbeses feuded with the Gordons, and this came to a head when Adam Gordon of Auchindoun and a force of his family ravaged through Forbes lands and besieged the castle. Corgarff was held by Margaret Campbell, wife of Forbes of Towie, and 26 others of her

household, women, children and servants; the men folk were away. Margaret, however, would not surrender the castle. Gordon of Auchindoun lost patience, had wood and kindling set against the building, and torched the place. The building went up in flames, killing all those inside: Margaret, her children and servants, all 27 of the household. The story is recounted in the ballad 'Edom o' Gordon', although Towie Castle is given as another possible site of the massacre. Ghostly screams have reportedly been heard in the castle, and the barrack room is supposed to be particularly haunted.

The castle saw much action in Covenanting times and the Jacobite Risings. It was burnt by Jacobites in 1689, and then in 1716 by Hanoverians. In 1748 it was altered into a barracks, and later used as a base to help prevent illicit whisky distilling.

Open daily Apr-Sep daily 9.30-18.30, last ticket 18.00; open wknds only Oct-Mar, Sat 9.30-16.30, Sun 14.00-16.30, last ticket 16.00.
Short walk to castle. Exhibition: one of the floors houses a restored barrack room.
Explanatory displays. Gift shop. Car and coach parking. Group concessions. £.
Tel: 01975 651460

Coroghon Castle

On NE of island of Canna, on N side of harbour.
NTS   (map ref: 1G)
Perched on the summit of a steep rock, Coroghon Castle is a ruinous stronghold of the Clan Ranald branch of the MacDonalds. The ghost of a woman imprisoned here by one of the Lord of the Isles reputedly haunts the site.

Ruin may be in a dangerous condition – view from exterior.

Corstorphine Castle, Edinburgh

Off A8, 3 miles W of Edinburgh Castle, Dovecote Road, Corstorphine, Edinburgh.
Ruin or site   (map ref: 9L)
The grounds around the site of the castle are said to be haunted by the ghost of Christian Nimmo, who was executed in 1679. She was in love with James Forrester of Corstorphine, 2nd Lord Forrester – they used to meet under an old tree which still grows at one end of Dovecot Road, supposedly planted in 1429. During an argument, Christian stabbed and killed Forrester, and she was quickly arrested, tried and sentenced to death. Christian managed to escape from prison dressed as a man, but was recaptured at Fala Moor and brought back to Edinburgh where she was executed by beheading. Her apparition, a 'White Lady', has reputedly been seen around the site of the castle.

Nothing remains of the ancient stronghold of the Forresters. The 16th-century doocot near the site has supernatural protection: it is said anyone demolishing it will die within a short time. Also nearby is Corstorphine Old Parish Church, dating from around 1426, which contains tombs of the Forresters.

Cortachy Castle
Off B955, 3.5 miles N of Kirriemuir, Angus.
Pri/LA   (map ref: 9I)
A phantom drummer – a harbinger of death – reputedly haunts Cortachy, an impressive courtyard castle dating from the 15th century, which has long been a property of the Ogilvie Earls of Airlie. Charles II spent a night here in 1650 in the 'King's Room', and the building was sacked by Cromwell in revenge.

The phantom drummer is said to be a spirit of a man who either had an affair with the laird's wife or did not raise the alarm when the castle was about to be attacked – depending on the version. The drummer was killed by dumping him into his drum and throwing him from the battlements of the castle. Before he died he cursed the family, saying that his drums would be heard whenever one of the family neared death.

It is said that the drums were heard several times in the 19th century, and heralded deaths in the family, including two of the Earls, their wives and relations. The drummer also appears to have been witnessed at Achnacarry, near Fort William, and also abroad, and was not bound to Cortachy. It is not recorded whether the drums have been heard recently.

Coull Castle
Off B9094, 2.5 miles N of Aboyne, Aberdeenshire.
Ruin or site   (map ref: 10G)
Coull Castle was held by the Durwards in the 13th century, hereditary 'door wards' to the kings of Scots. It saw action in the Wars of Independence, but may have been abandoned as early as the 14th century and is very ruinous. When one of the Durward family was near death, the bell of the church at Coull is said to have tolled by itself.

County Buildings, Ayr

Off A719, Wellington Square, Ayr.
Pri/LA (map ref: 6N)
The County Buildings were erected in 1818-22, and then extended in 1931. The site covers the former jail, and the buildings include the striking classical courthouse. The site is reputedly haunted by a headless apparition of a man thought to have been executed here.

County Hotel, Dumfries

Off A75, Dumfries.
Pri/LA (map ref: 8P)
Standing at the end of the High Street, the building dated from the 18th century but was closed in the 1980s. It was here that Bonnie Prince Charlie and his army stopped in 1745 on their way north after withdrawing from England. The Prince held court and slept in the inn, and in the 1936 a guest claimed they saw the apparition of a man, dressed in tartan, entering by a disused door, then returning the same way. The adjoining room is said to have been Bonnie Prince Charlie's bedroom. The hotel has been demolished and the site is occupied by shops.

County Hotel, Peebles

Off A72, High Street, Peebles, Borders.
Pri/LA (map ref: 8M)
The County Hotel is supposedly haunted by the ghost of a young woman, who was killed in a tunnel behind the dining room in the early 1900s. Her indistinct apparition has reputedly been seen, and objects have mysteriously disappeared or been moved. Ghostly whispers have also allegedly been heard.

Hotel. Open all year excluding Hogmanay and New Year's day.
Small family run hotel.
Tel: 01721 720595

Coylet Inn

On A815, Loch Eck, 8 miles N of Dunoon, Argyll.
Pri/LA (map ref: 5L)
Standing on the banks of Loch Eck, the Coylet Inn is a small family-run country inn. It is said to be haunted by the apparition of a 'Blue Boy', who reputedly searches through the building for his mother. Objects also mysteriously disappear only to reappear in new locations. Staff have also reported wet footprints in areas where nobody has been present. The story goes that a young lad staying

54

here walked in his sleep, and one night left the hotel and was drowned in Loch Eck. It is thought to be his ghost which causes the disturbances.

Hotel – open all year.
Three bedrooms. Refreshments and food. Open log fires. Boats for hire and fishing permits. Parking. $.
Tel: 01369 840322/426   Fax: 01369 840426

Craigcrook Castle, Edinburgh
Off A90, 2.5 miles W of Edinburgh Castle, Edinburgh.
Pri/LA   (map ref: 9L)

Nestling beneath Corstorphine hill, Craigcrook is a large castellated building which incorporates an old tower house. It was probably built by the Adamson family in the 16th century, and has been owned by many families down the centuries, including Archibald Constable, who started the publishing firm, and Lord Francis Jeffrey, the well-known judge, who died in 1850. It is his ghost that is said to haunt the building.

Many disturbances have been reported in recent times, including unexplained footsteps and noises, things being moved around and thrown, and the doorbell ringing when nobody is apparently present. The library is also reputed to be unnaturally cold at times.

Craighouse, Edinburgh
Off A702, 2 miles SW of Edinburgh Castle.
Pri/LA   (map ref: 9L)

Now in the campus of Napier University but long part of a mental institution, Craighouse incorporates a much-altered 16th-century tower house, which by 1712 was occupied by Sir Thomas Elphinstone.

Sir Thomas was married to Elizabeth Pittendale, a pretty girl much younger than her husband. Elizabeth is said to have become attracted to John, Sir William's son, and her feelings were reciprocated, although the couple appear to have acted honourably. Sir Thomas, however, caught them together and assuming the worst fell into a rage and stabbed Elizabeth to death. John escaped, and Sir Thomas was found dead the next day, having committed suicide.

John Elphinstone then inherited the property, and let the house, but a 'Green Lady', the spirit of Elizabeth, began to haunt the building. The hauntings only ceased when Elizabeth's remains were removed from the burial vault of her husband, and when John died he is said to have been buried beside her.

Part of Napier University.

Craignethan Castle

Off A72, 4.5 miles W of Lanark.
His Scot (map ref: 8M)
Standing above a deep and wooded ravine, Craignethan is a ruinous castle designed to withstand artillery, and was built by Sir James Hamilton of Finnart, who was beheaded for treason in 1540. There is an unusual caponier in the ditch.

Mary, Queen of Scots, is said to have spent the night here before the Battle of Langside in 1568. The Hamiltons formed the main part of her army, but were defeated by the Regent Moray and Mary fled to England. A headless ghost has been reported, identified by some as the spirit of Mary.

Other ghosts are said to have been witnessed in the later house in the courtyard, where the unexplained voices of women have been heard. The apparition of a woman wearing Stuart period dress has been witnessed in the courtyard in recent times, and other unexplained disturbances include mysterious pipe music.

Open daily Apr-Sep 9.30-18.30, Oct-Nov daily except closed Thu PM and Fri 9.30-16.30, last ticket 30 mins before closing.
Exhibition and explanatory boards. Gift shop. Tearoom. Car parking. Group concessions.
£.
Tel: 01555 860364

Cranshaws Castle
Off B6355, 0.5 miles W of Cranshaws, Borders.
Pri/LA   (map ref: 11M)
Cranshaws is an old tower house, dating partly from the 15th century but altered in later years, and was a property of the Douglases. The castle is supposed to have had a brownie, which used to gather and thresh the corn. One of the servants foolishly mentioned that it was not gathered neatly together, which angered the brownie. It left the castle during the night, and the grain was found two miles away, dumped in the Whiteadder river.

Crathes Castle
Off A93, 3 miles E of Banchory, Kincardine & Deeside.
NTS   (map ref: 11G)
A massive and magnificent castle, the upper storeys of Crathes are adorned with much corbelling, turrets, and decoration, while the lower storeys are very plain. The castle has original painted ceilings, and there is a splendid walled garden, consisting of eight separate areas with unusual plants.

Crathes was held from the 14th century by the Burnetts of Leys, their original stronghold being at Loch of Leys, which was also said to be haunted. The 'Horn of Leys', an ivory horn encrusted with jewels, was given to the family by Robert the Bruce in 1323.

One of the chambers, the Green Lady's room, is said to be haunted. The apparition, in a green dress, reportedly first appeared in the 18th century, and is seen crossing the chamber, with a baby in her arms, to disappear at the fireplace.

The young woman seems to have been a daughter of the then laird, and had been frolicking with a servant. It appears that she was murdered to hide her pregnancy. A skeleton of a young woman and baby – or just the baby, depending on the account – were reportedly found by workmen under the hearthstone

during renovations in the 19th century. The phantom is said to have been seen often, even in recent times.

Open Apr (or Good Friday if earlier)-Sep, daily 10.30-17.30, Oct, daily 10.30-16.30; last entry 45 mins before closing. Grounds and garden open all year 9.00-sunset. Timed ticket arrangement for castle; garden may be closed at short notice on very busy days (limited parking).
Collections of portraits and furniture. Gift shop. Restaurant. Gardens, grounds and adventure playground. Plant sales. Disabled facilities, including access to ground floor and WC. Car and coach parking. £££.
Tel: 01330 844525   Fax: 01330 844797

Crichton Castle
Off B6367, 2 miles E of Gorebridge, Midlothian.
His Scot   (map ref: 10M)
Standing above the River Tyne in an open and rugged location, Crichton Castle is a fabulous ruinous castle, dating from the 14th century, but much altered and extended in later centuries. Of special note is the diamond-studded facade of one of the ranges.

The castle was held by the Crichtons. Sir William Crichton, Chancellor of Scotland, entertained the young Earl of Douglas and his brother before having them murdered at the 'Black Dinner' at Edinburgh Castle in 1440. Outside the castle are the roofless stables, which are said to be haunted by Crichton. On the anniversary of his death, the story goes, he leaves the stables and enters the castle tower.

The Crichtons were forfeited for treason in 1488, and the property later passed to the Hepburns, one of whom was Patrick Hepburn, 4th Earl, third husband of Mary, Queen of Scots. Mary was present at a wedding here in 1562.

Crichton is also said to be haunted by a horseman, who enters the castle by the original gate, which is now walled up.

Open Apr-Sep, daily 9.30-18.30.
Walk to property. Car and coach parking. Group concessions. £.
Tel: 01875 320017

Cromarty Castle
Off A832, 0.5 miles SE of Cromarty, Highland.
Ruin or site   (map ref: 7E)
Nothing remains of Cromarty Castle, a once strong castle, which may have dated from as early as the 12th century. It was held by the Urquhart family from the 1450s. The Urquharts, however, lost everything as predicted by the Brahan Seer, and the property was sold in 1763 to the Murray Lord Elibank, then in 1771 to the Ross family. They demolished the castle, during which – it is said – a large quantity of human bones were recovered, including some headless skeletons, and built Cromarty House.

The old castle was said to be haunted by manifestations such as groans, cries and moans, and sightings of apparitions are also recorded.

Cross Keys Hotel, Peebles
Off A72, Northgate, Peebles, Borders.
Pri/LA (map ref: 8M)
The Cross Keys Hotel, which dates from 1693, was the town house of the Williamsons of Cardrona, but has been an inn from the 18th century. One of the innkeepers Marion Ritchie, who died in 1822, was used by Sir Walter Scott as Meg Dods in the novel *St Ronan's Well*. Marion is said to have run an excellent establishment with a rod of iron

Marion's ghost is thought to haunt the building. Disturbances have been reported, including items being moved about without being touched, electrical equipment being switched on and off, glasses broken, unexplained bangs and noises heard. Her apparition is also said to have been seen throughout the hotel, but bedroom five, where she died, is said to be the centre of activity.

Hotel.
Tel: 01721 724222

Culcreuch Castle
Off B822, 0.5 miles N of Fintry, Stirlingshire.
Pri/LA (map ref: 7L)
Set in 1600 acres of parkland below the Fintry Hills, Culcreuch Castle consists of a 15th-century keep, with later additions. The castle was built by the Galbraiths, whose chiefs lived here for 300 years. The Galbraiths were a lawless lot in medieval times, and were noted for their thievery, pillage, burning and rapine, but Robert, 17th chief, had to sell the property in 1630 because of debt. The fine building is now a hotel, and has the largest colony of bats in the UK living in the roof area above the dining room. The Chinese Bird Room, within the old part of the building, has hand-painted Chinese wallpaper dating from 1723, believed to be the only surviving example of this period in Scotland.

The castle is reputed to have several ghosts. The Phantom Harper of Culcreuch relates to events believed to have taken place in 1582. One of the Buchanan family was mortally wounded by Robert Galbraith, son of the 16th chief. The dying man was taken to what is now the Chinese Bird Room, accompanied by his mistress. When he died, to comfort herself she began to play a wire-strung harp, known as a clarsach in Gaelic – and it is said that her soft music has often been heard since, particularly in the dead of night. The music has been reported from this and the adjoining room, and also in the Laird's Hall.

The apparition of a severed animal head have also reported, which apparently flies around the battlements. Another manifestation is that of a cold grey mass, about the height and proportions of a human. This has been reported in all areas of the old castle.

Hotel – open all year and to non-residents.
8 rooms with ensuite facilities. Restaurant and 2 bars. Meetings, functions, weddings and parties. Gift shop. Self-catering lodges. Country park. Disabled access to function suite, ground-floor bar and WC, as well as ground-floor bedroom. Parking. $$.
Tel: 01360 860228   Fax: 01360 860556

Cullen House

Off A98, 0.5 miles SW of Cullen, Aberdeenshire.
Pri/LA   (map ref: 10E)
Said to have had 386 rooms, Cullen House is a large sprawling mansion which incorporates an old castle. It was long a property of the Ogilvies Earls of Findlater, but has been divided into flats.

The ghost of the 3rd Earl is said to haunt the building. Although well most of the time, he suffered from uncontrollable rages, and in 1770 murdered his factor during a frenzied episode. In remorse, the Earl committed suicide, reputedly by cutting his own throat. His ghost is said to have been seen, and footsteps from unoccupied areas have been reported often, including by newspaper journalists in 1964. Manifestations are said to take place mostly in the library, and in the pulpit and church rooms.

Culloden Moor

On B9006, 5 miles E of Inverness, Highland.
NTS   (map ref: 7F)
It was here on the bleak and windswept moor of Drumossie that on 16 April 1746 the Jacobite army of Bonnie Prince Charlie was crushed by Hanoverian forces led by the Duke of Cumberland – the last major battle to be fought on British soil. The Jacobites were tired and hungry, and the Hanoverians had a better equipped and larger army: the battle turned into a rout and many Jacobites were slaughtered after the battle. Sites of interest include Old Leanach Cottage, Graves of the Clans, Wells of the Dead, Memorial Cairn, Cumberland Stone,

and Field of the English. The visitor centre houses a Jacobite exhibition and historical display, and there is an interesting audio-visual programme.

It is said that many have witnessed visions of the battle or apparitions, especially from the Wells of the Dead and the clan memorials. The descendants of those killed here are supposedly particularly sensitive.

Nearby Culloden House, a property of Duncan Forbes of Culloden – a noted Hanoverian – is said to be haunted by a figure in clad green tartan, thought by some to the spirit of Bonnie Prince Charlie.

Site open daily all year; visitor centre and shop open Feb -Mar & Nov-30 Dec except 24/26 Dec 10.00-16.00; Apr-Oct daily 9.00-18.00; last admission to exhibition area 30 mins before closing; audio-visual show closes 30 mins before Visitor Centre.
Guided tours available in summer. Visitor centre with audio-visual programme. Gift shop. Restaurant. WC. Disabled access to visitor centre, WC and facilities. Car and coach parking.
Group concessions. £.
Tel: 01463 790607   Fax: 01463 794294

Culross Abbey

Off B9037, Kirk Street, Culross, Fife.
His Scot   (map ref: 8L)
Situated in the pretty town of Culross, the Cistercian Abbey was dedicated to St Serf and St Mary, and founded in 1217 by Malcolm, Earl of Fife. The abbey was dissolved at the Reformation and most of the buildings are ruinous, except the monk's choir, which has been used as the parish church since 1633. The remains of the domestic buildings are open to the public.

A piper is said to have been sent to explore a tunnel, the entrance to which was at the abbey – and which reputedly led to piles of gold and silver. The piper and his dog set off from a vault at the head of Newgate, followed by the locals, but when they reached West Kirk, some distance away, the pipes suddenly stopped. The piper was never seen again, although it is said that the faint sound of pipes can be heard at times.

Open all year at reasonable times.
WC. Sales area. Disabled access. Parking Nearby.
Tel: 0131 668 8800

Culzean Castle

Off A77, 4.5 miles W of Maybole, Ayrshire.
NTS   (map ref: 5O)
One of the foremost attractions in Scotland (and pronounced 'Cul-lane'), Culzean Castle is a magnificent sprawling castellated mansion of the Kennedy Earls of Cassillis. It was built between 1777 and 1792 by the architect Robert

Adam, and is now in the care of the National Trust for Scotland. There are caves in the cliffs below the castle.

A ghostly piper is said to herald a Kennedy marriage, and to play on stormy nights. His apparition has reportedly been seen in the grounds, particularly on a drive known as 'Piper's Brae' and near the ruinous Collegiate church. The piper is said to have been exploring caves beneath the castle when he disappeared.

Two other ghosts supposedly haunt the castle: one a young woman dressed in a ball gown – sightings of the ghost were reported in 1972. Another apparition has reportedly been seen on the main stair.

Castle, visitor centre, restaurants and shops open Apr (or Good Friday if earlier)-Oct 10.30-17.30, last admission 17.00; other times by appt. Park open all year daily 9.30-sunset.
Fine interiors. Collections of paintings and furniture. Gift shops. Two restaurants. WC. Picnic areas. Gardens and adventure playground. Country park and visitor centre – one of the foremost attractions in Scotland. Car and coach parking. Group concessions. £££.
Tel: 01655 884455   Fax: 01655 884503

Dalhousie Castle

Off B704, Bonnyrigg, 3 miles S of Dalkeith, Midlothian.
Pri/LA   (map ref: 9M)
Dating from the 13th century, Dalhousie incorporates an ancient castle into the large mansion. The castle was built by the Ramsays, who were made Earls of Dalhousie in 1630.

Sir Alexander Ramsay was active for the Scots against the English during the Wars of Independence. However, he was starved to death in Hermitage Castle in 1342 by Sir William Douglas after being abducted from St Mary's Church in Hawick. Ramsay's ghost is believed to haunt Hermitage.

Dalhousie saw much action in the following centuries, being besieged on at least two occasions, but in more peaceful times was remodelled into a fine mansion, and is now used as a hotel.

The castle is said to be haunted by a 'Grey Lady', an apparition of a Lady Catherine. She was mistress to one of the Ramsay lairds, but his vengeful wife had her locked up in one of the castle turrets, where she presumably perished. Her apparition has allegedly been seen on the stairs and in the dungeons, and other reported manifestations include the rustling of her gown and unexplained noises.

Hotel – open all year.
29 ensuite bedrooms in castle, 5 in lodge. Dungeon restaurant and library bar.
Conferences, banquets, meetings and weddings. Parking. $$.
Tel: 01875 820153   Fax: 01875 821936
Email: res@dalhousiecastle.co.uk   Web: www.dalhousiecastle.co.uk

Dalkeith House

Off A6094, 0.5 miles NW of Dalkeith, Midlothian.
Pri/LA   (map ref: 9M)
Standing in acres of parkland, Dalkeith House is a classical mansion which incorporates some of an old castle. It has been held by the Douglases since 1350.

James IV first met Margaret Tudor here in 1503, although the couple appear to have been less than happy once wed. Other famous visitors include James VI, Charles I and Bonnie Prince Charlie. The park was laid out in the 18th century, and includes working Clydesdale horses, adventure woodland play area, nature trails, 18th-century bridge, orangery and ice house.

The house is said to be haunted.

Gardens open Mar-Oct 10.00-18.00. House not open.
Explanatory displays. Gift shop. Restaurant. Tearoom. WC. Picnic area. Woodland walks.
Disabled access – cage, shop and toilets. Car and coach parking. Group concessions. £.
Tel: 0131 665 3277   Fax: 0131 654 1666

Dalmahoy

Off A71, 7 miles W of Edinburgh, Kirknewton, Edinburgh.
Pri/LA   (map ref: 9L)

Set in fine grounds commanding extensive views, Dalmahoy is a symmetrical mansion, which was built by the architect William Adam about 1720. The property was held from 1296 by the Dalmahoys of that Ilk, but was sold to the Dalrymples, then to the Douglas Earls of Morton.

The building is reputedly haunted by the ghost of Lady Mary Douglas, the daughter of the first Earl of Morton to own the property. Her portrait hangs in the hotel, and her apparition is said to be a 'White Lady'. The ghost has reportedly been witnessed in both the corridors and the bedrooms of the old part of the building, but is believed to be friendly.

Hotel – open all year.
151 bedrooms with ensuite facilities, 7 original. Restaurant, cafe and bars. Swimming pool, gym, sauna and health and beauty salon. Two golf courses. Conferences and meetings.
Parking. $$$.
Tel: 0131 333 1845   Fax: 0131 333 1433

Dalpeddar

Off A76, 3 miles SE of Sanquhar, Dumfries & Galloway.
Pri/LA   (map ref: 8O)

The area near Dalpeddar is said to be haunted by the apparition of a tall woman and sometimes young boy, dressed in white, and their figures have been recorded, appearing by the road.

They are said to be the ghosts of 'Lady Hebron' and her son. The story goes that, in the 16th century, Lady Hebron was heiress to the small estate of Dalpeddar. She was married in due course and had a son, but her husband died and she was left a widow. Her uncle, however, wanted the property, and Lady Hebron and her son disappeared. Much later the bones of a woman and child were found, buried near the road: the lady had had her skull split.

Dalry House, Edinburgh

Off A70, 1 mile W of Edinburgh Castle, Orwell Place, Edinburgh.
Pri/LA   (map ref: 9L)

Dalry House, standing in Orwell Place, dates from 1661 and was the country house of the Chiesly family. The building, with hexagonal stair-towers and fine plasterwork, is harled and whitewashed, and after renovation in 1965 is now an old people's day centre.

The house and area were said to be haunted by a ghost, 'Johnnie One Arm'. John Chiesly was executed for shooting and killing Sir George Lockhart of Carnwath, after Lockhart, Lord President of the Court of Session, found against Chiesly in a divorce settlement. Chiesly had his arm chopped off, before being hanged, but his dead body was removed from the gallows before it could be buried. His apparition, one armed, is then said to have been witnessed often, crying and screaming. In 1965 the remains of a one-armed man were said to have been found under a hearth, and his ghost has reputedly not been seen since the remains were buried.

View from exterior.
Parking Nearby.

Dalzell House

Off A721, 1.5 miles SE of Motherwell, Lanarkshire.
Pri/LA (map ref: 7M)
Standing on the edge of a rocky ravine, Dalzell House – other spellings can be Dalyell or Dalziel – incorporates an old castle in the large rambling mansion. The property belonged to the Dalziel Earls of Carnforth from the 13th century, but was sold to the Hamiltons of Boggs in 1649. Covenanters were sheltered in the grounds, and held illegal conventicles under a huge oak tree, now known as the 'Covenanter's Oak'. The north wing was used as a hospital during World War I.

The house is said to be haunted by three ghosts: 'Green', 'White' and 'Grey' Ladies.

Sightings of the 'Green Lady' have been reported in the Piper's Gallery, and other manifestations include unexplained flashing lights, footsteps and other noises. The smell of exotic perfume has also been recorded

The 'White Lady' is thought to be the ghost of a young female servant. Although unmarried, she became pregnant and in despair threw herself to her death from the battlements.

The 'Grey Lady' was said to haunt the north wing, and to date from when the house was used as a hospital. Her apparition is believed to be seen wearing a grey nurse's uniform.

Dalzell Park open dawn-dusk.

Dean Castle

Off B7038, 1 mile NE of Kilmarnock, Ayrshire.
Pri/LA   (map ref: 6N)
Standing in acres of parkland, Dean Castle dates from the 14th-century or earlier, and was long a property of the Boyd Earls of Kilmarnock. Robert Boyd was Guardian of James III, and for a time very powerful in Scotland. He fell from favour and had to flee abroad, while his brother was executed.

The 4th Earl was Privy Councillor to Bonnie Prince Charlie during the Jacobite Rising of 1745, and the ghost story relates to him. Well before the Rising, servants were terrified by an apparition of Boyd's severed head rolling about the floor. When Boyd joined the Jacobite Rising, he told the Earl of Galloway about the haunting. Boyd was a Colonel in the Prince's guard, but was captured after the Battle of Culloden in 1746 and – as predicted by the apparition – executed by beheading.

The castle now houses a museum, containing a collection of armour and musical instruments.

Open daily Apr-Oct 12.00-17.00; open end Oct to end Mar wknds only; closed Christmas and New Year; park open daily dawn-dusk.
Guided tours. Explanatory displays. Gift shop. Restaurant. WC. Picnic area. Disabled access – but not into castle. East Ayrshire residents free. Car and coach parking. Group concessions. £ (castle).
Tel: 01563 522702

Deer Abbey

Off A950, 2 miles W of Mintlaw, Aberdeenshire.
His Scot   (map ref: 11E)
Deer Abbey, a Cistercian house, was founded in 1219 by William Comyn, Earl of Buchan, and dedicated to the Blessed Virgin Mary. The lands passed in 1587 to Robert Keith, Lord Altrie, and not much of the church remains except foundations, although the infirmary, Abbot's House and the southern cloister range are better preserved. The University Library at Cambridge now houses the beautifully illustrated Book of Deer.

The spectre of a monk has reputedly been seen on the nearby main road, the apparition dressed in a dark robe and hood and with a blur for a face.

Open at all reasonable times.
Parking.
Tel: 0131 668 8800 Fax: 0131 668 8888

Delgatie Castle

Off A947, 2 miles E of Turriff, Banff & Buchan.
Pri/LA (map ref: 11E)

Delgatie Castle, an ancient pile, is a strong castle which has been held by the Hays since the 14th century. It is said to be haunted by a the ghost of a spirited young woman, traditionally called Rohaise.

She supposedly haunts a bedroom off the main stair, which now bears her name, and is said to visit men who stay in the chamber. Rohaise is believed to have defended the castle from an attack. The ghost would appear to be quite frightening, however, as soldiers stationed at Delgatie twice fled outdoors after unexplained disturbances and a search made of the building revealed nothing.

The Hays were made Earls of Errol in 1452, and Mary, Queen of Scots, spent three days here in 1562. Sir William Hay of Delgatie was standard bearer to the Marquis of Montrose. Although defeated at Philiphaugh, Hay managed to return the standard to Buchanan Castle, but he was executed at Edinburgh in 1650, and buried beside Montrose in St Giles Cathedral.

Open daily Apr-Oct 10.00-17.00.
Many rooms, two with original painted ceilings of 1592 and 1597. Collection of portraits.
Guided tours available. Explanatory boards. Gift shop. Tearoom. WC. Picnic area. Disabled
access to tearoom and front hall only. Accommodation available. £.
Tel: 01888 563479 Fax: 01888 563479

Devanha House, Aberdeen
Off A956, off Holbourn Street, Ferryhill, Aberdeen.
Pri/LA   (map ref: 12G)
Named after a Roman camp believed to be at the mouth of the Denburn, Devanha is a small mansion, built in 1813, but later remodelled. The once extensive grounds were broken up in the late 19th century.

The house is said to be haunted by the apparition of a woman, although only the upper half of her body is seen. This may be because of a change in floor levels rather than any dismemberment.

Discovery Point, Dundee
Off A92, Discovery Quay, Dundee.
Pri/LA   (map ref: 10K)
Discovery Point is the home of RRS *Discovery*, Captain Scott's Antarctic ship. Within the complex are eight exhibition areas, using lighting, graphics and special effects to recreate key moments in the *Discovery's* history. The ship has been extensively restored below deck.

Discovery is said to be haunted, by unexplained footsteps on deck and other disturbances. Suggested identities for the ghost include Ernest Shackleton; or Charles Bonner, a member of the crew who fell from the craw's nest to his death in 1901.

Open all year: Apr-Oct Mon-Sat 10.00-17.00, Sun 11.00-17.00; Nov-27 Mar last admission 16.00; closed 25 Dec & 1/2 Jan.
Guided tours available. Explanatory displays. Gift shop. Cafe. WC. Disabled access. Car and coach parking. Group concessions. ££.
Tel: 01382 201245   Fax: 01382 225891

Dolphinston Tower
Off A68, 4 miles SE of Jedburgh, Borders.
Ruin or site   (map ref: 11N)
Nothing remains of an old tower house, which is said to have had a brownie. The brownie left when it was given a mean present, a course shirt, reputedly saying:

'Since ye've gien me a harden ramp,
   Nae mair o' your corn I will tramp.'

Doune
Off B970, 2 miles S of Aviemore, Highland.
Pri/LA   (map ref: 8G)
Doune, a mansion dating from the late 18th century, is a property of the Grants of Rothiemurchus. It was home to Elizabeth Grant, author of *Memoirs of a Highland Lady*.

The house was said to be haunted by the son of a laird, who suffered from episodes of madness. During one of these he reputedly strangled a servant girl on the stairs, then died himself after falling over the balustrade. His ghost reportedly haunts the house, and activity is said to be concentrated in one of the bedrooms.

Drumlanrig Castle

Off A76, 3 miles NW of Thornhill, Dumfriesshire.
Pri/LA (map ref: 7O)

The large towered mansion, dating mostly from the 17th century, incorporates part of an ancient castle. It was held by the Douglases, later Earls and Dukes of Queensberry, from the 14th century or earlier. The 2nd Duke was instrumental in getting the Act of Union passed in 1707, which abolished the separate parliaments of England and Scotland. Bonnie Prince Charlie stayed at the castle in 1745, after his retreat from Derby, and his men ransacked the building, including stabbing a picture of William of Orange, since repaired.

Drumlanrig passed to the Scott Dukes of Buccleuch in 1810.

Three ghosts are believed to haunt the castle. One is reputed to be the spirit of Lady Anne Douglas, dressed in white, with her fan in one hand and her head in the other; another that of a young woman in a flowing dress; and the third of a monkey, ape or other creature, witnessed in the Yellow Monkey Room. Another story is that someone was murdered in one of the corridors, the 'Bloody Passage', and that the blood could not be washed off the floor.

There is also a prophecy by Thomas the Rhymer about the castle – House of Hassock is another name for Drumlanrig:

'When the Marr Burn runs where never man saw
 The House of the Hassock is near to a fa''

This is said to have been fulfilled when Charles 3rd Duke diverted the Marr Burn to make a fountain south of the castle. His two sons died young.

The Burn has since been returned to its original course.

Open Easter Sat-Sep, Mon-Sat 11.00-16.00, Sun 12.00-16.00 – phone to confirm; country park, gardens & adventure woodland 24 Apr-1 Sep 11.00-17.00; other times by appt only.
Fine collection of pictures, including paintings by Rembrandt, Holbein and Leonardo, as well as many other works of art. Guided tours. Gift shop. Tearoom. Visitor centre. Parkland, woodland walks and gardens. Visitor centre. WC. Picnic area. Adventure woodland play area. Working craft centre. Demonstrations of birds of prey (except Thu). Disabled access. Car and coach parking. Group concessions. ££.
Tel: 01848 330248   Fax: 01848 331682   Email: bre@drumlanrig.org.uk

Dryburgh Abbey

Off B6356, 5 miles SE of Melrose, Borders
His Scot   (map ref: 10N)
A picturesque and substantial ruin by the banks of the Tweed, the Abbey was founded by David I as a Premonstratensian establishment, dedicated to St Mary. Most of the buildings date from the 12th and 13th centuries, and part of the church survives, as do substantial portions of the cloister, including the fine chapter house, parlour and vestry. The Abbey was burnt by the English in 1322, 1385 and 1545. Sir Walter Scott and Earl Haig are both buried here.
   The abbey ruins are said to be haunted by ghostly monks.

Open all year: Apr-Sep daily 9.30-18.30; Oct-Mar Mon-Sat 9.30-16.30, Sun 14.00-16.30, last ticket 30 mins before closing; closed 25/26 Dec & 1-3 Jan.
Gift shop. WC. Picnic area. Disabled access. Car and coach parking. Group concessions. £.
Tel: 01835 822381

Dryburgh Abbey Hotel

Off A68, 3 miles SE of Melrose, Borders.
Pri/LA   (map ref: 10N)
Dryburgh Abbey Hotel, a castellated mansion formerly known as Mantle House, was remodelled in 1892, but stands on the site of a much older building. It was home to Lady Grizel Baillie, and has recently undergone a major renovation.
   The ghost story, however, dates from the 16th century or earlier. Before the nearby abbey was dissolved, a young lady of the house fell in love with a monk, and they became close. The abbot, on hearing of the monk's earthly love, had the poor man killed. When the young lady found out she was devastated, and threw herself into the Tweed and was drowned. Her apparition, a 'Grey Lady', has reputedly been seen on the chain bridge and in outbuildings of the hotel. Disturbances apparently increased during building work.

Hotel – open all year.
37 luxury bedrooms. Restaurant and bar. Swimming pool. Conferences, meetings, weddings and dinners. Parking. $-$$.
Tel: 01835 822261   Fax: 01835 823945
Email: enquiries@dryburgh.co.uk

Duchal Castle

Off B788, 1.5 miles W of Kilmacolm, Ayrshire.
Ruin or site   (map ref: 6M)
Little remains of Duchal Castle, a 13th-century stronghold of the Lyles, who were later made Lord High Justiciars of Scotland. The building was said to have been haunted by the spirit of a monk, who was excommunicated in the 13th century, apparently a very 'corporeal' ghost. The monk would stand on the walls of Duchal and shout and swear at the occupants. The ghost could not be vanquished – arrows melted away before they hit it – until a son of the laird, a particularly goodly youth, cornered it in the great hall. In the ensuing battle the son was killed and the hall wrecked, but the ghost was banished and not witnessed again.

Dunnottar Castle

Off A92, 2 miles S of Stonehaven, Kincardine & Deeside.
Pri/LA   (map ref: 11H)
Perched on a spectacular cliff-top promontory 160 feet above the sea, Dunnottar Castle is an extensive ruinous stronghold of the Keith Earls Marischal. External shots of the castle were used, along with Dover and Blackness, in the making of the film *Hamlet* with Mel Gibson.

Famous visitors include Mary, Queen of Scots, Charles II, and William Wallace – although the latter was uninvited and is said to have burnt 4000 Englishmen here. In 1651 the Scottish crown jewels were brought to Dunnottar during

Cromwell's invasion. Roundheads besieged the castle in 1652, but before the garrison surrendered, the regalia and state papers were smuggled out and hidden in nearby Kinneff Church.

In 1685 Covenanters, numbering some 167 women and men, were packed into one of the cellars during a hot summer and nine died while 25 escaped.

Sightings of several ghosts have been reported here. The apparition of a girl, thought to be about 13 years old and dressed in a dull plaid-type dress, is said to have been witnessed in the brewery. She allegedly leaves by the doorway next to the brewery, and then vanishes.

Other ghosts witnessed here are said to include a young deer hound, which faded away near the tunnel; a tall Scandinavian-looking man going into the guardroom at the main entrance, who then vanished; and noises of a meeting coming from Benholm's Lodging when nobody was apparently present.

Open Easter-Oct Mon-Sat 9.00-18.00, Sun 14.00-17.00; winter Mon-Fri only 09.00 to sunset.
Getting to the castle involves a walk, steep climb, and a steeper one back. Sales area. WC.
Car and coach parking. Group concessions. Parking.
Tel: 01569 762173

Dunphail Castle

Off A90, 6.5 miles S of Forres, Moray.
Ruin or site   (map ref: 8E)
Little remains of Dunphail Castle, a once strong castle of the Comyns. The Comyns tried to waylay the Regent Andrew Moray, but were themselves ambushed and fled back to Dunphail, pursued by Moray. They were besieged here but had few supplies. Moray seized five of the garrison, including Alasdair Comyn of Dunphail, who had sneaked out of the fortress to forage for food. Moray had the men beheaded and their severed heads flung over the walls into the castle, reputedly with the cry 'Here's beef for your bannocks'. The rest of the Comyn garrison fled, but were hunted down and slaughtered by the Regent's men. In the 18th century, five headless skeletons were found buried near the castle. Dunphail is said to be haunted by the spectres of the Comyns, and tales of the sound of fighting and groans have also been reported.

Dunrobin Castle

Off A9, 1.5 miles NE of Golspie, Sutherland.
Pri/LA   (map ref: 8D)
Set in fine grounds overlooking the sea, Dunrobin dates from the 1300s and is a splendid 'fairy-tale' castle. There are fine formal gardens. The Sutherland family were created Earls of Sutherland in 1235, and had a castle here in the 13th century: Dunrobin may be called after Robert or Robin, the 6th Earl. The property passed by marriage to the Gordons, then to the Trentham Marquis of Stafford in the 18th century.

The upper floors of the old part of the castle are reputedly haunted by the spectre of Margaret, daughter of the 14th Earl of Sutherland, who himself died in 1703. She fell in love with one Jamie Gunn, younger son of one of the Earl's tacksmen. But her father, who considered the man too low in station to marry his daughter, found out, and had her imprisoned in one of the attic rooms so that she could not see Jamie. Margaret pined in the attic room and despaired; and Gunn decided to rescue her as her health was failing. A rope was smuggled to her attic room and she tried to escape, but her father burst into her room and surprised her, and she fell to her death. It is said that one of the rooms she haunted has since been disused, although her moans and cries still come from the chamber where she was imprisoned.

Open daily 1 April to mid October: Apr, May & Oct Mon-Sat 10.30-16.30, Sun 12.00-16.30; Jun & Sep Mon-Sat 10.30-17.30, Sun 12.00-17.30; Jul & Aug daily 10.30-17.30; last entry 30 mins before close.

Collections of furniture, paintings and memorabilia. Museum, which features a collection of Pictish stones. Formal gardens. Museum. Guided tours. Explanatory displays. Gift shop. Tea room. WC. Disabled access: phone to arrange. Car and coach parking. Group concessions. £££.

Tel: 01408 033177   Fax: 01408 634081

Duns Castle

Off A6112, 1 mile NW of Duns, Borders.
Pri/LA   (map ref: 11M)
Duns Castle incorporates a 14th-century keep, later altered to an L-plan, then much altered and extended in the 18th and 19th centuries. The castle may have been built by Thomas Randolph, Earl of Moray, in 1320, but had passed to Home of Ayton by 1489. It was damaged by the Earl of Hertford in 1547, and in 1639 used by the Covenanter General David Leslie, who later went on

to defeat the Marquis of Montrose at the Battle of Philiphaugh in 1645. It passed to the Cockburns, then the Hays of Drumelzier, who had the architect James Gillespie Graham remodel and extend the house.

The ghost of Alexander Hay, who was killed at the Battle of Waterloo in 1815, is said to haunt the castle and to have been seen in the Yellow Turret room.

Accommodation available.
Tel: **01361 883211**   Fax: **01361 882015**

Dunskey Castle

Off A77, 0.5 miles SE of Portpatrick, Dumfries & Galloway.
Ruin or site   (map ref: 5P)
Set on a windswept and oppressive headland above the sea, Dunskey Castle is

ruinous tower house of the 16th century. It was held by the Adairs, and it was here that the abbot of Soulseat Abbey was imprisoned and tortured in the castle to force him to sign away the abbey lands. The castle has been ruinous since the end of the 17th century, but has recently been put up for sale.

The castle was said to have had a brownie, and also reported to be haunted by the ghost of a careless nursemaid, who dropped her charge from one of the windows to its death on the seashore far below.

View from exterior – climb and walk to castle.
Parking Nearby.

Dunstaffnage Castle

Off A85, 3.5 miles NE of Oban, Argyll.
His Scot   (map ref: 4J)
On a promontory in the Firth of Lorn, Dunstaffnage Castle consists of a massive curtain wall, with round towers, and an altered gatehouse.

A stronghold here was held by the kings of Dalriada in the 7th century, and was one of the places that the Stone of Destiny was kept. The present castle was built by the MacDougalls, but later passed to the Campbells after the castle was seized by Robert the Bruce in 1309. Other well-known visitors include James IV, and Flora MacDonald, who was imprisoned here after helping Bonnie Prince Charlie.

The castle is said to be haunted by a ghost in a green dress, the 'Ell-maid of Dunstaffnage' and her appearance heralds events, both bad and good, in the lives of the Campbells. When she was seen to be smiling then there were happy events to come, but if she wept or was sad it augured trouble. She is said to be a *gruagach*, a spirit woman who was closely associated with the fortunes of her family. Ghostly footsteps are also been reported, as well as bangs and thumps, although the spirit was also said to be able to hand on handicraft skills.

Open daily Apr-Sep 9.30-18.30; Oct-Mar Mon-Sat 9.30-16.30, Sun 14.00-16.30, except closed Thu PM and Fri; last ticket 30 mins before closing.
Explanatory panels. Gift shop. WC. Car and coach parking. Group concessions. £.
Tel: 01631 562465

Duntrune Castle

Off B8025, 6.5 miles NW of Lochgilphead, Argyll.
Ruin or site   (map ref: 4L)
Standing in a picturesque location on a rocky hillock by the banks of Loch Crinan, Duntrune was a property of the Campbells and dates from the 13th century. In 1792 it passed to the Malcolms of Poltalloch, who still own it.

The castle is allegedly haunted by a ghostly piper. A MacDonald had been sent as a spy to try to capture the castle in 1615, but was discovered, and the only way he could warn his companions was to play the pipes. The Campbells had both his hands or fingers chopped off, and he was buried under the kitchen flagstones. From that time on the sound of ghostly bagpipes was often reported.

The ghost was thought to have been exorcised in modern times, when part of the basement was used as a church. A handless or fingerless skeleton was found sealed beneath the floor about 1870, and the remains were buried. However, the ghost became active in the 1970s, and unexplained knockings on doors were reported, as well as furniture and other objects being thrown about the rooms. Or so it is said.

Duntulm Castle

Off A855, 6.5 miles N of Uig, Skye.
Ruin or site   (map ref: 2E)
On a commanding headland overlooking the sea and the Outer Hebrides, not much now remains of Duntulm Castle, once a fine stronghold of the MacDonalds. The family later moved to Monkstadt, itself now ruinous, reputedly because of the many ghosts here.

Hugh MacDonald was imprisoned and starved to death in a dungeon at Duntulm after he had tried to seize the lands of Trotternish from his kin. He was given salted beef and no water, and is reported to have died insane and raving. His ghostly groans have reputedly been heard.

The ghost of one of the chiefs, Donald Gorm, brawling and drinking with spectral companions, has also been recorded in many tales. Another apparition was that of Margaret, a sister of MacLeod of Dunvegan, who was married to one of the MacDonalds. She had lost an eye in an accident, but her husband threw her out, sending her back to Dunvegan on a one-eyed horse with a one-eyed servant and one-eyed dog. Her weeping ghost is said to haunt the castle.

A nursemaid also reputedly dropped a baby out of one of the windows, onto the rocks below. Her terrified screams are said to be heard sometimes as the poor woman was murdered in reprisal.

View from exterior – care must be taken as dangerously ruined.
Parking Nearby.

Dunure Castle

Off A719, 5 miles NW of Maybole, Ayrshire.
Ruin or site   (map ref: 5N)
Perched on a rock on the banks of the Firth of Clyde, Dunure Castle is now very ruinous but was a property of the Kennedys. In 1570 Allan Stewart, Commendator of Crossraguel Abbey, was roasted in sop here until he signed away the lands of the abbey. Ghostly cries have reputedly been heard emanating from the torture chamber.

View from exterior.
Parking Nearby.

Dunvegan Castle
Off A850, 1 mile N of the village of Dunvegan, Skye.
Pri/LA (map ref: 1E)
Continuously occupied by the chiefs of MacLeod since 1270, Dunvegan Castle is a large mansion and castle, which dates from the 13th century. It is the home

of the Fairy Flag, said to have been given to one of the chiefs by his fairy wife, who he had married thinking she was a mortal woman. The flag is supposed to give victory to the clan, whenever unfurled, and reputedly has done so both at the battles of Glendale in 1490 and Trumpan – also said to be haunted – in 1580. It may actually have been captured from a Saracen on a crusade, and was also believed to make the marriage of the MacLeods fruitful, when draped on the wedding bed, and to charm the herrings in the loch when unfurled.

Other interesting items include a drinking horn, 'Rory Mor's Horn', holding several pints of claret, which the heir of the MacLeods had to empty in one go; and the Dunvegan Cup, gifted to the clan by the O'Neils of Ulster in 1596. There are mementoes of Bonnie Prince Charlie and Flora MacDonald.

Open daily mid-Mar-end-Oct 10.00-17.30; Nov-mid-Mar, castle and gardens, 11.00-16.00; closed 25/26 & 31 Dec & 1 Jan; last entry 30 mins before closing.
Guides in each of the public rooms. Explanatory panels and displays. Audio-visual theatre. Gift shops. Restaurant. WC. Gardens. Boat trips to seal colony. Pedigree Highland cattle fold. Car and coach parking. Group/student/OAP concessions. Holiday cottages available.
£££.
Tel: 01470 521206   Fax: 01470 521205
Email: info@dunvegancastle.com   Web: www.dunvegancastle.com

Durris House
Off B9077, 6.5 miles E of Banchory, Kincardine & Deeside.
Pri/LA (map ref: 11G)
Durris House, an altered and extended tower house, was held by the Frasers from the 13th until the end of the 17th century. The house, divided into three, is still occupied.

A 'Green Lady' is said to haunt the castle, reputedly the wife of the Fraser lord when Montrose torched the house on 17 March 1645. The poor woman is said to have been distraught, feeling that she was responsible after having cursed Montrose, and she drowned herself in a nearby burn. Her curse may have had some effect, however, as Montrose was finally defeated in 1650, captured, and taken to Edinburgh where he was executed.

Earlshall

Off A919, E of Leuchars, Fife.
Pri/LA (map ref: 10K)

Earlshall, a fine courtyard castle, was built by Sir William Bruce in 1546. He had survived the Battle of Flodden in 1513.

Another occupant was Sir Andrew Bruce of Earlshall, known as 'Bloody Bruce' as he and his men killed Richard Cameron, a noted Covenanter and leader of the Cameronians, at Airds Moss in July 1680. Bruce then hacked off Cameron's head and hands, and took them back to Edinburgh. The castle is thought to be haunted by the ghost of Sir Andrew. Sightings of his apparition have been recorded, and the ghostly sound of heavy footsteps have reputedly been heard on one of the turnpike stairs when nobody is about.

Another apparition is allegedly that of an old woman.

The castle and gardens are NOT open to the public.

Eden Court Theatre, Inverness

Off A82, Inverness.
Pri/LA (map ref: 7F)

On the west bank of the River Ness, the Eden Court Theatre, which was opened in 1976, stands on the site of the Bishop's Palace, and incorporates part of the old building. A 'Green Lady' has reputedly been witnessed here, the wife of one of the Bishops who hanged herself in the palace. The unexplained sounds of feet in unoccupied areas have also been reported.

Theatre.
Diverse programme of theatre, dance, variety, opera and cinema. Restaurant and bar.
Parking.
Tel: 01463 39841   Fax: 01463 713810

Edinample Castle

Off A84, 1 mile SE of Lochearnhead, Perthshire.
Pri/LA (map ref: 7K)

Edinample Castle, a fine Z-plan tower house, was built by Sir Duncan Campbell of Glenorchy – Black Duncan of the Castles – around 1584. The story goes that Campbell had ordered that the castle should have a parapet walk. The mason forgot to add this feature, but tried to show that it was possible to walk around the roof, as Campbell refused to pay him. Campbell,

however, shoved him from the roof, so saving himself the fee. The apparition of the mason can reputedly be seen occasionally, still clambering around the roof.

Edinburgh Castle

Off A1, in the centre of Edinburgh.
His Scot (map ref: 9L)

Standing on a high rock in the middle of Scotland's capital, Edinburgh Castle was one of the strongest and most important castles in Scotland, and has a long

and bloody history – little of which can be related here. The castle is the home of the Scottish crown jewels, and the Stone of Destiny, once held at Dunstaffnage then Scone – on which the Kings of Scots were inaugurated – and is an interesting complex of buildings with spectacular views over the city.

The oldest building is the small 12th-century chapel, dedicated to St Margaret, wife of Malcolm Canmore, probably built by her son David I. The castle held an English garrison during the Wars of Independence, but was recaptured in 1313 when the Scots, led by Thomas Randolph, climbed the rock, surprised the garrison, and retook it. After the murder of the young Earl of Douglas and his brother at the 'Black Dinner' here in 1440, it was attacked and captured by the Douglases. In 1566 Mary, Queen of Scots, gave birth to the future James VI in the castle. It also saw much action in Covenanting times and during the Cromwellian invasion and Jacobite Risings.

The castle is reputedly haunted by several ghosts.

A drummer, sometimes reported as being headless, has allegedly been witnessed. His apparition is said to be a warning that the castle is about to be besieged, and was first seen in 1650 before Cromwell attacked. Drums are reputedly heard more often than an apparition is seen. Manifestations were reported in 1960, although it is not clear who was about to besiege the castle.

A piper was sent to search a tunnel, believed to travel from the castle to Holyroodhouse one mile away at the end of the Royal Mile, but was never seen again. It is said that sometimes the faint sound of his pipes can still be heard.

The spectre of a dog, whose remains are buried in the pets' cemetery, reportedly haunts the battlements.

Open daily all year: Apr-Sep 9.30-17.15; Oct-Mar 9.30-16.15, castle closes 45 mins after last ticket is sold; times may be altered during Tattoo and state occasions; closed Christmas & New Year. Explanatory displays. Guided tours. Gift shop. Restaurant. WC. Disabled access. Visitors with a disability can be taken to the top of the castle by a courtesy vehicle; ramps and lift access to Crown Jewels and Stone of Destiny. Car and coach parking (except during Tattoo). *£££.*
Tel: 0131 225 9846

Edinburgh Festival Theatre, Edinburgh
On A7, 13-29 Nicolson Street, Edinburgh.
Pri/LA (map ref: 9L)
The theatre here is said to be haunted by the apparition of the Great Lafayette, Sigmund Neuberger. Lafayette was killed when part of the Empire Palace Theatre, dating from 1892, burned down in 1911, probably due to an electrical fault. The theatre was out of action for several months, but was restored, then remodelled in 1928 and latterly used for bingo. The theatre was virtually rebuilt in the 1990s, and in 1994 reopened as the Edinburgh Festival Theatre. Since

the renovation, however, an apparition of a black figure, believed to be Lafayette, has been seen several times.

Theatre.
Parking Nearby. Bar.
Tel: 0131 529 6000

Edzell Castle

Off B966, 6 miles N of Brechin, Angus.
His Scot (map ref: 10H)
Standing by the magnificent walled garden, ruinous Edzell Castle dates from the 16th century and was built by the Lindsay Earls of Crawford. Mary, Queen of Scots, held a Privy Council at Edzell in 1562. One story is that a Lindsay laird hanged the sons of a gypsy woman for poaching and she cursed him. His pregnant wife died that day, while he himself was devoured by wolves – all as foretold of course.

The castle is said to be haunted by a 'White Lady', reputedly the spirit of Catherine Campbell, second wife of David Lindsay, 9th Earl of Crawford. She was thought to have died in 1578, but was only in a coma and was interred alive in her family vault. She eventually regained consciousness, after a sextant

had tried to steal her rings by cutting off her finger, but died of exposure at the castle gates. The ghost has been witnessed in recent times, described as being quite small with a white dress and blur for a face, and is also said to exude a sickly smell or faint odour of scent.

Open daily all year: Apr-Sep 9.30-18.30; Oct-Mar Mon-Sat 9.30-16.30, Sun 14.00-16.30 except closed Thu PM & Fri; last ticket 30 mins before closing; closed 25/26 Dec & 1-3 Jan.
Visitor centre. Exhibition and explanatory panels. WC. Garden. Picnic area. Reasonable disabled access and WC. Car and coach parking. Group concessions. £.
Tel: 01356 648631

Eilean Donan Castle

On A87, 8 miles E of Kyle of Lochalsh, Highland.
Pri/LA   (map ref: 4F)

One of the most picturesque strongholds in the country, Eilean Donan Castle stands in a spectacular unspoilt location at the mouth of Loch Duich. A strong tower stands within an enclosing wall on a small island joined to the mainland by a bridge. Although once quite ruinous, it was completely rebuilt in the 20th century.

Eilean Donan was long held by the Mackenzies, and sheltered Robert the Bruce in 1306. In 1331 Randolph, Earl of Moray, executed 50 men at Eilean Donan and spiked their heads on the castle walls. In 1509 the MacRaes became constables of the castle.

William Mackenzie, 5th Earl of Seaforth, garrisoned it with Spanish troops during the Jacobite Rising of 1719, but three frigates battered it into submission. The Spaniards were defeated at nearby Glenshiel, and the site is marked by an information board. The ghost of one of the Spanish troops, killed at the castle or the battle, is said to haunt the castle, and has been seen in the gift shop. The ghost is said to carry his head under his arm.

Another apparition, Lady Mary, reputedly haunts one of the bedrooms.

Open Apr-Oct daily 10.00-17.30.
Guided tours available. Visitor centre. New exhibitions.. Gift shop. Tearoom. WC. Car and coach parking. Group concessions. ££.
Tel: 01599 555202   Fax: 01599 555262

Ethie Castle

Off A92, 5 miles NE of Arbroath, Angus.
Pri/LA   (map ref: 10J)

Ethie Castle, dating from the 15th century, was a property of the Beatons, and used by Cardinal David Beaton when Abbot of Arbroath in the 1530s, and Archbishop of St Andrews until his murder in 1546. He was married to Marion Ogilvie, whose apparition is said to be seen at Claypotts, and had seven children, although his marriage was later annulled. His ghost is thought to haunt the house – as well as St Andrews and Melgund – and the

83

sound of phantom footsteps climbing a stair have reportedly been heard. Other unexplained noises include the sound of something heavy being dragged across the floor.

Another ghost was apparently that of a child, and activity was centred in a room where a skeleton of a child was said to have been found. When the bones were buried, this haunting is believed to have stopped.

A further apparition seen here is reputedly a 'Green Lady'.

Fairburn Tower

Off A832, 4 miles W of Muir of Ord, Highlands.
Pri/LA   (map ref: 6F)
An impressive castle, Fairburn Tower is a 16th-century tower house of the Mackenzies. It features in one of the Brahan Seer's prophecies, when a cow managed to climb all way to the watch-chamber at the top of the tower. It could not be brought down again until it had calved – an event, predicted by the Seer, along with the end of the Mackenzies of Fairburn. The line died out in 1850.

One ghost story involves one of the lairds. His apparition is said to have crossed the Conon Ferry, accompanied by the unfortunate ferryman, some hours after his death.

Falkland Palace

Off A912, 4 miles N of Glenrothes, Fife.
NTS   (map ref: 9K)
A magnificent Renaissance Palace of the Stewart monarchs, Falkland consists of a gatehouse range of the 15th century and a ruinous adjoining block. The impressive Chapel Royal has an unusual 16th-century oak screen and a painted

ceiling of 1633. There is also the fine tapestry gallery, which is said to be haunted by a 'White Lady', and access to the keeper's apartments.

The restored cross house contains a refurbished room, reputedly the King's Room, where James V died in 1542, as well as the Queen's Room on the first floor.

David, Duke of Rothesay, heir of Robert III, was imprisoned here in 1402 and starved to death, or murdered, by his uncle, Robert Duke of Albany. Falkland became a favourite residence of the Stewart monarchs, and was visited by James III, James IV, James V, Mary, Queen of Scots, James VI, Charles I and Charles II, but afterwards little used. The National Trust for Scotland assumed responsibility for the building in 1952.

Open Apr (or Good Friday if earlier)-Oct 11.00-17.30, Sun 13.30-17.30; last admission to Palace 16.30, garden 17.00; groups at other times by appt.
Explanatory displays. Gift shop. Visitor centre. Picnic area. Extensive gardens. Real tennis court. WC. Disabled access. Tape tour for visually impaired. Car parking nearby. ££.
Tel: 01337 857397   Fax: 01337 857980

Fasque
Off B974, 5 miles NW of Laurencekirk, Kincardine & Deeside.
Pri/LA   (map ref: 10H)
Fasque, a castellated mansion built in 1809, passed to the Gladstones in 1829, one of whom, William Ewart Gladstone, was Prime Minister four times between 1830 and 1851. The house is said to be haunted by the ghost of Helen Gladstone, youngest sister of the Prime Minister, as well as the spirit of a butler called MacBean.

Open May-Sep daily 11.00-17.30; last admission 17.00.
William Gladstone library, state rooms, kitchen, extensive domestic quarters and family church. Guided tours. Explanatory displays. Gift shop. Tearoom. WC. Picnic area. Collections of farm machinery. Deer park with Soay sheep and walks. Car and coach parking. ££.
Tel: 01561 340569   Fax: 01561 340569

Fedderate Castle
Off A981, 2 miles NE of New Deer, Aberdeenshire.
Ruin or site   (map ref: 11E)
Little remains of Fedderate Castle, which dates from the 13th century, a stronghold of the Crawford family then the Gordons. It was probably the last stronghold to hold out for the Jacobites in the Rising of 1689-90. The castle is said to be haunted.

Fernie Castle

On A914, 4 miles W of Cupar, Fife.

Pri/LA   (map ref: 9K)

Situated in 17 acres of woodland, Fernie Castle is a 16th-century tower house with later additions and extensions. It was held by many families, and is now a hotel.

The west tower of the building is said to be haunted by a 'Green Lady', a girl who ran off with her lover. They sought refuge in the castle, but were discovered by her father's men – her father disapproving of her lover. The poor woman fell three floors from the west tower to her death, and her apparition is said to have been seen in some of the bedrooms. Other manifestations include electrical equipment and lights switching themselves on and off.

Hotel – open all year round.
15 bedrooms with ensuite facilities. Restaurant, bar and lounge. Dinners, meetings and corporate entertaining. Parking. $$.
Tel: 01337 810381   Fax: 01337 810422

Ferniehirst Castle

Off A68, 1.5 miles S of Jedburgh, Borders.

Pri/LA   (map ref: 11N)

Ferniehirst Castle is an impressive Border stronghold, which dates from the 16th century, but was altered in later centuries. It was a property of the Kerrs of Ferniehirst, but seized by the English in 1523, and only recaptured 25 years later when the captain of the English garrison was beheaded. James VI attacked the castle in 1593 because of help given to the Francis Stewart, Earl of Bothwell, who was accused of witchcraft among many other things.

A 'Green Lady' is said to haunt a bedroom in the old part of the castle, and

unusual occurrences were reported during the time the castle was used as a youth hostel – although the story is refuted.

Open daily Jul 13.00-16.00 except Mon.
Collection of portraits. Turret library. Guided tours. Explanatory displays. Gift shop. WC.
Riverside walk. Sheep of Viking origin. Car and coach parking. £.
Tel: 01835 862201   Fax: 01835 863992

Fetteresso Castle

Off A92, 1.5 miles W of Stonehaven, Kincardine & Deeside.
Ruin or site   (map ref: 11H)
Fetteresso Castle, a mansion dating from the 17th century, stands on the site of a 15th-century castle. It was built by the Keith Earls Marischal, but was torched by the Marquis of Montrose in 1645. James VIII, the old Pretender, stayed here over Christmas 1715 during the Jacobite Rising.

The castle is believed by some to be haunted.

One ghost is reputedly a 'Green Lady', whose apparition is said to have been witnessed, as well as the sounds of her feet and the swish of her skirt on the stairs. On one occasion the ghost is said to have had a baby in its arms, and to have disappeared into a wall, later shown to be a sealed-up doorway. On another occasion the sound of feet, followed by the dragging of something metallic along the floor of a passage, was also reported.

The ghost is also reputed to haunt a house on the High Street of Stonehaven, and there is an unlikely tale of a tunnel linking Fetteresso, this house and Dunnottar Castle – one of many such tales.

Finavon Castle

Off A94, 4.5 miles NE of Forfar, Angus.
Ruin or site   (map ref: 10I)
Only ruins remain of Finavon Castle, once the strong and splendid castle of the Lindsay Earls of Crawford. David, 3rd Earl, and his brother-in-law Ogilvie of Inverquharity – badly wounded at Battle of Arbroath in 1446 – were brought back to the castle. The Earl soon died, and his wife suffocated Ogilvie, her brother, with a pillow to ensure the succession of her own son. Alexander Lindsay, this son, was the 4th Earl, and called 'The Tiger' or 'Earl Beardie', a cruel and ruthless character. On the Covin Tree, grown from a chestnut dropped by a Roman soldier, Crawford hanged Jock Barefoot as an example for cutting a walking stick from the one of its branches. Jock's ghost is said to have been seen here. Crawford himself is said to haunt Lordscairnie and Glamis, where one tale recounts he played cards with the devil.

'When Finavon Castle runs to sand
The end of the world is near at hand.'

A large 16th-century doocot stands nearby, built by the Earls of Crawford, which could house 2400 birds.

Finavon Doocot open to the public all year: key from the Finavon Hotel.

Floors Castle

Off A6089, 1 mile NW of Kelso, Borders.
Pri/LA   (map ref: 11N)
Said to be the largest inhabited mansion in Scotland, Floors Castle dates from 1721, and was originally designed by William Adam for the 1st Duke of Roxburghe: Floors is still the home of the Duke and Duchess of Roxburghe. There is a walled garden, with fine herbaceous borders.

  One story relates that the house is haunted by the ghost of a gardener, who is said to be experienced – rather than seen – outside the main entrance. In the grounds is a holly tree, reputedly where James II was killed by an exploding cannon while besieging Roxburgh Castle. The apparition of a horseman has allegedly been seen riding towards the site of the old stronghold.

Open daily Easter to end Oct 10.00-16.30; last admission 16.00.
Collections of furniture, tapestries, works of art and porcelain. Gift shop. Licensed restaurant. WC. Playground. Walled garden and park. Disabled access to house; lift for wheelchairs; WC. Car and coach parking. Group concessions. ££.
Tel: 01573 223333   Fax: 01573 223333

Fordell

Off B981, 1.5 miles N of Inverkeithing, Fife.
Pri/LA   (map ref: 9L)
Standing on the edge of a ravine, Fordell Castle is a 16th-century Z-plan tower house, long a property of the Hendersons.

  A nearby mill – although the location may be at Fordel near Kinross – was said to be occupied by Cromwell's troops following the Battle of Inverkeithing in 1651. The soldiers interfered with the miller's wife and daughter, and the man poisoned them then fled with his family. When the dead troops were discovered, the assistant miller was hanged for the crime although he had nothing to do with the killings. On some nights it is said that an apparition of his corpse can still be seen swinging from an old oak tree.

Fort George

Off B9006, 10 miles NE of Inverness, Highland.
His Scot   (map ref: 7E)
An outstanding example of a Georgian artillery fort, Fort George was built after the failure of the Jacobite Rising at the Battle of Culloden in 1746 and named after the king. It was designed by the architect William Skinner, with

work also by William and John Adam. By the time the work was finished in 1769 it was not needed – the Duke of Cumberland had 'pacified' the Highlands efficiently in a bloody campaign 20 years earlier. The fort could house nearly 2000 troops, and covers 16 acres.

The fort is said to be haunted by a ghostly piper.

Open all year: Apr-Sep daily 9.30-18.30; Oct-Mar 9.30-16.30, Sun 14.00-16.30; last ticket 45 mins before closing; closed 25/26 Dec & 1-3 Jan.
Reconstruction of barrack rooms in different periods, and display of muskets and pikes. Visitor centre with explanatory panels. Gift shop. Tearoom. WC. Picnic area. Disabled access and WC. Car and coach parking. Group concessions. £.
Tel: 01667 462777

Fortingall

Off B846, 5 miles W of Aberfeldy, Perthshire.
Pri/LA   (map ref: 8J)
Fortingall is reputed to be the birthplace of Pontius Pilate, the son of a Roman emissary and a local girl. In the churchyard is a 3000-year-old yew tree, and in the church itself a bell said to have been used by St Adamnan, biographer of St Columba, and a 7th-century font. Fortingall, a picturesque village with thatched cottages, was a religious centre from the 6th century, and the village is reputedly haunted by a procession of nuns.

Access to churchyard at all reasonable times.
Car parking.

Fountainhall, Aberdeen

Off A92, Blenheim Place, Aberdeen.
Pri/LA   (map ref: 12G)
Fountainhall, an 18th-century house, is said to be haunted. It was home to Dr Patrick Copland, an eminent Professor at Marischal College in Aberdeen, who died in 1822.

Manifestations were reported, including the sounds of heavy footsteps and unexplained knockings, crashes and banging. One account of the haunting is that one of the owners murdered his wife, said to be the mistress of a Scottish noble, and hid her body here.

Frendraught Castle

Off B9001, 6 miles E of Huntly, Aberdeenshire.
Pri/LA   (map ref: 10F)
Frendraught dates mostly from the 17th century and later, but may incorporate part of an old castle of the Crichtons. It is the scene of an infamous fire in 1630.

It was during a time when the Crichtons and Gordons were feuding over land. Several of the Gordons were staying at the castle when it mysteriously caught fire. John Gordon, Lord Rothiemay, and John Gordon, Viscount Aboyne, were burned and killed, as well as others of their kinsfolk and servants, although Sir James Crichton escaped with his family.

Sir James was tried for their murder, but acquitted, although one of his servants was executed. Lady Rothiemay certainly believed in Crichton's involvement: she employed Highlanders to attack and plunder his lands and family. Lady Rothiemay was eventually imprisoned in 1635, although she was later released.

The castle is believed to be haunted by the ghost of Crichton's wife, Lady Elizabeth Gordon, daughter of the Earl of Sutherland, who may have been involved in the torching of the castle. Her ghost has reportedly been seen, most often on the stairs, in the 18th and 20th centuries, and her apparition has been described as a dark woman wearing a white dress edged with gold. Other activity includes arguing, footsteps coming down the stairs and crashing sounds, as well as doors being locked and unlocked, opened or shut.

The castle passed to the Morisons, who still occupy the building.

Fulford Tower

Off A702, 2.5 miles N of Penicuik, Midlothian.
Ruin or site   (map ref: 9M)
Site of an old mansion, which incorporated part of a 14th-century castle, and was built with materials from Old Woodhouselee. It was completely demolished in 1965.

It is said that the mansion was haunted by a ghost of Lady Hamilton, apparently transferred from Old Woodhouselee, although this may be a confusion.

Fyvie Castle

Off A947 1 mile N of Fyvie village, Banff & Buchan.
NTS   (map ref: 11F)
One of the most splendid castles in Scotland, Fyvie Castle consists of a large tower house with very long wings. Famous visitors include William the Lyon, Alexander II, Edward I of England, Robert the Bruce and the Marquis of Montrose.

The property was originally held by the Lindsays, but passed to the Prestons, then to the Meldrums, then the Seton Earls of Dunfermline, then to the Gordons and finally to the Leith family, each of whom added to the castle. It is now owned by The National Trust for Scotland.

The castle is reputedly haunted by a 'Green Lady', the spectre of Lilias Drummond, wife of Alexander Seton, who died on 8 May 1601 at Seton's house in Fife. Lilias had several children, but all were daughters, and her husband may have hankered after a son and heir. One theory is that she was starved to death by her husband, or she may have died of a broken heart, or she simply grew ill and died. Whatever the truth of it, Seton married Grizel Leslie only months after Lilias's death.

It is said that Lilias's ghost carved her name on the stone window sill of the newlyweds' bedroom – the 'Drummond Room' – soon after they were married – and the

writing can certainly be seen 'D[ame] LILIAS DRUMMOND'. Her appearance bodes ill for the family, and she is recorded as often appearing on the main turnpike stair. She is thought to have appeared before the death of Cosmo Gordon in 1879, and Alexander Gordon a few years later.

The castle is also reported to have a 'Grey Lady', believed to be the spirit of a lady starved to death here. The ghost was at its most active in the 1920s and 1930s. When workmen were renovating one of the chambers, the gun room, in the castle, they found a secret chamber behind a wall in which they uncovered the remains of a woman. When the skeleton was removed, disturbances increased until the bones were returned to the secret room – or so it is said. These two ghosts may be one and the same, depending on the account.

Some say the castle also has a ghostly drummer, while others a trumpeter, the ghost of Andrew Lammie. He is said to have fallen in love with Agnes, daughter of a local miller, but her parents had him banished or abducted. His ghost is said to return and blow a trumpet when one of the Gordons is near death.

Thomas the Rhymer is recorded as having made a prophecy concerning Fyvie and the 'weeping stones'. When the castle was first being built stones were removed from church lands by demolishing a nearby monastery, but fell into a river. The then laird refused Thomas shelter in the castle, and the Rhymer is said to have prophesied that unless the three stones were recovered the castle and estate would never descend in direct line for more than two generations. Only two of the stones were found, and the prophecy is said to have come true.

One is in the charter room, while another is reported to be built into the foundations – and are said to 'weep' when tragedy is going to strike the owners.

*Open Good Friday-Easter Monday, then May-Sep; weekends only in Oct 13.30-17.30; Jul-Aug daily
11.00-17.30, last admission 16.45. Tearoom and shop as castle but open 12.30 when castle open
13.30. Grounds open all year daily 9.30-sunset.*
Collections of portraits, arms and armour and tapestries. Gift shop. Tearoom. WC. Picnic
area. Garden and grounds. Plant sales. Disabled access to tearoom & WC. Car parking. *££.*
Tel: 01651 891266

Gairnshiel Lodge

On B976, 4 miles NW of Ballater, Kincardine & Deeside.
Pri/LA   (map ref: 9G)
Standing in a wild and picturesque location, Gairnshiel Lodge, a fine building, was used as a hunting lodge by Queen Victoria, and is now a family-run hotel. It is said to be haunted by the apparition of an old woman, reputedly the ghost of one of the former owners.

The old military road, built because of the Jacobite Risings, runs past the building. The sound of feet, horses, carts and marching men have allegedly been heard here, although there is apparently nobody to be seen.

Hotel – open all year to residents.
Friendly family-run hotel. Accommodation. Refreshments, food and dinners. Good
location for castles, malt whisky trail, skiing, golf and hill walking. $.
Tel: 01339 755582   Fax: 01339 755105

Galdenoch Castle

*Off B738, 6 miles W of Stranraer,
Dumfries & Galloway.*
Ruin or site   (map ref: 5P)
Galdenoch Castle, a ruinous tower house, was built by Gilbert Agnew, who was killed at the Battle of Pinkie in 1547.

The castle was reputedly haunted in the 17th century. The spirit is recorded as having grabbed old women and tossed them into a nearby river, as well as many other disturbances. It was apparently eventually exorcised by the mighty singing of a priest, after all else had failed.

Garleton Castle

Off B1343, 1.5 miles N of Haddington, East Lothian.
Pri/LA (map ref: 10L)
Nestling under the picturesque Garleton Hills, Garleton Castle is a partly ruinous courtyard castle, once a property of the Lindsays. Sir David Lindsay of the Mount, the well-known 16th-century playwright who wrote *The Satire of the Three Estates*, is thought to have been born here.

The building was said to be haunted by the apparition of a man at one time, and the sounds of heavy footsteps were also reported.

Garth Castle

Off B846, 6 miles W of Aberfeldy, Perthshire.
Pri/LA (map ref: 8J)
Standing on a steep crag, Garth Castle, a plain 14th-century tower, was built by Alexander Stewart, the Wolf of Badenoch

Nigel Stewart of Garth was by all accounts a wicked fellow. He seized Sir Robert Menzies in 1502 from nearby Weem and imprisoned him in the dungeon at Garth, threatening to torture him unless he signed away some of his lands. Stewart was also suspected of murdering his wife, Mariota, who died in suspicious circumstances: a stone apparently struck her on the head in the ravine below the castle. Sightings of her apparition have been reported in the area. Stewart was imprisoned in Garth until his death in 1554.

Gartloch Hospital

Off A8, Gartcosh, Glasgow.
Pri/LA (map ref: 7M)
The hospital is allegedly haunted by the apparition of a woman dressed in black. She appeared at the top of the stair of Ward 1's dormitory, and passed through a passage to disappear through a sealed-up door. The temperature was said to drop when the spectre was witnessed. The hospital has been closed.

Gight Castle

Off B9005, 4 miles E of Fyvie, Aberdeenshire.
Ruin or site (map ref: 11F)
Pronounced 'Gecht', Gight Castle is a ruined castle of the Gordons, who were reputedly a wicked lot: bad enough indeed to have practised the black arts – one account states that a nearby pool is where the devil still cavorts with phantoms of the Gordons.

Catherine Gordon, heiress of Gight, married John Byron, but in 1787 had to sell the property to pay off his gambling debts. Their son was the poet Lord Byron.

Ghostly pipes can reputedly be heard from a piper sent to explore a subterranean passage under the castle. His progress could be followed by the music of his pipes, which eventually died away, and although the unfortunate piper was never seen again, it is said that his bagpipes can sometimes still be heard.

Gight House Hotel, Methlick

Off B999, Methlick, Aberdeenshire.
Pri/LA   (map ref: 11F)
The hotel here, once a manse, is said to be haunted. The apparition of a man, thought to be the Reverend John Mennie who died in 1886, has been seen in the bedrooms and bar, which are in the former manse. Ghostly footsteps have reputedly been heard from unoccupied parts of the hotel, and a bathroom door was locked from the inside when nobody was in it.

Hotel – open all year except New Year's day.
3 rooms. Refreshments. Parking.
Tel: 01651 806389   Fax: 01651 806389

Glamis Castle

Off A928, 5.5 miles SW of Forfar, Angus.
Pri/LA   (map ref: 10J)
One of the most famous, and reputedly haunted, castles in Scotland, Glamis Castle is a splendid building, which incorporates a massive 15th-century keep. The property has long been held by the Lyon family, from whom the Queen Mother is descended.

Malcolm II is said to have been slain here in 1034, although if he was it was in an earlier building. Glamis is traditionally associated with Macbeth, and in the

old keep is 'Duncan's Hall', but any connection is probably only based on Shakespeare's play.

On 3 December 1537 Janet Douglas, the young and beautiful widow of John Lyon 6th Lord Glamis and sister of the Earl of Angus, was burned to death on Castle Hill in Edinburgh on a false charge of witchcraft, which was fabricated by James V who hated the Douglases. Her apparition, the 'Grey Lady of Glamis' is said to haunt the building, and has been seen in the chapel and clock tower.

The ghost of Alexander Lindsay, 4th Earl of Crawford, 'Earl Beardie', is said to haunt a walled-up room where he played cards with the devil. A similar tale is related about Lindsay's castle at Lordscairnie, where the Tiger Earl is reputed to be seen on Hogmanay.

Other stories of ghosts include that of the spirit of a little African boy, which along with many other tales appear to have no foundation.

Open 2 Apr-12 Nov, daily 10.30-17.30 (from 10.00 Jul & Aug); Nov, daily 10.30-16.00 – confirm by tel; last tour 45 mins before closing; at other time groups by appt.
Collections of historic pictures, porcelain and furniture. Guided tours. Two additional exhibition rooms. Four shops. Licensed restaurant. WC. Picnic area. Play park. Garden. Nature trail. Disabled access to gardens and ground floor; WC. Car and coach parking. Group concessions. £££.
Tel: 01307 840393 Fax: 01307 840733 Email: glamis@great-houses-scotland.co.uk

Glasgow Infirmary

Off A8, Castle Street, Glasgow.
Pri/LA   (map ref: 7M)
Glasgow Infirmary, dating from 1792, stands on the site of Glasgow Castle, the bishop's residence, with the fine medieval cathedral nearby – a stone marks the site of the old castle in the grounds.

The surgical block is reputedly haunted by a 'Green Lady', one story being that she is the spectre of a nurse who fell to her death down a stairwell while trying to prevent a patient from committing suicide. The ghost is said to be helpful, and to have been witnessed on numerous occasions.

Glencoe

On A82, 17 miles S of Fort William.
NTS   (map ref: 5I)
One of the most picturesque parts of Scotland, Glencoe is the site of the infamous massacre in 1692, executed by government forces under Campbell of Glenlyon. Thirty eight members of the MacDonalds of Glencoe, including their chief MacIain, were slaughtered by men from the garrison at Fort William, who had been billeted on the MacDonalds. One of the sites of the massacre at Inverglen can be visited; as can the Signal Rock, reputedly where the signal to begin the massacre was given.

The glen is reported to be haunted by ghosts of the slaughtered MacDonalds.

Site open all year; visitor centre, shop and snack bar open Apr (or Good Friday if earlier)-Oct 10.00-17.00; open 19 May-Aug daily 9.30-17.30; last admission 30 mins before closing.
Video programme on the massacre. Exhibition on the history of mountaineering. Guided walks in glen. Gift shop. Snack bar. WC. Picnic area. Disabled access to visitor centre. Walks. Climbing. Car and coach parking. Group concessions. £ (visitor centre).
Tel: 01855 811307   Fax: 01855 811772

Glenlee

Off A762, 2 miles NW of New Galloway, Dumfries & Galloway.
Pri/LA   (map ref: 7P)
Glenlee, much enlarged in 1822, was the home of the Miller family in the 18th century, two of whom were eminent judges, but by the end of the 19th century had passed to the Smiths.

The house is said to be haunted by a 'Grey Lady', the spirit of a Lady Ashburton. She may have been murdered, or involved in a plot to kill her husband. The apparition, clad in a grey silk dress, has reportedly been witnessed on several occasions, as have the sounds of her footsteps.

Glenluce

Off A75, Glenluce, Dumfries & Galloway.
Pri/LA   (map ref: 5P)
The house of Gilbert Campbell, in the village, was said to be haunted by a poltergeist in 1655. Disturbances included objects being thrown at the house,

clothes being shredded, bedclothes being pulled from the beds, all when nobody was apparently present. The activity stopped as suddenly it had started.

Campbell is thought to have been cursed by Alexander Agnew, a tinker, after he had insulted him, and the activity apparently stopped at the same time that Agnew was hanged.

Glenmallan

On A814, 3 miles N of Garelochhead, Argyll.
Pri/LA   (map ref: 5L)
A house here was said to have been haunted by the apparition of a woman, lying on a bed with her face turned to the wall. The ghost was witnessed by a girl staying in the house in 1875. The story goes that the woman was the wife of a former owner. He was a drunkard and beat his wife, and she died of her injuries.

Grandtully Castle

Off A827, 2.5 miles NW of Aberfeldy, Perthshire.
Pri/LA   (map ref: 8J)
An impressive and well-preserved fortress, Grandtully Castle consists of a Z-plan tower house of the Stewarts, later altered and extended. The castle was visited by the Marquis of Montrose and Bonnie Prince Charlie.

After defeat at the Battle of Killiecrankie in 1689, a soldier serving in the forces of William and Mary killed an officer in one of the turrets. The blood staining the floor is said to be impossible to wash off.

Grange House, Edinburgh

Off A7, 1.5 miles S of Edinburgh
Castle, Edinburgh.
Ruin or site   (map ref: 9L)
Grange House was a splendid old mansion, dating from the 16th century or earlier, but it was completely demolished in 1936. Bonnie Prince Charlie stayed here in 1745.

The old house reputedly had many ghosts, one of whom was a miser, who rolled a phantom barrel of gold through the corridors and passageways.

Greenlaw House

Off A701, N of Penicuik, Glencorse, Midlothian.
Pri/LA (map ref: 9M)
Greenlaw House, which incorporated a 17th-century laird's house, was remodelled from 1804 into a large barracks and prison which could hold up to 6000 prisoners from the Napoleonic wars. The building served as the military prison for Scotland from 1845 to 1888. In 1875 it was extended to become the army depot for south-east Scotland, but was completely demolished and the site is occupied by later buildings.

The ghost of a young woman is reported to have been seen at a spot called 'Lover's Leap' at a gorge above the River Esk. The story goes that she had been cavorting with one of the French prisoners held at Greenlaw. Her father had her imprisoned, and while incarcerated her French lover was murdered, died or moved elsewhere. When the girl was released, she found her lover gone, and then threw herself into the river at 'Lover's Leap'.

Haddo House

Off B9005, 10 miles NW of Ellon, Aberdeenshire.
NTS (map ref: 11F)
Haddo House, a massive classical mansion with two sweeping wings, was first built in 1731-6 and designed by William Adam, although it was later altered. The apparition of Lord Archibald Gordon is said to have been seen in the Premier's Bedroom. He was the youngest son of the 1st Marquis of Aberdeen and Temair, and was killed in a car accident, one of the first to die in such a way.

The house stands on the site of an old castle. In 1644 Sir John Gordon of Haddo, who had been active with the Marquis of Montrose, was captured after being besieged here for three days. He was imprisoned in 'Haddo's Hole' in St Giles Cathedral before being executed by beheading. The castle was then destroyed.

Open Good Friday-Easter Monday, May-Sep, wknds only in Oct 13.30-17.30, last admission 16.45.
Garden and country park open all year daily 9.30-sunset.
Exhibition of paintings. Explanatory displays. Gift shop. Restaurant. WC. Adjoining country park. Disabled access. Car and coach parking. Group concessions. ££.
Tel: 01651 851440 Fax: 01651 851888

Hallgreen Castle

Off A92, east of Inverbervie, Kincardine.
Pri/LA (map ref: 11H)
Several ghosts are said to haunt Hallgreen Castle, including a woman who reputedly killed herself after the death of her child, a cloaked man, and two servant girls witnessed in the basement.

Hallgreen Castle, held by the Dunnet family then the Raits, is an L-plan tower house, which incorporates work from the 14th century, with later alterations and extensions.

Hawkhead Hospital
Off A726, 1 mile E of Paisley, Renfrew.
Pri/LA   (map ref: 7M)
Hawkhead, built 1932-5 as an infectious diseases hospital, is said to be haunted by a 'Grey Lady', the spectre of a ward sister murdered by one of the patients.

The hospital stands on the site of a castle, once surrounded by wooded parks and gardens, a property of the Ross family from the middle of the 15th until the 19th century.

Hermitage Castle
Off B6357, 5 miles N of Newcastleton, Borders.
His Scot   (map ref: 10O)
A foreboding fortress in a windswept location, Hermitage, a massive brooding castle, stands near to the English Border.

The castle was held by the De Soulis family, around the turn of the 14th century. William de Soulis was said to be a warlock, and he reputedly seized and slaughtered many local children within the walls. According to one account, the local population eventually rebelled and Soulis was wrapped in lead and boiled in a cauldron in Nine Stane Rig, a stone circle. He may actually have been imprisoned in Dumbarton Castle for supporting the English. The family were forfeited in 1320. Ghostly screams and cries have reportedly

heard from the victims of Lord Soulis, and his own ghost is said to haunt the castle and vicinity.

The castle later passed to the Grahams, then by marriage to the Douglas family. William Douglas, 'The Knight of Liddesdale', was prominent in resisting Edward Balliol in 1330s. He seized Sir Alexander Ramsay of Dalhousie while at his devotions in St Mary's Church in Hawick, and imprisoned him in a dungeon at the castle and starved him to death. The ghost of Ramsay is said to have been seen and heard within the walls. Ramsay's own castle of Dalhousie is also said to be haunted.

In 1353 Douglas was murdered by his godson, another William Douglas, after he had tried to block his claim to the lordship of Douglas. In 1492 Archibald, 5th Earl of Angus, exchanged Hermitage for Bothwell with Patrick Hepburn, Earl of Bothwell.

In 1566 James Hepburn, 4th Earl of Bothwell was badly wounded in a fight with the Border reiver 'Little Jock' Elliot of Park, and was paid a visit on his sick bed by Mary, Queen of Scots. Mary and Bothwell were later married, but after she fled Scotland in 1568, he escaped to Norway. Bothwell was eventually imprisoned in the Danish castle of Dragsholm until his death – his mummified body is said to still be preserved there. An apparition of Mary, Queen of Scots, clad in a white dress, has allegedly been witnessed here.

The castle and title passed from the Hepburns to Francis Stewart, Earl of Bothwell, then – after he was forfeited – to the Scotts of Buccleuch.

The castle was recently the focus for a thorough and state-of-the-art investigation by the American 'supernatural headhunter' Bob Schott. The results are very interesting, and the video is available in PAL format from Global Media Productions, PO 36773, Los Angeles, CA90036, USA.

Open daily Apr-Sep daily 9.30-18.30, last ticket sold 18.00.
Sales area. Car and coach parking. Group concessions. £.
Tel: 01387 376222

His Majesty's Theatre, Aberdeen
Off A956, Rosemout Viaduct, Aberdeen.
Pri/LA   (map ref: 12G)
His Majesty's Theatre, a fine building dating from 1906, was fully renovated in the 1980s. It is said to be haunted by the spirit of a former stagehand known as 'Jake' who was killed in 1942 by a stage hoist. Objects have mysteriously moved by themselves, and an apparition has also reputedly been seen. The foyer is said to be haunted by a 'Grey Lady'.

Theatre.
Tel: 01224 641122   Fax: 01224 632519

Holyroodhouse, Edinburgh
Off A1, at foot of Royal Mile, in Edinburgh.
Pri/LA   (map ref: 9L)
Standing near Holyrood Park and the impressive mass of Arthur's Seat, Holyroodhouse is a fine palace, set around a courtyard, and incorporates a

16th-century block built out of the guest house of the Abbey. Original 16th-century interiors survive in the old block, and the ruins of the abbey church adjoin.

Holyrood Abbey was founded by David I around 1128 as an Augustinian establishment dedicated to the Holy Cross. It was sacked in 1322, 1385, 1544 and 1547 by the English. David Rizzio, Mary, Queen of Scots's secretary, was murdered here in her presence by men led by her husband, Lord Darnley, and a plaque marks the spot. Bonnie Prince Charlie stayed here in 1745 during the Jacobite Rising, and Butcher Cumberland later made it his headquarters. The palace is the official residence of the monarch in Scotland.

A 'Grey Lady', thought to be the spirit of one of Mary's companions, has reputedly been seen in the Queen's Audience Chamber. Ghostly footsteps are said to have been heard in the long gallery, which has portraits – most of them entirely fictitious – of Scottish monarchs.

Open all year (except when monarch is in residence, Good Friday, 7-16 May, 24 Jun-12 Jul & 25/26 Dec): Apr-Oct daily 9.30-17.15; Nov-Mar daily 9.30-15.45.
Guided tours Nov-Mar. Gift shop. WC. Garden. Disabled access. Car and coach parking.
Group concessions (10% groups of 15 or more). £££.
Tel: 0131 556 1096   Fax: 0131 557 5256

Hopetoun House
Off A904, 2.5 miles W of Forth Road Bridge, West Lothian.
Pri/LA   (map ref: 9L)
Standing in extensive parkland by the Firth of Firth, Hopetoun House is a large palatial mansion, which dates from 1699, and was built by the architect William Bruce for the Hope family. Sir Charles Hope, made Earl of Hopetoun in 1703, had the house remodelled by William Adam from 1721, the work being continued by John and Robert Adam.

101

The ghost of a dark-cloaked man is said to have been seen on one of the paths in the grounds, and to be a harbinger of death or misadventure in the Hope family.

Open daily 2 Apr-26 Sep 10.00-17.30; wknds only in Oct; last admission 16.30; other times closed except for group visits by prior appt.
Fine interiors. Collections of furniture and pictures. Gift shop. Restaurant. WC. Picnic area. Exhibitions. Park land. Croquet. Car and coach parking. Group concessions. ££.
Tel: 0131 331 2451 Fax: 0131 319 1885

Houndwood House

Off A1, 3 miles SE of Granthouse, Borders.
Pri/LA   (map ref: 11M)
Houndwood House incorporates a 16th-century tower house, but was remodelled and castellated in the 19th and 20th centuries.

The lands were originally held by Coldingham Priory – the monks are believed to have had a hunting lodge here – but were acquired by the Homes after the Reformation.

The house was said to be haunted by a ghost called 'Chappie', and manifestations were reported in the 19th century, including unexplained heavy footsteps, knocking and rapping, and deep breathing and moans. The apparition of the lower part of a man, dressed in riding breeches, was said to have been witnessed in the grounds outside the house. The story goes that a man was killed by a party of soldiers in the 16th century, and then apparently cut in half.

The sounds of ghostly horses have also been reported here.

Howlet's House

Off A702, 3 miles NW of Penicuik, Midlothian.
Ruin or site   (map ref: 9M)
Site of old house, with thick walls and a vaulted basement. One tale recounts that one of the owners, although old, returned unexpectedly with a young and fetching new wife. For a while they appear to have been happy, but eventually the attractions of a young servant lad tempted her. The young wife and servant lad then disappeared, with a sum of money, but soon afterwards phantoms of the couple were reported in the area. The bodies of the young woman and lad were eventually unearthed, and when they were properly buried in consecrated ground the disturbances stopped. It seems the old farmer murdered them, then fled the area.

Hunter's Tryst, Edinburgh

Off B701, Oxgangs, Edinburgh.
Pri/LA   (map ref: 9L)
Hunter's Tryst, an old coaching inn much altered and extended in recent years, is said to be haunted by a 'White Lady'.

Public house and restaurant.
Tel: 0131 445 3132   Fax: 0131 445 3159

Huntingtower Castle

Off A85, 2 miles NW of Perth.
His Scot   (map ref: 9K)
Standing on the outskirts of Perth, Huntingtower is an impressive pile which dates from the 15th century and was long held by the Ruthvens. Some rooms have fine original painted ceilings, mural paintings and plasterwork, as well as decorative beams in the hall.

   Mary, Queen of Scots, visited the castle in 1565. In 1582 William Ruthven, 1st Earl of Gowrie, abducted the young James VI – in what became known as

the 'Raid of Ruthven' – and held him at Huntingtower. James escaped during a hunting trip and had the Earl beheaded in 1585. Gowrie's ghost is said to haunt the West Bow in Edinburgh.

   In 1600 the 3rd Earl of Gowrie and his brother, Alexander, Master of Ruthven, were slain at Gowrie House in Perth by James VI and his followers, following the 'Gowrie Conspiracy', a possible plot to murder the king. Their bodies were posthumously hanged, drawn and quartered, which must have been messy.

The Ruthvens were forfeited, their name proscribed, and the castle renamed Huntingtower.

The castle and grounds are said to be haunted by a 'Green Lady', also known as 'My Lady Greensleeves'. Her footsteps have reputedly been heard, along with the rustle of her gown, and she has reportedly appeared on several occasions, sometimes as a warning of death, sometimes to help passers-by – including an ill child and a man being robbed.

Open daily all year: Apr-Sep, 9.30-18.30; Oct-Mar Mon-Sat 9.30-16.30, Sun 14.00-16.30 except closed Thu PM & Fri; last ticket sold 30 mins before closing; closed 25/26 Dec & 1-3 Jan.
Gift shop. Picnic area. Car parking. Group concessions. £.
Tel: 01738 627231

Inchdrewer Castle
Off B9121, 3 miles SW of Banff, Aberdeenshire.
Pri/LA   (map ref: 10E)
Inchdrewer Castle was built by the Ogilvies of Dunlugas in the 16th century, who were made Lords Banff. The then Lord Banff was murdered here in 1713 after returning home from Edinburgh. He was probably slain by his own servants, who had been robbing him. The castle was torched to destroy the evidence.

The castle is said to be haunted by the spirit of a lady, who reputedly takes the form of a white dog.

India Street, Edinburgh
Off A90, 0.5 miles N of Edinburgh Castle, Edinburgh.
Pri/LA   (map ref: 9L)
One of the houses in the street, dating from the 1820s, is reputedly haunted. An apparition has often apparently been seen in the hall a few feet above the present floor level, but it is ill-defined and transparent.

Inverawe House
Off A85, 1 mile NE of Taynuilt, Argyll.
Pri/LA   (map ref: 5K)
The later mansion may incorporate a castle of the 14th century. It was a property of the Campbells, and Mary, Queen of Scots, is said to have visited.

The house is thought to be haunted by a 'Green Lady', believed to be the ghost of Mary Cameron of Callart, who married the then laird, Diarmid Campbell. Campbell died in 1645 of wounds received at the Battle of Inverlochy, while fighting against the Marquis of Montrose, and is buried at Ardchattan Priory. Mary died after him, and her ghost is said to haunt the house. It has supposedly been seen in the Ticonderoga Room, and there are reports of the ghost in the 20th century.

Another ghost is said to be that of Duncan Campbell, who died at Ticonderoga in Canada in 1758.

Inverey Castle
Off A93, 4.5 miles W of Braemar, Kincardine & Deeside.
Ruin or site   (map ref: 8G)
Site of a tower house, which was demolished in 1689 after the Battle of Killiecrankie.

John Farquharson of Inverey, the 'Black Colonel' was a Jacobite, and in 1689 defeated a force attacking Braemar Castle, which he then burnt. He is said to have summoned servants by firing a pistol.

After being interred in St Andrew's churchyard at Braemar – despite wanting to be buried at Inverey – his coffin reputedly appeared above ground three times before finally being taken back to Inverey. His ghost is said to have been seen at Braemar Castle.

Invergarry Castle
Off A82, 7 miles SW of Fort Augustus, Highlands.
Ruin or site   (map ref: 5H)

Perched on the 'Rock of the Raven', the slogan of the family, Invergarry Castle is an impressive ruinous tower house of the Clan Ranald branch of the MacDonalds. It has an eventful history, and was burnt in 1654 by Cromwell, changed hands several times during the Jacobite Risings, and was finally torched by the 'Butcher' Duke of Cumberland after being visited by Bonnie Prince Charlie. The Glengarry Castle Hotel stands on the site of a later mansion.

The old castle is said to have had a brownie.

Glengarry Hotel – open 26 Mar-8 Nov. Ruins can be seen from grounds of hotel – the interior of castle is in dangerous condition.
Tel: 01809 501254   Fax: 01809 501207

Inverquharity Castle

Off B955, 3.5 miles NE of Kirriemuir, Angus.
Pri/LA (map ref: 9I)

Inverquharity Castle was built by the Ogilvies about 1420. One of the family, Alexander, was smothered at Finavon Castle by his sister in 1446, while another Alexander was captured after the Battle of Philiphaugh in 1645, while fighting for the Marquis of Montrose, and beheaded in Glasgow.

Inverquharity is said to have been haunted by a Sir John Ogilvie. Desiring the beautiful daughter of the local miller John White, Ogilvie had her father hanged when she refused him, then raped the girl and her mother. The local priest prayed for vengeance, and Ogilvie was struck down dead, although his ghost is said to have so plagued the castle it had to be abandoned – at one time, anyway.

Iona Abbey

Off A849, Iona, Argyll.
Pri/LA (map ref: 2K)

Situated on the beautiful and peaceful island of Iona, the Abbey occupies the site of St Columba's monastery, founded in 563. Columba converted the Picts of mainland Scotland to Christianity, and died in 597. His shrine, within the Abbey buildings, dates from the 9th century.

The abbey was abandoned after raids by Norsemen, and one ghost story dates from this time. It is said that apparitions of longships and marauding Norsemen have been seen at White Sands, reputedly the spot where Vikings slew the abbot and 15 monks in 986. They then went on to plunder and burn the abbey buildings.

The Abbey was re-established by Queen Margaret, wife of Malcolm Canmore, in the 11th century. Some of the surviving abbey buildings date from the early 13th century after it had been refounded as a Benedictine establishment by Reginald, son of Somerled, Lord of the Isles. The abbey church and cloister were rebuilt in 1938 for the Iona Community. Ghosts of brown-robed monks have apparently been seen around the island and within the abbey.

The 9th-century St Martin's Cross and St John's Cross – the latter a replica – stand just outside the church, and the museum houses a splendid collection of sculptured stones and crosses, one of the largest collections of early Christian carved stones in Europe. Between the abbey and the nunnery is MacLean's Cross, a fine 15th-century carved stone cross.

Many of the early Kings of Scots are buried in 'Reilig Odhrain' – the 'Street of the Dead' – as well as kings of Ireland and Norway. The 12th-century chapel of St Oran also survives.

The nearby Augustinian nunnery of St Mary was founded in 1208, also by Reginald, and is a fine consolidated ruin.

Open at all times – ferry from Fionnphort (£), no cars on Iona. Walk to abbey.
Day tours from Oban in summer. Explanatory displays. Gift shop. Tearoom. WC. Car and coach parking at Fionnphort. £ (ferry).
Tel: 01681 700404

Jedburgh Castle
Off A68, Castlegate, in Jedburgh, Borders.
Ruin or site   (map ref: 11N)
The Castle Jail stands on the site of an ancient castle, occupied by the English from 1346 until 1409, when it was retaken by the Scots and demolished. The Castle Jail, built in 1823 and now a museum, is a Howard reform prison, and the only one of its kind now remaining in Scotland. The museum recreates life in the jail using costumed figures and replica prison furniture, and there are displays on local history in the Gaoler's House.

Malcolm the Maiden died at the old castle in 1165. Alexander III was married to the young and beautiful Yolande of Druix in the hall of the castle in 1285 after his first wife and children had predeceased him. A ghostly apparition at the marriage feast warned of his impending death – which came true when Alexander fell, with his horse, from a cliff at Kinghorn on his way to see his new bride. The ghostly apparition was apparently witnessed several times, and was always the harbinger of death.

Castle Jail open Apr-Oct daily Mon-Sat 10.00-16.45, Sun 13.00-16.00; open on Bank Holidays.
Explanatory displays. Gift shop. WC. Picnic area. Disabled access. Car and coach parking.
Group concessions. £.
Tel: 01835 863254

Johnstone Lodge, Anstruther
Off A917, Kirk Wynd, Anstruther, Fife.
Pri/LA   (map ref: 10K)
Johnstone Lodge, a town house of 1829, was said to be haunted. In the 19th century it was the home of a George Dairsie, who married Princess Tetuane Marama, a Tahitian princess. The two lived here, although Tetuane found the climate inhospitable, and when she died she was buried in the town's kirkyard, a memorial on the south wall of the church commemorating her.

After her death, the apparition of Tetuane was reported in many of the rooms of Johnstone Lodge, as well as on a balcony. The building has been converted into flats.

Kellie Castle

Off B9171, 4 miles N of Elie, Fife.
NTS   (map ref: 10K)

A splendid castle with a magnificent garden, Kellie dates from the 16th and 17th centuries and was built by the Oliphants. It passed to the Erskines, then in 1878 was leased by James Lorimer, who proceeded to restore it. The ghost of Lorimer is said to have been seen, seated in one of the corridors. Robert Lorimer, his son, the famous architect, spent most of his childhood here.

A turnpike stair in the castle is reputedly haunted by the ghost of Anne Erskine, who died when she fell from one of the upstairs windows. Her apparition is rarely reported, but it is said that her footsteps have often been heard on the stair.

In 1970 Kellie passed into the care of The National Trust for Scotland.

Open Good Friday-Easter Monday, then May-Sep, open wknds only Oct, 13.30-17.30 last admission
16.45. Grounds and garden open all year 9.30-sunset.
Victorian nursery, old kitchen, and audio-visual show. Explanatory displays. Giftshop.
Tearoom. Magnificent walled garden. WC. Disabled access to ground floor & grounds. Car
park. ££.
Tel: 01333 720271   Fax: 01333 720326

Kilchrenan

Off B845, 1 mile E of Kilchrenan, N of minor road, Argyll.
Ruin or site   (map ref: 5K)
A cup-marked stone here is reputedly where a monk was sacrificed in early Christian times. An apparition of his decapitated body has been reported.

Killiecrankie

On B8079, 3 miles N of Pitlochry, Perthshire.
NTS (map ref: 8I)

Set in a fine and picturesque wooded gorge, it was on 27 July 1689 that the Jacobites, led by John Graham of Claverhouse, Viscount Dundee, defeated a government army. Claverhouse was mortally wounded at the battle, and the

Jacobites disbanded after failing to capture Dunkeld. At Killiecrankie is the 'Soldier's Leap', where one government soldier escaped from Jacobite forces by jumping across the River Garry. An exhibition in the visitor centre features the battle, with models and maps, and there are also displays on natural history.

There are many reports of manifestations here, including a red glow that covers the area on the anniversary of the battle. Others claim to have had visions of the battle or its aftermath. Dundee, himself, is said to have had a visitation of a bloodied man, gore dripping from his head, on the night before the battle. The apparition apparently said: 'Remember Brown of Priesthill!' Brown of Priesthill was executed by Dundee in 1685 because he was a Covenanter who refused to acknowledge the authority of James VII. This was taken afterwards to be a warning of Dundee's impending death.

Dundee's apparition, itself, is said to have appeared to Lord Balcarres, about the time he died. Incidentally, Dundee was said to be a warlock by his Covenanter enemies, and therefore could only be killed by a silver bullet. Similar 'quirks' were given to other enemies, including Mackenzie of Rosehaugh, Bruce of

Earlshall, Grierson of Lag and Tam Dalziel of the Binns. In Tam's case at the Battle of Rullion Green in 1666 musket balls were said just to bounce off him.

Site open all year; visitor centre, shop and snack bar open 1 Apr (or Good Friday if earlier)-Oct 10.00-17.30.
Exhibition. Gift shop. Tearoom. WC. Disabled WC. Car park. £.
Tel: 01796 473233

Kindrochit Castle, Braemar
Off A93, to S of Braemar, Kincardine & Deeside.
Ruin or site   (map ref: 8G)
Little remains of a once strong castle, for many years held by the Drummonds. It was reputedly destroyed by cannon in the 17th century, after the plague had struck, so that the occupants could not escape.

  The story goes that during the Jacobite Rising a way into one of the old vaults was found. A Hanoverian soldier was lowered in, hoping to find treasure, but fled when he found a phantom party seated around a table piled with skulls. Excavations failed to reveal a ghostly company – strangely – but the Kindrochit Brooch was unearthed.

Open all year.
Parking.

Kingcausie
Off B9077, 1.5 miles SE of Peterculter, Aberdeenshire.
Pri/LA   (map ref: 11G)
Pronounced 'Kincowsie', Kingcausie, a modern mansion, incorporates a 16th-century tower house of the Irvines of Kingcausie, and is still owned by the same family.

  The house is said to be haunted by the ghost of a two-year-old child. James Turner Christie, the infant, fell down the stair from his nanny's arms and was killed. The pattering of child's footsteps have reputedly been heard several times when there is nobody about. The Chinese Room is also reputedly haunted. The bedclothes are said to have been flung off one of the occupants.

King's Arms Hotel, Dumfries
Off A75, Dumfries.
Ruin or site   (map ref: 8P)
Standing near the junction of English Street with the High Street, the King's Arms Hotel was haunted by the ghost of a young woman in Victorian garb, a 'Grey Lady'. The building has been demolished, and the site is occupied by shops.

Kinnaird Castle

Off A934, 5.5 miles W of Montrose, Angus.
Pri/LA (map ref: 10I)

Kinnaird, a 19th-century mansion, incorporates part of an ancient castle, long a property of the Carnegie Earls of Southesk, who still live here.

One story connected with the castle is that the corpse of James Carnegie, the 2nd Earl of Southesk, who died in 1669, was reportedly taken by a ghostly black coach driven by black horses. Carnegie is said to have studied in Padua, where he allegedly learnt black magic, and to have lost his shadow to the devil. A similar story is told of Alexander Skene of Skene House.

Kinnaird Head Castle, Fraserburgh

Off A98, N of Fraserburgh, Banff & Buchan.
His Scot (map ref: 11E)

Kinnaird Head Castle consists of an altered white-washed tower house, dating from the 15th century, with a lighthouse on top. The lighthouse was built in 1787, and the outbuildings clustered around it were added in 1820 by Robert Stevenson, grandfather of Robert Louis Stevenson. It now forms part of a lighthouse museum.

The Wine Tower, standing about 50 yards away, is a lower tower, probably used as a chapel at one time.

The castle was a property of the Frasers of Philorth. Sir Alexander Fraser built the harbour at Fraserburgh – the town had been called Faithlie – and came near to bankrupting himself: he had to sell much of his property in 1611.

Sir Alexander is said to disapproved of his daughter Isobel's lover, and had the poor man chained in a sea cave below the Wine Tower to teach him a lesson. Fraser miscalculated, however, and the poor man drowned. When Isobel found her lover, she threw herself to her death in the water. An apparition is said to been seen by the Wine Tower whenever there is a storm.

Open daily all year as Lighthouse Museum, Apr-Oct , Mon-Sat 10.00-18.00, Sun 12.30-18.00; Nov-Mar, Mon-Sat 10.00-16.00, Sun 12.00-16.00; closed 25/26 Dec & 1/2 Jan – joint entry ticket.
Visitor centre with explanatory displays and audio-visual display. Gift shop. Tearoom. WC.
Disabled access. Car and coach parking. Group concessions. £.
Tel: 01346 511022   Fax: 01346 511033

Kinneil House

Off A993, 1 mile SW of Bo'ness, West Lothian.
His Scot   (map ref: 8L)
Set in a public park, Kinneil House, dating from the 16th-century, is a fine old mansion with original tempera paintings in two rooms. The lands were long held by the Hamiltons, although the building was occupied by Cromwell's forces in 1650, from when the ghost story is said to originate.

Kinneil is said to be haunted by the ghost of the young wife of a Roundhead officer billeted here. After having tried to escape several times, as she was homesick, she was imprisoned in one of the upper chambers. In despair, she threw herself from the window into the Gil Burn, nearly 200 feet below. Her screams and wails are still said to be heard on dark winter nights.

Open all year – view from exterior.
Car parking.

Knockderry Castle

Off B833, 1 mile N of Cove, Loch Long, Argyll.
Pri/LA   (map ref: 5L)
Perched at the edge of a rocky outcrop, Knockderry Castle, a 19th-century mansion, is said to have been built on the site of a tower dating from the 13th century. The house is reputedly haunted.

Kylesku Hotel

Off A894, 9 miles SE of Scourie, Kylesku, Highlands.
Pri/LA   (map ref: 5B)
By the sea in a unspoilt, remote and rugged location, the Kylesku Hotel is a comfortable establishment near the former ferry – the road now crosses by a bridge. Boat trips can be arranged to take guests to the highest waterfall in Britain, the 685-foot 'Eas Coul Aulin'.

The inn is said to be haunted by the apparition of an old man. The story goes that a party was being held in the attic, above the bar, after a barrel of whisky had been washed ashore following a wreck. Father and son brawled, and the older man fell down the ladder from the attic and broke his neck. An apparition is said to appear near the entrance to the snug on the anniversary of his death, the last recorded appearance was said to be in 1950.

Hotel – open all year and to non-residents.
Ensuite accommodation. Restaurant and bar. Ideally situated for hill walking, climbing fishing, sea trips and wildlife. Parking. $-$$.
Tel: 01971 502231/200   Fax: 01971 502313

Largie Castle

Off A83, 17 miles SW of Tarbert, Argyll.
Ruin or site   (map ref: 4M)
Site of castle of the MacDonalds, replaced by a mostly 19th-century mansion, nothing of which remains. It was held by the family until the 20th century, and is reported to have had a brownie.

Laudale House

Off A884, S side of Loch Sunart, Highland.
Pri/LA   (map ref: 3I)
Laudale House, a three-storey mansion, is said to be haunted. The sounds of something heavy, perhaps a body in armour, being dragged across the floor are reportedly heard, but nothing can be found to explain the noises. One tale is that it was to Laudale that the body of Angus Mor was brought. Angus had murdered the young chief of the MacIans, and was himself slain in battle in Glen Dubh, near Kinlochaline, by a force of Camerons and MacLeans.

Lauriston Castle, Edinburgh

Off B9085, 3 miles W of Edinburgh Castle.
Pri/LA   (map ref: 9L)
Set in 30 acres of a parkland and gardens near the picturesque village of Cramond, Lauriston Castle consists of tower house and mansion, and dates from the 16th century. The castle has a fine Edwardian-period interior.

It was built by the Napiers of Merchiston in the 1590s, one of whom, John Napier, was the inventor of logarithms. It passed through several families, until the last owners, the Reids, gave it to the city of Edinburgh in 1926.

The ghostly sound of feet have reportedly been heard in the castle.

Open Apr-Oct except Fri 11.00-13.00 & 14.00-17.00; wknds only Nov-Mar 14.00-16.00; grounds open all year.
Good collections of Italian furniture, Blue John, Grossley wool mosaics, Sheffield plate, mezzotint prints, Caucasian carpets, and items of decorative art. Guided tours of house only. WC. Disabled access to grounds & WC. Car and coach parking. Group concessions.
££ (castle).
Tel: 0131 336 2060   Fax: 0131 557 3346

Learmonth Hotel, Edinburgh

Off A90, 18-20 Learmonth Terrace, Edinburgh.
Pri/LA   (map ref: 9L)
Standing on Queensferry Road, the Learmonth Hotel is said to be haunted by a poltergeist. Doors reputedly open and close, and even unlock, themselves. Electrical equipment, such as kettles and hairdryers, have been known to switch themselves on and off, and unexplained whistling is said to have been heard in empty corridors.

Hotel – open all year.
Accommodation. Refreshments and meals.
Tel: 0131 343 2671   Fax: 0131 315 2232

Leith Hall

Off B9002, 3.5 miles NE of Rhynie, Aberdeenshire.
NTS   (map ref: 10F)
Set in 286 acres of grounds, Leith Hall is a courtyard mansion with yellow-washed walls and small drum towers. It was a property of the Leith family from 1650, or earlier, until 1945, when it was given to The National Trust for Scotland.

Guests in 1968 reported manifestations in their bedroom, including the sounds of a woman's laugh and a party going on when nobody else was apparently there. Sightings of the apparition of a man, bandaged about the head, were also reported. The ghost is thought to be John Leith, who was killed in a brawl in 1763.

Open Good Friday-Easter Monday, then May-Sep, then wknds Oct 13.30-17.30, last admission 16.45. Garden and grounds open all year 9.30-sunset.
Explanatory sheets. Exhibition. Tearoom. WC. Picnic area. Gardens. Disabled facilities and WC. Car and coach parking. Group concessions. *££*.
Tel: 01464 831216   Fax: 01464 831594

Liberton House, Edinburgh

Off A701, 3 miles SE of Edinburgh Castle, Edinburgh.
Pri/LA   (map ref: 9L)

Liberton House, built by William Little, Provost of Edinburgh, around 1605 is an L-plan tower house, now harled and orange-washed. The name Liberton comes from 'leper's town': the leper colony which was once located near here. The house is reputedly haunted, and a photograph taken at the beginning of the century purports to show the image of a man not apparently present when the photograph was taken.

Linlithgow Palace

Off A803, in Linlith-gow, West Lothian.
His Scot   (map ref: 8L)

Once a splendid palace and still a spectacular ruin, Linlithgow Palace consists of ranges of buildings around a rectangular courtyard, and may include 12th-century work. There is a fine carved fountain in the courtyard. The palace was used by the Stewart monarchs, and has a long and eventful history.

115

A castle here was captured by Edward I of England in 1301 during the Wars of Independence, but was recaptured by the Scots driving a cart under the portcullis. It was rebuilt by James I at the beginning of the 15th century, and the work continued under James III and James IV. Mary, Queen of Scots, was born here in 1542. It was last used by Charles I in 1633 although his son, James, Duke of York, stayed here before succeeding to the throne in 1685. In 1746 General Hawley retreated here after being defeated by the Jacobites at Falkirk. The soldiers started fires to dry themselves, and the palace was accidentally set blaze. It was never restored.

The palace is said to be haunted by a 'Blue Lady', who walks from the entrance of the palace to the door of the nearby parish church of St Michael.

Queen Margaret's bower, at the top of one of the stair-towers, is reputed to be haunted by the ghost of either Margaret Tudor, wife of James IV, or Mary of Guise, wife of James V.

Open daily all year: Apr-Sep 9.30-18.30; Oct-Mar Mon-Sat 9.30-16.40, Sun 14.00-16.30; last ticket sold 30 mins before closing; closed 25/26 Dec & 1-3 Jan.
Explanatory panels and exhibition. Gift shop. WC. Picnic area. Disabled access. Car parking. Group concessions. £.
Tel: 01506 842896

Littledean Tower

Off A699, 6.5 miles W of Kelso, Borders.
Ruin or site   (map ref: 11N)
Littledean Tower has a sinister tale regarding one of the Kerr lords of the 17th century. The ruinous castle consists of a 16th-century block to which was added a large D-plan tower.

A ghostly horsemen, the spirit of one of the Kerr lords, the 'Deil of Littledean', is said sometimes to be seen near the castle.

The story goes that he was a cruel man – as in many other ghost stories he was a persecutor of Covenanters – who scorned his wife and his servants, and spent his nights and drinking and brawling with others of like mind. One night, while out riding after an argument with his wife, he came to a clearing in the woods, where there was the cottage of an attractive young woman. In brief, the laird began cavorting with the girl, but it turned out she was a witch, whose severed arm strangled him in his bed.

Loch of Leys

Off A980, 1 mile N of Banchory, Aberdeenshire.
Ruin or site   (map ref: 11G)
Once on an island which has since been drained, nothing remains of a castle of the Burnetts. Alexander Burnett of Leys married Janet Hamilton in 1543, and

acquired a sizeable dowry of church lands. With this new wealth, they built Crathes Castle, which has its own ghost story, and abandoned Leys.

The old castle was reputedly haunted. Alexander Burnett fell in love with Bertha, a relative who was staying with his family. His mother, Agnes, was dismayed for she had other plans for her son and poisoned Bertha. But Bertha did not rest after her death, and Agnes was apparently frightened to death by Bertha's spectre – or perhaps by her own conscience. A phantom is said to still appear on the anniversary of Bertha's death.

Lochailort Inn

Off A830, 22 miles W of Fort William, Highlands.
Pri/LA   (map ref: 3H)
The Lochailort Inn was said to be haunted, and manifestations included the apparition of a woman in a blue dress. There has been an inn on the site from 1650, but after a fire in 1994 and the rebuilding of the hotel, there have been no further reported disturbances. Ghostly bagpipes are allegedly heard in the glen from a phantom piper of the Jacobite Rising of 1745.

Hotel - open all year and to non-residents.
Ensuite accommodation. Refreshments and food. Parking. Ideally situated for touring, fishing, cruises and hill walking. Railway station 600 yards.
Tel: 01687 470208

Lochleven Castle

Off B996, 1 mile E of Kinross, Perth & Kinross.
His Scot   (map ref: 9L)
Standing on an island in the picturesque Loch Leven, the castle consists of a tower house and courtyard, dating from the 14th century. Andrew of Wyntoun wrote his 'Chronicle of Scotland' at the priory of St Serf's on the largest island in the loch.

During the Wars of Independence, having been seized by the English, the castle was stormed by William Wallace, who swam out to the island and surprised the garrison. Mary, Queen of Scots, was imprisoned here from 1567 until she escaped the next year. She signed her

abdication here, and she is also said to have miscarried – her ghost reputedly still haunts the castle.

Open Apr-Sep daily 9.30-18.30, last ticket 30 mins before closing – includes boat trip from Kinross.
Gift shop. WC. Picnic area. Car parking at Kinross. £.
Tel: 01786 450000

Lochnell House
Off A828, 4 miles N of Oban, Argyll.
Pri/LA (map ref: 4J)
Lochnell House, a modern mansion, was built by the Campbell family and suffered a serious fire about 1859. It is now held by the Earl of Dundonald. The house is said to have had a brownie, and ghostly music has reportedly been heard here.

Logie House, Dundee
Off A85 or A923, 1 mile S of Dundee Law, Dundee.
Ruin or site (map ref: 10K)
Site of a mansion, designed by James Black, but demolished at the beginning of the 20th century. It was a property of the Read family at the beginning of the 19th century. It was thought to be haunted by a 'Black Lady', reputedly an Indian princess captured by one of the family while working for the East India Company. Read had brought her to Logie, but kept her imprisoned, and there she died. Her ghost was then reported to have haunted the area.

Lordscairnie Castle
Off A913 or A914, 3 miles NW of Cupar, Fife.
Ruin or site (map ref: 10K)
Once standing on an islet in a loch, Lordscairnie Castle is a stark ruinous tower, dating from the 15th century and later. It was a property of the Lindsay Earls of Crawford from about 1350, and probably built by the 4th Earl, 'Earl Beardie' also known as the 'Tiger Earl'. His ghost can reputedly be seen playing cards here

with the devil on the stroke of midnight on New Years' Eve – although this may be a translation from Glamis.

There are stories of treasure being buried here.

Loudon Castle

Off A719, 1 mile N of Galston, Ayrshire.
Ruin or site   (map ref: 7N)
Loudon Castle, a large ruined castellated mansion, incorporates an old tower house. The property was owned by John Campbell, Chancellor of Scotland, who was made Earl of Loudon in 1641. The building was accidentally torched and gutted in 1941, and is now the centre piece of a theme park.

The castle was reputedly haunted by a 'Grey Lady', who was apparently often seen before its destruction in 1941, and is said to have been witnessed since. The ghost of a hunting dog, with glowing eyes, is also believed by some to roam the area.

Loudon Castle Park open Easter-Oct from 10.00.
Guided tours for school parties. Gift shop. Restaurant. Tearoom. WC. Picnic area. Disabled limited access and WC. Car and coach parking. Group concessions. £££.
Tel: 01563 822296   Fax: 01563 822408

Luffness House

Off A198, 1 mile E of Aberlady, East Lothian.
Pri/LA   (map ref: 10L)
Standing by he sea near the picturesque village of Aberlady, Luffness House consists of an old tower house, although parts date from the 13th century, with later additions and modifications. It was once a large strong castle.

The property was given to the Church in memory of the 8th Earl, a crusader, and a Carmelite friary was built nearby before 1293. Some of the church survives, including the stone effigy slab of a crusader, probably of the founder himself. The property passed to the Hepburn Earls of Bothwell, after the Reformation, and was visited by Mary, Queen of Scots. Luffness was sold to the Hope Earls of Hopetoun in 1739, and remains with their descendants.

119

One story is that the massive door of one of the angle towers – the only way into the chamber – is said to have locked itself. When the room was investigated through one of the gunloops, the key was found to be on a table in the middle of the room. There was no other way into the room.

Macduff's Castle

Off A955, E of East Wemyss, Fife.
Ruin or site   (map ref: 9L)
Macduff's Castle, a ruinous 14th-century castle, was held by the Wemyss family in the 17th century, and in 1666 the Countess of Sutherland, who was a daughter of the 2nd Earl of Wemyss, lodged her children here during the plague in

Edinburgh. The castle is said to be called after the MacDuff Thanes or Earls of Fife, who may have had an older stronghold here.

The ghost of a woman, the 'Grey Lady' reputedly haunts the castle. She is thought to be Mary Sibbald, who ran off with a gypsy laddie but was accused of thievery. A court found her guilty, and she was sentenced to be whipped, but the punishment appears to have killed the poor woman. Her ghost is also said to haunt Wemyss Caves, as the trial took place in the Court Cave.

Other caves in the complex include Doo Cave, Sliding Cave and Jonathan's Cave, and the walls are inscribed with a variety of Bronze Age, Norse, Pictish and early Christian symbols, many defaced and vandalised. Some of the caves have been sealed.

View from exterior.

Mains Castle

Off B873, 1 mile N of East Kilbride, Lanarkshire.
Pri/LA   (map ref: 7M)
Mains Castle was a property of the Lindsays of Dunrod until 1695. One of the family, along with Kirkpatrick of Closeburn, helped 'mak siccar' by slaying John Comyn after he had been stabbed by Robert the Bruce in 1306.

The castle is reputedly haunted by the ghost of a woman strangled by her jealous husband. The poor woman is said to have been a sister of William the Lyon, the 12th-century King of Scots. Her husband found her with her lover, and slew her in a rage.

Marlfield House
Off B6401, 5.5 miles S of Kelso, Borders.
Pri/LA   (map ref: 11N)
Marlfield House was remodelled in the mid 18th century and later, possibly by William Adam, but is said to incorporate part of an ancient castle. The house is reputed to be haunted by a ghost which pushes past people in one of the passageways. It is said to have been active in recent years.

Mary King's Close, Edinburgh
Off A1, High Street, under City Chambers, Edinburgh.
Pri/LA   (map ref: 9L)
Lying beneath the City Chambers, which was designed by the architects John and Robert Adam in 1753, lies Mary King's Close, a narrow old Edinburgh close which is said to be haunted, indeed believed by some to be the most haunted place in the capital. The population of the Close was devastated by the plague of 1645, and the buildings were abandoned and sealed off. Some years later, they were reoccupied, but had reputedly become haunted. Apparitions were allegedly seen frequently, including that of a small girl in a dirty dress and a dog, and eventually the close was abandoned again. The upper floors were then demolished, while the lower ones were sealed over, and the City Chambers constructed on the site.

Tours of the close are available, and the spirit of the young girl and dog have reportedly been seen, as well as that of a tall thin woman, garbed in a black dress, witnessed recently. Other disturbances include cameras flashing for no apparent reason, and not working in parts of the close.

Guided tours of Mary King's Close are available at 10.30, 11.30, 14.30, 15.30, 19.30, 20.30 &
21.30.
Booking essential. £££. Combined tours with vaults available. Concessions. Group
discounts.
Tel: 0131 225 6591   Fax: 0131 225 6591
Email: info@mercat-tours.co.uk   Web: www.mercat-tours.co.uk

Maryculter House
Off B9077, South Deeside Road, 8 miles SW of Aberdeen.
Pri/LA   (map ref: 11G)
Picturesquely situated on the banks of the Dee, Maryculter House is substantially a 17th-century house of the Menzies family, later altered and extended, who

held the property from the 14th century. There was a preceptory of the Knights Templars here, founded by Walter Bisset between 1225 and 1236, which passed to the Knights of St John of Jerusalem about 1309. Vaulted cellars from the preceptor's house are built into the hotel, notably the cocktail bar. The foundations of the nearby Templar's church, which was used by the parish until 1782, can also be traced

It is recorded that one of the Templars brought his Saracen lover to Maryculter, and the couple were executed. When the execution took place, the Preceptor is said to have been stuck down by lightning. The hollow, 'The Thunder Hole', which was formerly much deeper, is traditionally the site of his death.

Hotel – open all year.
23 bedrooms with ensuite facilities. Dining room and bars. Banquets, weddings and conferences. Parking. $$-$$$.
Tel: 01224 732124   Fax: 01224 733510

Medwyn House

Off A702, 0.25 miles NW of West Linton, Borders.
Pri/LA   (map ref: 9M)
Medwyn House, a modern mansion, incorporates parts of a 15th-century building, which was used as a coaching inn – the main road to Edinburgh used to follow a course nearer to the house.

The unexplained sounds of horses and a coach are said to have been heard near the house.

Meggernie Castle

Off B846, 8 miles N of Killin,
Perthshire.
Pri/LA   (map ref: 7K)
Meggernie Castle, an extended 16th-century tower house, was built by Colin Campbell of Glenlyon, but passed to the Menzies of Culdares, then the Stewarts of Cardney.

The rather grim ghost story dates from when the castle was held by the Menzies family. One of the lairds had a beautiful wife, but he was a jealous husband and suspected his wife of straying. In a fit of rage, he attacked and then murdered the

122

poor woman in one of the chambers in the ancient part of the castle. Menzies chopped her body in two, hoping to dispose of it later, and hid her remains under the floorboards or disposed of it in a chest in a closet, depending on the version. Menzies then left for the continent, and when he returned excused his wife's disappearance by claiming she had drowned when they were away.

He then returned to the gruesome task of disposing of her body. He managed to bury her lower half, but was then apparently murdered himself.

From then on odd things began to happen at Meggernie. The apparition of top half of a woman's body was said to haunt the upper floors; while the lower half was reputedly seen on the ground floor and in the grounds near the family burial ground. During renovation, the upper bones of skeleton were reportedly discovered, but the haunting continued even after the skeleton was buried. There are also said to have been other disturbances such as knockings and banging in the building. The ghost is also said to have kissed visitors to Meggernie, waking them from sleep, but this particular story was a matter of some debate and doubt was thrown on the credibility of at least one of the witnesses.

Megginch Castle

Off A85, 8 miles E of Perth.
Pri/LA   (map ref: 9K)
Surrounded by woodlands, Megginch Castle has been a property of the Drummonds from 1646, although the building dates from the 15th century. There are extensive gardens with 1000-year-old yews, a 16th-century rose garden, kitchen garden, topiary and a 16th-century physic garden. The courtyard of the castle was used for filming part of the film version of 'Rob Roy' with Liam Neeson in 1994. This is a little ironic as the Drummonds of Megginch tried to hunt down Rob Roy MacGregor, but were – of course – unsuccessful.

One of the rooms in the old part of the castle is said to be haunted by the whispering of two gossiping women.

Castle not open; gardens open Apr-Oct Wed 14.00-17.00; Aug daily 14.00-17.00.
Guided tours by arrangement and extra charge. Disabled partial access. Car and coach parking. £.
Tel: 01821 642222   Fax: 01821 642708

Meldrum House

Off A947, 1 mile N of Oldmeldrum, Aberdeenshire.
Pri/LA   (map ref: 11F)
Located in 15 acres of landscaped parkland, Meldrum House, an impressive sprawling mansion with round towers, incorporates an ancient castle. It was a property of the Meldrums until about 1450, then the Setons, then from 1670 the Urquharts, but is now used as a hotel.

The house is said to be haunted by a 'White Lady', and her apparition has been reported several times, as recent as in 1985 when she reputedly gave a male guest a cold kiss during a thunder storm. It was thought she only appeared to children, who when left alone would subsequently report seeing a lady in a white dress who took care of them.

Hotel – open all year.
9 bedrooms with ensuite facilities. Restaurant and private bar. Functions, small conferences and weddings. Own 18-hole golf course available to residents. Parking.
Tel: 01651 872294   Fax: 01651 872464

Melgund Castle

Off B9134, 4.5 miles SW of Brechin, Angus.
Ruin or site   (map ref: 10I)
Melgund Castle, an L-plan tower house and hall-block, was built in the 16th century by Cardinal David Beaton, Archbishop of St Andrews and Chancellor of Scotland. Beaton was murdered in 1546 at St Andrews,
and his ghost is said to have been witnessed here, as well as at Ethie and St Andrews. The castle passed to other families, and is currently being restored.

Melrose Abbey

Off B6361, in Melrose, Borders.
His Scot   (map ref: 10N)
An elegant and picturesque ruin, Melrose Abbey was founded as a Cistercian house by David I about 1136, and dedicated to the Blessed Virgin Mary. The church is particularly well preserved, while the domestic buildings and the cloister are very ruinous.

The Abbey was sacked by the English in 1322, 1385 and 1545. The heart of Robert the Bruce is buried in the nave, as is Alexander II and Joanna, his wife, as well as many of the powerful Douglas family. Sir Michael Scott of Balwearie, the 13th-century scholar and reputed warlock, is also said to be interred on the south side of the chancel. The area is supposed to radiate unease.

The spirit of a monk was reputed to haunt the cloister area. This wicked fellow is said to have led a life of violence and sin, despite his vows, and to have become a vampire, who returned to his tomb each night after venturing abroad for blood. The monk apparently attacked the abbess of a nearby convent. He was finally laid to rest when another monk waited for him to emerge from the tomb, then beheaded him with an axe.

Open all year: Apr-Sep, daily 9.30-18.30, Nov-Mar Mon-Sat 9.30-16.30, Sun 2.00-16.30; last ticket sold 30 mins before closing.
Audio guide and explanatory displays. Gift shop. WC. Picnic area. Museum in former Commendator's House. Car and coach parking. Group concessions. £.
Tel: 01896 822562

Melville Grange
Off A720, 1 mile W of Dalkeith, Edinburgh.
Pri/LA   (map ref: 9M)
The farmhouse here is said to be haunted, and the apparition of a girl dressed in white has been reported. The story goes back 700 years to when there was a farm here, belonging to Newbattle Abbey. It was used as a rendezvous by a young noble women and a monk from the abbey. The girl's father learned of their dallying, and forbad them to meet. The girl met the monk for the last time at the farm to part from him forever, but her father followed her, and when she would not respond to his threats, burnt the farm down around them, killing them both.

Menie House

Off A92, 2 miles N of Balmedie, Aberdeenshire.
Pri/LA   (map ref: 12F)
Menie House is said to be haunted by a 'Green Lady', who is reported to have been seen during the night in the basement of the old part of the house. Menie dates from the 18th century, and stands on the site of an ancient castle. It was a property of the Forbeses.

Mercat Cross, Edinburgh

Off A1, Royal Mile, W of St Giles Cathedral, Edinburgh.
Pri/LA   (map ref: 9L)
It was at Edinburgh's Mercat Cross, parts of which date from the 15th century, that ghostly apparitions are reported to have read the lists of dead at the Battle of Flodden, some months before the disastrous battle or on the eve, depending on the account. The list began with James IV, then went through the nobles and commoners. This was witnessed by a Richard Lawson, a merchant in the burgh, but the poor man collapsed on hearing his own name and appealed to be spared. If this was a warning, it remained unheeded, as was a similar portent at Linlithgow. James IV led his large army into England, and was killed at Flodden with 15 earls, 70 lords, 100s of lairds and 10000 men. Lawson, however, is said to have survived.

The sighting of the apparition of one of the old town guard, a Highlander with a grey beard, has been reported in Parliament Square.

Accessible at all times.

Moncrieffe Arms, Bridge of Earn

Off A912, Bridge of Earn, Perth and Kinross.
Pri/LA   (map ref: 9K)
The hotel here is said to be haunted. Manifestations include the sound of footsteps on floorboards, even though areas are carpeted, and the sound of weeping coming from unoccupied areas, thought to be one of the upstairs passages. In the 1970s the owner reported finding a bathroom door locked with sounds of someone having a bath, only to find some seconds later that the door was open and nobody was in the room.

Hotel – open all year except Christmas day, Boxing day, New Year's day + day after!
Tel: 01738 625670

Montrose Air Station Museum
Off A92, Waldron Road, Broomfield, NW of Montrose on Links, Angus.
Pri/LA   (map ref: 11I)
The airfield here was established in 1913, making it one of the oldest in the country. It was bombed by German bombers in 1940, and hangers and a mess were destroyed. The airfield was abandoned by the RAF after the war in 1957, and a museum, housed in the buildings, displays wartime memorabilia, comprising artefacts, pictures, models and uniforms relating to the site. Aircraft are also on display, including a Seahawk 131, as well as a Bofors gun.

The aerodrome is said to be haunted. There were several reports of a phantom biplane here, thought to be from a crash which happened soon after the airfield was opened. Other manifestations include the apparition of an airman, again reported several times, and the unexplained sounds of footsteps around the aerodrome.

Open all year, Sun 12.00-17.00; parties other times by arrangement.
Guided tours. Explanatory displays. Gift shop. WC. Car and coach parking. £.
Tel: 01674 673107
Email: 106212.152@compuserve.com   Web: //ourworld.compuserve.com/homepages/
AirspeedNews

Monymusk Castle
Off B993, 6.5 miles SW of Inverurie, Aberdeenshire.
Pri/LA   (map ref: 11G)
Monymusk Castle, a tower house dating from the 16th century, is said to be haunted by several ghosts.

One is a 'Grey Lady', who reputedly appears from a cupboard in the nursery to check children sleeping there. Another reported apparition is that of a man reading in the library who vanishes when approached. The 'Party Ghost' is described as a red-haired man in a kilt, laced shirt and jacket. This ghost is said to push through party guests, and other manifestations include cavorting and footsteps on the stairs when apparently nobody is about.

The lands were originally owned by the priory of Monymusk, and the Monymusk Reliquary, a casket containing the relics of Saint Columba, was long kept here. The Reliquary was carried before the Scottish army at the Battle of Bannockburn in 1314, and is now held at in the National Museum of Scotland. The lands were held by the Forbes family after the Reformation, and then by the Grants from 1711.

127

Moy Castle

Off A849, 10 miles SW of Craignure, Mull.
Ruin or site   (map ref: 3K)

In a beautiful situation on a rocky crag by the seashore, Moy Castle is a plain somewhat dour tower house, which is ruinous but complete to the wallhead. It was long a property of the MacLaines, who were kin to the MacLeans of Duart.

Iain the Toothless, the chief, and his son and heir, Ewen of the Little Head, fought in 1538 over the latter's marriage settlement: apparently Ewen's wife was not satisfied with their house on a crannog in Loch Squabain, and desired something more luxurious. Ewen was slain in the subsequent battle, his head being hewn off and his horse riding away for two miles with the decapitated body. His ghost, the headless horseman, is said to been seen riding in Glen Mor when one of the MacLaines is about to die.

MacLean of Duart seized his opportunity to gain the lands of Lochbuie as Iain the Toothless now had no heir. Iain was imprisoned on the isolated castle of Cairnburg, on one of the Treshnish Isles, to prevent him producing a new heir. Iain's only female companion was reputedly a deformed and ugly woman – although Iain the Toothless hardly conjures a picture of great beauty – but Iain contrived to make her pregnant. MacLaine himself was soon slain, but the woman escaped and in due time produced a son, Murdoch the Stunted, who eventually regained the castle and the lands.

View from exterior.
Walk to castle.

Muchalls Castle

Off A92, 4 miles NE of Stonehaven, Kincardine & Deeside.
Pri/LA   (map ref: 11H)

Muchalls Castle was built by the Burnetts in the early 17th-century and is a fine courtyard castle, which incorporates earlier work. James VIII stayed here in 1716 during the Jacobite Rising, although by then the cause was deemed hopeless and he soon fled back to France.

The castle is thought to be haunted by the ghost of young woman, a 'Green Lady', who is said to have been drowned in a cave used for smuggling, which formerly could be reached by an underground stair from the wine-cellar. She had been awaiting her lover, one of the crew of a ship, in the cave, but fell into the water and was

drowned. Her ghost, a 'Green Lady' clad in a green gown, has reportedly been seen in one of the rooms, sitting in front of a mirror, one sighting being in the 1970s.

Neidpath Castle

Off A72, 1 mile W of Peebles, Borders.
Pri/LA   (map ref: 9N)
Standing on a steep bank of the River Tweed in a picturesque wooded gorge,

Neidpath Castle dates from the 14th century and is a substantial tower house with a small courtyard. The property belonged to the Frasers, then the Hays, Douglas Duke of Queensberry and the Earl of Wemyss and March. Mary, Queen of Scots, stayed here, as did James VI.

Neidpath is reputedly haunted by the ghost of a young woman, the 'Maid of Neidpath', said to be Jean Douglas, youngest of three daughters of Sir William Douglas, Earl of March. She was born in 1705, and fell in love with the son of the laird of Tushielaw, which was owned by the Scott family.

129

Her father did not think the man good enough for an Earl's daughter, forbade them to marry, and the lad was sent away. The girl pined and eventually died of a broken heart after she became so ill that her lover did not recognise her. Her ghost then began to haunt Neidpath, waiting for her lover to come for her.

The apparition is said to be dressed in a floor-length brown gown with a large white collar. Doors are said to open and close by themselves, unexplained noises have also been reported, and objects move by themselves including a plank.

Open daily Thu before Easter-Sep 11.00-17.00; Sun 13.00-17.00.
Gift shop. Museum. Display about Mary Queen of Scots and tartan collection. WC. Disabled access only to museum and ground floor of castle (up 5 steps). Picnic area. Group concessions. Car and coach parking. £.
Tel: 01721 720333

New Century Theatre, Motherwell

Off, Windmillhill Street, Motherwell, Lanarkshire.
Pri/LA   (map ref: 7M)
The Rex Cinema dates from 1936 but incorporates part of the New Century Theatre, and is now used as a snooker club. The New Century was said to be haunted by a ghost, 'Oscar', the story going that a man had committed suicide by jumping from the gallery into the stalls. The ghost has not been reported in recent times.

New Lanark

Off A70, 1 mile S of Lanark.
Pri/LA   (map ref: 8N)
Surrounded by woodlands and close to the Falls of Clyde, this cotton-spinning village was founded in 1785 by David Dale, and made famous by the social pioneer Robert Owen, his son-in-law. The innovative audio-visual exhibition 'Annie McLeod Experience', gives a glimpse early 19th-century life under Owen's paternalistic management. Entrance to the mills, Millworker's House, Village Store and Robert Owen's House is also included. Fine walk to Falls of Clyde.

The house, located over the village shop, was reputedly haunted by the apparition of young woman, dressed in a tartan cloak and black hat. She was witnessed by several children on different occasions, and is said to have disappeared through a sealed door.

Access to village at all times. Visitor centre open all year, daily 11.00-17.00 except closed Christmas and New Year.
Walk from car park. Guided tours. Explanatory displays. Gift shop. Tearoom. WC. Picnic areas. Special needs guided tours and information. Partial disabled access and WC. Car and coach parking. Group concessions. Accommodation available. ££ (exhibition).
Tel: 01555 661345   Fax: 01555 665738

130

Newark Castle

Off A708, 3 miles W of Selkirk, Borders.
Ruin or site   (map ref: 10N)
Standing in the grounds of the mansion of Bowhill, Newark Castle is a ruinous 15th-century castle with the remains of a courtyard. It has an eventful history, but is the site of a cruel massacre in 1645.

The Marquis of Montrose was defeated at the Battle of Philiphaugh, and while he escaped most of his small army was slaughtered by the forces of the Covenanter General David Leslie. This was not enough for the Covenanters.   Camp followers were brought to Newark – mostly Irish women, many of them pregnant – and were then shot, stabbed, slashed or bludgeoned to death. The castle and area are said to be haunted by the folk butchered here, and their cries and moans have reputedly been heard.

Other prisoners, again mostly women and children, were taken to the market place in Selkirk, and there later also shot.

Park open 24 Apr-30 Aug, except closed Fri apart from Jul; Bowhill open Jul 13.00-16.30; other times by appt for educational groups.
[Bowhill] Fine collections of paintings and artefacts, including the Duke of Monmouth's saddle and execution shirt. Audio-visual presentation. Restored Victorian kitchen. Restaurant. WC. Garden and country park. Disabled facilities; wheelchair visitors free. Ruins of Newark Castle in grounds. ££ (Bowhill). £ (country park).
Tel: 01750 22204   Fax: 01750 22204

Newbattle Abbey

Off B703, 1 mile SW of Dalkeith, Midlothian.
Pri/LA   (map ref: 9M)
Newbattle Abbey was founded in 1140 by David I, as a Cistercian house dedicated to the Blessed Virgin Mary, and became a very rich establishment. It was visited by Alexander II – Marie de Coucy, his wife, was buried here. It was burned by the English in 1385, 1544 and 1548. The Kerrs acquired the abbey after the Reformation, having been Commendators, and were made Lords Newbattle in 1591, and Earls of Lothian in 1606. They demolished most of the abbey, and greatly altered the little that was left – the vaulted undercrofts of the dormitory and reredorter survives, as well as the warming house. The

131

building is now an adult education college. Fine plasterwork and wood carving survives.

Newbattle has a reputation for being haunted, and it is said that few folk like to stay in the building after dark.

Adult education college.

Newton Castle

Off A923, NW of Blairgowrie, Perthshire.
Pri/LA   (map ref: 9J)
Newton and Ardblair Castles are said to share the same ghost, Lady Jean Drummond. Newton was a property of the Drummonds, who feuded for many years with the Blairs of Ardblair.

A 'Green Lady' reputedly haunts Newton, the sad and tragic apparition of Lady Jean, dressed in green silk, who searches for her love. Lady Jean fell in love with one of the Blairs of Ardblair, but appears to have died of a broken heart when she was betrothed to another man,

drowning herself in a local marsh. An old and long ballad recounts the tale, and has Jean involved with fairies, who gave her the green gown, the colour of the fairies and generally believed to be unlucky.

The castle was plundered in 1644 by the Marquis of Montrose, then burnt by Cromwell in the 1650s, although the garrison is said to have survived by sheltering in the vaulted basement while the castle burned around them. Newton later passed to the Macphersons, is in good condition and still occupied.

Niddry Street, Edinburgh

Off A1, off the Royal Mile, Niddry Street, Edinburgh.
Pri/LA   (map ref: 9L)
The vaults here are said to be haunted by several ghosts, and can be entered through various ghost tours. Sightings of apparitions include that of a young woman, dressed in white, but with numerous bloody wounds; a very tall man in dressed 18th-century fashion with appears to be knee-length leather boots; a small lad in blue with a high-starched collar; and a short middle-aged gentleman wearing a leather apron and knee-length trousers. Photographs have allegedly been taken of some of the ghostly figures.

Ghost tours give access to the vaulted chambers, including Mercat Tours and Auld Reekie Tours.

Nivingston House Hotel

Off B9097, Cleish, 3 miles SW of Kinross, Perth & Kinross.
Pri/LA   (map ref: 9L)
Standing in 12 acres of secluded gardens, the Nivingston House Hotel is housed in an elegant mansion dating from 1725. The building is said to be haunted by the spectre of an old woman.

Hotel – open all year and to non-residents.
17 rooms. Restaurant and bar. Car parking. $$-$$$.
Tel: 01577 850216   Fax: 01577 850238
Email: 100414.1237@compuserve.com

Noltland Castle

Off B9066, NE side of island of Westray, Orkney.
His Scot   (map ref: 10C)
A strong and grim stronghold in a remote location, Noltland Castle is a large ruined 16th-century Z-plan tower

house, built by Gilbert Balfour.

Balfour was Master of the Household to Mary, Queen of Scots. He acquired the property by marrying Margaret Bothwell, whose brother was Bishop of Orkney and granted the lands to Balfour. He had been involved in the murders of Cardinal Beaton in 1546, for which he was imprisoned and became a galley slave, and Lord Darnley in 1567. He supported Mary after she fled to England, but when her cause became hopeless he fled Scotland, and served in the Swedish army until his death, being executed for treason against the Swedish king, in 1576. The castle was abandoned about 1760 and is ruinous.

A death in the Balfour family was reputedly heralded by a ghostly howling dog, the 'Boky Hound', while births and marriages were announced by eerie spectral lights. The castle is also said to have had a brownie, the spirit of an old man which helped folk at need, beaching boats or clearing roads, and is said to have been well liked by the Balfour family. The brownie is reported to have left when the castle was abandoned.

Open all year at reasonable times.
Tel: 0131 668 8800   Fax: 0131 668 8888

Norwood Hall, Aberdeen

Off A93, Garthdee Road, Cults, Aberdeen.
Pri/LA   (map ref: 12G)
Set in seven acres of wooded grounds, Norwood Hall, built in 1887 for the Ogston family, stands on the site of Pitfodels Castle. Pitfodels was held by the Reids, but passed by marriage in the 16th century to the Menzies family.

The building is reputedly haunted by two ghosts. One is said to be the apparition of the wife of James Ogston. The poor woman despaired after Ogston would not leave his mistress. The other is reputedly Ogston himself, and an apparition has been seen twice in the dining room in recent times.

Hotel – open all year.
21 bedrooms with ensuite facilities. Dining room, restaurant and bar. Seminars, conferences, meetings, weddings, murder mystery meals, BBQs and haggis hunts. Disabled access to restaurant only. Parking. $$-$$$.
Tel: 01224 868951   Fax: 01224 869868

Old Manse, Lairg

Off A836, Lairg, Highland.
Pri/LA   (map ref: 7D)
The Old Manse, which has been demolished, was said to have been haunted by the Reverend Thomas MacKay, who had been the minister. He died peacefully in his sleep in 1803, but his apparition is alleged to have been seen in 1827, and his ghost is believed to still haunt the site.

Old Post Horn Inn, Crawford

Off M74, Crawford, Lanarkshire.
Pri/LA   (map ref: 8N)
The inn here, which dates from 1744 but was closed some years ago and is now derelict, is said to be haunted by two ghosts. One is that of a young girl, who was killed by a coach in Main Street and was the daughter of a former innkeeper. Her apparition had reputedly been seen in the dining room, which was originally the stables, and she is said to have moved the chairs around and to be heard singing to herself. Another phantom is reportedly that of a coachman, who wears a dark cloak, believed to have died in snows of 1805.

A third ghost is that of a five-year-old girl, said to have been hanged for stealing bread. Her phantom was reportedly seen in the neighbouring countryside, and occasionally in the inn.

Ghostly Roman legionnaires are also said to have been seen, marching up the main street. However, they can only be seen from the knees up as the level of the road in Roman times was much lower than it is today.

Old Woodhouselee Castle

Off B7026, 1.5 miles NE of Penicuik, Midlothian.
Ruin or site   (map ref: 9M)
An old castle here, which is very ruinous, was owned by the Hamiltons, and has a tragic ghost story.

One winter night a favourite of the Regent Moray turned up at Woodhouselee, and threw Lady Hamilton and her infant out into the snow in only their night wear. The infant died from the cold and Lady Hamilton went mad with despair and wept herself to death. Her sad ghost, dressed in white, was then frequently reported, searching through the castle and countryside, trying to find her baby. At one time her ghost is said to have been seen often on cold moonlit nights.

Her husband, James Hamilton of Bothwellheugh, shot and killed Regent Moray at Linlithgow in 1570, possibly as an act of revenge – although another account has Lady Hamilton alive as late as 1609. James Hamilton then fled Scotland,

The castle was demolished in the late 17th century, and much of the stone was used to build Woodhouselee at Fulford, itself now gone. Lady Hamilton's ghost is said to have translated to the new house, but this may be a confusion over names.

Pannanich Wells Hotel, Ballater

On B976, South Deeside Road, 1.5 miles E of Ballater, Kincardine & Deeside.
Pri/LA   (map ref: 9G)
The hotel here, which dates from 1760, and the neighbouring area are said to be haunted by a 'Grey Lady', a young woman dressed in a grey blouse and long

dark skirt, as is the neighbouring area. The ghost is said to have been seen quite often. Other disturbances include unexplained noises and the moving of furniture and opening of doors when nobody is apparently present, as well as the smell of scent. This latter manifestation may be from a separate spirit, said to have been experienced in Room One.

Hotel.
Tel: 01339 755018 Fax: 01339 756364

Penkaet Castle

Off A6093, 1 mile SW of Pencaitland, East Lothian.
Pri/LA (map ref: 10M)
Standing in a walled garden, Penkaet Castle has been the property of several families, but was held by the Lauders from 1685 until 1922. The castle, although altered and extended in later centuries, incorporates a 16th-century tower house.

The castle is reputedly haunted by several ghosts.

One is said to be the spectre of Alexander Hamilton. He was a beggar, who

was accused of witchcraft after cursing the lady of the house and her eldest daughter. They both died from a mysterious illness, after they had thrown Hamilton off their property. He was executed in Edinburgh, and his ghost is said to have been witnessed near the castle.

Another is reported to manifest itself by banging doors and moving furniture. It may be the spirit of John Cockburn, who had apparently committed – or been the victim of – a murder. The sounds of footsteps and the dragging of a heavy object have also apparently been heard.

A four-poster bed, once slept in by Charles I, is reportedly haunted as it often appears to have been used – some say by a manifestation of the king himself – although it has not actually been slept in.

Manifestations were reported in the 20th century – the house was investigated, when and unexplained noises and events were recorded, although the investigation was not as thorough or rigorous as it would be today.

Perth Theatre

Off M90, 185 High Street, Perth.
Pri/LA   (map ref: 9K)
The theatre, Scotland's most successful repertory theatre established in 1935, is reputedly haunted by a 'Grey Lady', seen since a fire in 1924. Other manifestations included seats slamming down and then springing back up.

Theatre.
Bar and restaurant. Box office 01738 621031. Bar and restaurant 01738 472709.

Pinkie House

Off A199, Loretto School, Musselburgh.
Pri/LA   (map ref: 10M)
Now part of a private school, Pinkie House has an L-plan tower house of the 16th century at its core, and has been altered and extended in later centuries. Noteworthy visitors include Charles I and Bonnie Prince Charlie.

   The ghost story dates from when the house was held by the Setons. Alexander Seton was 1st Earl of Dunfermline and Chancellor to James VI. He altered the house in 1613, and died here in 1622. The house is said to be haunted by a 'Green Lady', Lilias Drummond, his first wife, who died in 1601 after giving Seton four daughters but no son as an heir. The manner of her death is a matter of some debate, but Seton did marry again only months after her death. Her appearance bodes ill for the family, and she also reputedly haunts Fyvie. Her ghost, or another, is sometimes said to be sometimes accompanied by a child.

School.

Pitcaple Castle

Off A96, 4 miles NW of Inverurie, Aberdeenshire.
Pri/LA   (map ref: 11F)
Pitcaple Castle, a Z-plan tower house dating from the 15th century, but later altered and extended, was a property of the Leslies from 1457 until 1757. Famous visitors include James IV, Mary, Queen of Scots, the Marquis of

Montrose – who was imprisoned here on his way to execution in Edinburgh – and Charles II.

When a robin is found in the castle it is reputedly the harbinger of bad news and the herald of death. A robin was discovered when Montrose was executed, and another when the laird, Sir John Leslie of Pitcaple, was killed at the Battle of Worcester in 1651. A recent recorded instance was in 1978, when a robin apparently heralded the death of one of the family.

Pittodrie House

Off A96, 5 miles NW of Inverurie, Aberdeenshire
Pri/LA   (map ref: 11F)
Set in 200 acres in the foothills of the impressive and foreboding hill of Bennachie, Pittodrie House was once a property of the Erskines, and incorporates an old tower house. The building was extended in later centuries, and after it had become a hotel.

A chamber, formerly used as a nursery, is said to be haunted.

Hotel – open all year.
27 bedrooms with private facilities. Dining room and bar. Hill walking and sports.
Functions, conferences, corporate events and meetings. Parking. $$-$$$$.
Tel: 01467 681444   Fax: 01467 681648
Email: **info@pittodrie.macdonald-hotels.co.uk**   Web: **www.macdonald-hotels.co.uk**

Place of Bonhill

Off A8, S of Alexandria, Dunbartonshire.
Ruin or site   (map ref: 6L)
Place of Bonhill, a later mansion, incorporated an old house or castle. The whole building was demolished in 1950, and the site appears to now be occupied by a school.

The property was originally held by the Lennox family, but Bonhill passed to the Lindsays in the 15th century, then to the Smolletts in the 17th century.

It is said that a tunnel led down from a hidden entrance behind the drawing room fireplace to the banks of the River Leven. A piper was sent to explore the passage, but vanished without trace. Afterwards it was said that faint pipe music was often be heard within the walls.

Playhouse Theatre, Edinburgh

On A1, 18-22 Greenside Place, Edinburgh.
Pri/LA   (map ref: 9L)
The theatre, which was built in 1927-9 and can hold 3000 people, is said to be haunted by a ghost called 'Albert'. His apparition has been seen, apparently often, and his ghost is said to be friendly but mischievous. It is believed that Albert is the ghost of a maintenance man killed in a backstage accident.

The theatre stands near Gallowlea, where Major Thomas Weir, whose house was in the West Bow, was strangled and burnt for witchcraft.

Theatre.
Tel: 0131 557 2590

Princes Street, Edinburgh
On A1, Edinburgh.
Pri/LA   (map ref: 9L)
The West End is said to be haunted by a weeping woman, one Moira Blair. The story goes that her husband had been murdered in the area. The poor woman found his body, and in distress stumbled into the road and was killed by a coach and horses. Sounds of her weeping have also been reported in Princes Street Gardens and in St John's Church, and her apparition has also allegedly been seen.

Rait Castle
Off B9101, 2.5 miles S of Nairn, Highland.
Ruin or site   (map ref: 8E)
Rait Castle consists of a ruinous 13th-century hall-house, much altered in later centuries, and is the scene of a gruesome haunting.

The tale goes that in 1524, when the castle was held by the Cummings, they invited the Mackintoshes here for a feast, possibly a wedding banquet, but planned to murder their guests. The Mackintoshes apparently learned of the plan and came heavily armed, and managed to flee from Rait after killing many

of their treacherous hosts. The Cumming laird was furious – he suspected his daughter had betrayed his plan as she was in love with one of the Mackintoshes – and pursued the terrified girl through the building. She tried to escape out of an upstairs window, but her father hacked off her hands with his sword as she

hung from a window ledge, and she plunged to her death. Her ghost, a handless phantom in a blood-stained dress, then began to haunt Rait.

The Cumming laird and his followers were, themselves, apparently slain at Balblair in retribution.

Rammerscales House

On B9020, 3 miles S of Lockerbie, Dumfries & Galloway.
Pri/LA (map ref: 9P)
Standing on a high slope of the Torthorwald Hills, Rammerscales is a fine 18th-century mansion, with magnificent views over Annandale. In Adam style and mostly unaltered, the mansion was built for Dr James Mounsey by the architect William Craik in the 1760s, but is now a property of the Bell Macdonald family. It houses rare contemporary art and a library with 600 volumes.

The house is said to be haunted by the ghost of Dr James Mounsey, who had been physician to Peter Czar of Russia and died in 1773. Disturbances are said to be centred in the library, and evacuees from Glasgow, during World War II, were so scared of the ghost that they chose to sleep in the stables.

Last week in Jul; 1st three weeks in Aug: daily except Sat 14.00-17.00.
Guided tours for parties. Picnic area. Extensive and attractive grounds with walled gardens.
Car and coach parking. Group concessions. ££.
Tel: 01387 810229/811988   Fax: 01387 810940

Rathen Church

Off A92, 3 miles S of Fraserburgh, Banff & Buchan.
Ruin or site (map ref: 12E)
The present church, dating from 1870, replaced a much older building, of which the south and west wall and the remains of an aisle survive. The church here was given to the Abbey of Arbroath by the Countess of Buchan, and in 1328 Robert the Bruce granted the benefice to the College of Old Machar.

The old church was believed to be haunted at one time, the story originating from the 1640s. The sounds of singing and musical instruments were heard coming from the loft of the building, when there was nobody present. The phenomena was attributed to the ongoing battle between the Marquis of Montrose and Earl of Argyll.

Open at all reasonable times.

Ravenswood Hotel, Ballater

Off A93, Ballater, Kincardine & Deeside.
Pri/LA (map ref: 9G)
Set in large grounds by the picturesque River Dee, the Ravenswood Hotel dates from around 1820 and was a private residence until the 1970s. It is reputedly haunted: one ghost is said to be that of a woman, who is only apparently heard over an intercom when babies are staying in the hotel – she may have been a nursemaid. The other is said to be the apparition of an old

man with a white beard, dressed like a sailor, sightings of which have been reported on the stair and in two of the bedrooms.

Hotel – open all year.
Family-run hotel. 11 rooms, 5 with ensuite facilities. Restaurant and bar. Weddings and small functions. Parking. $.
Tel: 01339 755539   Fax: 01339 755539

Ring Croft of Stocking, Auchencairn
Off A711, near Auchencairn, Dumfries and Galloway.
Pri/LA   (map ref: 8Q)
The haunting of Ring Croft of Stocking near Auchencairn in the parish of Rerrick, the house of Andrew Mackie, is a well documented case of poltergeist activity, recorded in 1695 and witnessed by many people. The activity did not last for very long but was very intense. His cattle were let out of his cow shed, stones and other objects were thrown about, items disappeared only to be found later. The disturbances became even more intense: Mackie and others were hit with an invisible stick and dragged across the floor, stones and other items were thrown at folk, there were thumps and bangs, peats were cast about, and a rough voice was heard. After several months, however, the haunting suddenly ceased.
   The house was reputedly built where a body had been found, believed to be a victim of murder.

Rockhall
Off A75, 6 miles E of Dumfries.
Pri/LA   (map ref: 9P)
Rockhall, a much-altered 16th-century tower house, was occupied at the end of the 17th century by Sir Robert Grierson, an infamous persecutor of Covenanters. His pet monkey, killed by his servants after his death, is said to haunt the house and reputedly can be heard blowing a whistle. One story is that a phantom black coach and horses were sent by the devil to fetch Grierson to hell after his death, all this witnessed by a ship on the Solway Firth.

Rosslyn Castle, Roslin
Off B7006, 2 miles S of Loanhead, Midlothian.
Pri/LA   (map ref: 9M)
Standing in the picturesque glen high above the River Esk, Roslin Castle was once the magnificent fortress of the Sinclair Earls of Orkney and Caithness. Although much is now ruinous, part of the building is still habitable.
   A ghost story dates from the Wars of Independence in 1303, when an English army was heavily defeated by the Scots near the castle. A spectre of a dog, the

141

'Mauthe Dog', killed with its English
master after the battle, reputedly
haunts the castle, and its howling has
been reported. Sir William Sinclair was
one of the knights who set out on a
Crusade with Robert the Bruce's
heart, and killed fighting the Moors
in Granada in 1330. A wondrous
treasure is said to be buried beneath
the vaults of the castle.

The apparition of a knight in black
armour, riding a black horse, is said
to have been seen in recent times.

Rosslyn Chapel, Roslin

*Off A701, in Roslin, 6 miles S of Edin-
burgh, Midlothian.*

Pri/LA   (map ref: 9M)

Situated in the wooded Roslin
Glen and overlooking the River
Esk, Rosslyn Chapel, dedicated
to St Matthew and once a
Collegiate Church, was founded
by William Sinclair, Earl of
Caithness and Orkney, in 1446.
It was never completed: only the
choir and parts of the transepts
were built. The roof is vaulted
and there are a mass of flying
buttresses to carry the weight.

The chapel is richly carved with
Biblical stories, and has the
largest number of 'Green Men'
found in any medieval building.
In the burial vault are ten of the
lairds of Roslin and their kin, said
to be laid out in full armour
without coffins. Ghostly flames
were said to be seen here when

one of the Sinclairs was about to die.

The chapel is also reputedly haunted by the ghost of the apprentice, who carved the famous Apprentice Pillar and traditionally was murdered by his teacher. The apparition of a monk has also been reported in recent times, both in the chapel and the vicinity.

Rosslyn Castle is nearby, and there are picturesque walks through the Glen.

Open all year Mon-Sat 10.00-17.00, Sun 12.00-16.45.
Guided tours available. Explanatory displays. Gift shop. Tearoom. WC. Disabled access.
Car and coach parking. Group concessions. £.
Tel: 0131 440 2159   Fax: 0131 440 1979
Email: rosslynch@aol.com   Web: rosslynchapel.org.uk

Rothesay Castle
Off A886, in Rothesay, Bute.
His Scot   (map ref: 5M)
Standing in the seaside town on the island of Bute, Rothesay Castle, dating from 12th-century, consists of a circular curtain wall with four round towers. The ruinous stronghold is surrounded by a wet moat, and a large gatehouse block was added in the 15th century.

The castle was attacked and captured by Norsemen in the 1230s, and a ghost story dates from this time. According to a 19th-century ballad, the castle is haunted by a Lady Isobel, her apparition seen on the 'Bloody Stair', behind the chapel. Her family were killed by Norsemen and, rather than submit to marriage with a Viking, she stabbed herself to death.

Rothesay was long held by the Stewarts, and was besieged on many occasions. Robert II and Robert III, who died here in 1406, both visited often. In 1401 Robert III made his son, David, Duke of Rothesay, a title since taken by the eldest son of the kings of Scots and currently held by Prince Charles. It did not do David much good – he was starved to death at Falkland Palace by his uncle, Robert, Duke of Albany.

Open daily all year: Apr-Sep 9.30-18.30; Oct-Mar Mon-Sat 9.30-16.30 except closed Thu PM and Fri, Sun 14.00-16.30; last ticket sold 30 mins before closing; closed 25/26 Dec & 1-3 Jan.
Explanatory panels. Car parking nearby. Group concessions. £.
Tel: 01700 502691

Roxburgh Castle

Off A699, 1 mile W of Kelso, Borders.
Ruin or site   (map ref: 11N)
This was once one of the most important strongholds in Scotland, although not much now remains, and saw much action in the long wars with England. Mary, sister of Robert the Bruce, was hung in a cage, suspended from the walls, by the English, although she was eventually released. In 1460 James II was killed when one of the cannons, with which he was bombarding the castle, blew up beside him, although Roxburgh was then stormed and demolished. A holly tree between Floors and the River Tweed is said to mark the spot where James was killed.
   A ghostly horsemen is reputedly sometimes seen riding towards the castle.

Open at all times.

Roxburghe House

Off A608, 3 miles S of Kelso, Borders.
Pri/LA   (map ref: 11N)
Situated in a peaceful location in 200 acres of gardens and wooded parkland, Roxburghe House – formally known as Sunlaws – dates mostly from 1853 after the previous house was destroyed by fire. This old house may have dated from the 15th century. It was a property of the Kerrs of Chatto, and Bonnie Prince Charlie was entertained here in November

1745. The house was used to hold German prisoners of war during World War II, acquired by the Duke of Roxburghe in 1969, and is now an exclusive hotel.

The building is said to be haunted by the apparition of a woman, a 'Green Lady', seen late at night crossing the entrance hall of the house from the stair, through the lounge and conservatory up to the Chinese bridge. The story goes that she is searching for her baby, but there is no clue as to her identity.

Another ghost is reputedly that of a soldier, possibly one of those imprisoned here during the war, which has been witnessed on the top floor of the house. This floor is currently only used as storage space.

The administration offices, housed in the old laundry in the oldest part of the building, are also said to be haunted.

Hotel - open all year except closed 23-29 Dec.
22 bedrooms. Restaurant. Conferences and wedding receptions. Championship golf course, fishing and other sports facilities. Disabled access to public rooms on ground floor & WC. Parking. $$-$$$$.
Tel: 01573 450331   Fax: 01573 450611
Email: sunlaws.roxgc@virgin.net

Royal Hotel, Cupar
Off A91, Cupar, Fife.
Pri/LA   (map ref: 10K)
The former hotel is said to be built on the site of a graveyard associated with the Dominican friary of St Katherine, founded in 1348 by Duncan Earl of Fife but decayed by 1517. The lands were given to the burgh in 1572, and a small part of the church survived in the 19th century, but nothing now remains. The building was said to be haunted by the ghost of one of the friars, seen most often in the function rooms. The hotel is now used as flats for old folk.

Royal Lyceum Theatre, Edinburgh – see next page.

145

Royal Lyceum, Edinburgh

Off A1, Grindlay Street, Edinburgh.

Pri/LA   (map ref: 9L)

The Royal Lyceum Theatre, dating from 1883 but remodelled in 1992 with a glass foyer, has a fine Victorian interior. The building is said to be haunted by the apparition of a woman in a blue dress, seen in an upper gallery not open to the public during the performance of a play.

Theatre.
Bar and restaurant. Access for wheelchairs to all front-of-house areas. Audio-described performances and induction loop. Parking Nearby.
Tel: 0131 248 4848
Email: royallyceumtheatre@cableinet.co.uk   Web: www.ifoser.com/infotheatre/lyceum
[illustration see above]

Ruthven Castle

Off A9, 1 mile S of Kingussie, Highland.

His Scot   (map ref: 7G)

The present building, a barracks built to defend against the Jacobites, stands on the site of an ancient stronghold. It was held by Alexander Stewart, Earl of Buchan and the Wolf of Badenoch, at the end of the 14th century. Stewart,

who was an unruly fellow, was one of the sons of Robert II. When he was excommunicated by the Bishop of Moray, he burnt Forres and Elgin in revenge, including the cathedral.

One tale has him as an even darker character. The story goes that Stewart practised witchcraft, but in 1406 a dark visitor challenged Stewart to a game of chess. In the morning he and his men were found dead, for Stewart had played with the devil and lost. The phantoms of Stewart and his followers reputedly repeat their grisly doom and haunt the place. So the story goes. Stewart, however, was buried in Dunkeld Cathedral, having died in his sixties, and his stone effigy survives.

Open all year.
Car parking.
Tel: 0131 668 8800   Fax: 0131 668 8888

Saddell Castle

Off B842, 8 miles N of Campbeltown, Kintyre.
Ruin or site   (map ref: 4N)

Saddell Castle consists of an altered 15th-century keep, and a range of 18th-century outbuildings, which replaced the original courtyard. The castle stands on what were the lands of Saddell Abbey, founded by Reginald, son of Somerled. Angus Og MacDonald is said to have sheltered Robert the Bruce here in 1306.

Saddell is said to be haunted. A 'White Lady' is reputed to walk the battlements, and the castle also reportedly has a ghostly monk, who appears to have translated, with much of the stone, from Saddell Abbey.

Saltoun Hall

Off B6355, 5 miles SW of Haddington, East Lothian.
Pri/LA   (map ref: 10M)

Saltoun Hall incorporates part of a strong castle, dating from as early as the 12th century. It was a property of the Abernethy Lords Saltoun, but was sold in the 17th century to Sir Andrew Fletcher, who was prominent in resisting the Union of Parliaments of Scotland and England of 1707.

The hall is reputedly haunted by a 'Grey Lady'.

Salutation Hotel, Perth

Off M90, 34 South Street, Perth.
Pri/LA   (map ref: 9K)

One of the oldest hotels in Scotland dating from 1699, the Salutation Hotel was visited by Bonnie Prince Charlie in 1745 during the Jacobite Rising. His

147

apparition, wearing green tartan, is said to have been seen in one of the
bedrooms.

Hotel – open all year and to non-residents.
85 bedrooms with ensuite facilities. Restaurant and bar. Conferences and meetings. $-$$.
Tel: 01738 630066   Fax: 01738 633598

Sandwood Bay

Off B801, 8 miles N of Kinlochbervie, Highland.
Pri/LA   (map ref: 5A)
The picturesque sands here are reported to be haunted by a bearded sailor, as is
a nearby cottage on Sandwood Loch, the apparition having been witnessed on
several occasions, including in recent times. The phantom is clad in a brass-
buttoned dark tunic, sailor's cap and boots. One story suggests that the ghost
is that of a seaman drowned when his ship sank and his body was washed up in
the bay.

Accessible at all times.
Long walk.

Sanquhar Castle

Off A76, 0.25 miles S of Sanquhar, Lanarkshire.
Ruin or site   (map ref: 8O)
Sanquhar Castle is a ruinous 13th-century castle of the Crichton family, and
two ghosts reputedly haunt the crumbling walls.

One is the 'White Lady', which is believed to be the spirit of a young golden-
haired woman, Marion of Dalpeddar, who is said to have disappeared in 1590.
She may have been
murdered by one of
the Crichton lords,
and a skeleton of a
girl was reportedly
found in 1875-6,
face down in a pit,
during excavations.
Her appearance was
said to bode ill for the
Crichtons.

The other ghost is
allegedly that of John
Wilson, who was
hanged unjustly in 1597 by Robert Crichton, 6th Lord Sanquhar. It manifests
itself with groans and the rattling of chains.

148

The headless body of a man was also found around the 1840s, under the floor of one of the castle vaults.

Dalpeddar itself has its own ghost – and the two may be linked.

Open all year.

Scone Palace

Off A93, N of Perth.
Pri/LA   (map ref: 9K)

Standing in 100 acres of fine gardens and woodlands, Scone Palace is a magnificent mansion, dating from 1802, although it incorporates older work, possibly part of the Abbot's Lodging. The property has long been owned by the Murray Earls of Mansfield.

The palace stands on the site of an abbey founded here in the 12th century, and the Kings of Scots were inaugurated at the Moot Hill from the 9th century up to Charles I in 1651. The Stone of Destiny, also called the Stone of Scone, was kept here, until taken to Westminster Abbey by Edward I in 1296 – although this was returned to Edinburgh Castle in 1996.

The palace is said to be haunted by ghostly footsteps heard in the south passage.

Open Good Friday-4th Mon Oct daily 9.30-17.15; last admission 16.45; other times by appt.
Fine collections of furniture, clocks, needlework and porcelain. Gift shops. Restaurant. Tearoom. WC. Picnic area. 100 acres of wild gardens. Maze. Adventure playground. Meetings and conferences. Disabled access to state rooms & restaurant. Car and coach parking. Group concessions. £££.
Tel: 01738 552300   Fax: 01738 552588
Email: SCONEPALACE@CQM.CO.UK

Shieldhill

Off B7016, 3 miles NW of Biggar, Quothquan, Lanarkshire.
Pri/LA   (map ref: 8N)

Set in rolling hills and farmland, Shieldhill, a sprawling mansion, incorporates an ancient castle at its core, said to date from as early as 1199, which was extended often in following centuries. The building stands in six acres of wooded parkland.

It was a property of the Chancellor family. The building is said to be haunted by a 'Grey Lady', the ghost of a daughter, wrapped in a grey cloak, of one of the Chancellor lords. One story relates how she was raped by soldiers returning from a battle in the 1650s, and became pregnant, but the child was cruelly taken from her at birth and left to die. The more credited version is that the events date from the 14th century and she was made pregnant by a gamekeeper's son, and her baby was born dead then buried without her permission. The girl wept herself to death.

Her ghost has reputedly been seen in recent times, walking towards the burial place in the grounds of the hotel, in one of the rooms, as well as on the patio , the roof of the hotel, and in the car park. Unexplained footsteps and thumps during the night have also been reported, as have chairs moving by themselves and television channels changing independently. Her apparition is said to appear mostly to children staying at the hotel.

Hotel – open all year and to non-residents.
16 rooms with ensuite facilities. Restaurant and bistro. Weddings, conferences, private parties and meetings. Parking. $$.
Tel: 01899 220035   Fax: 01899 221092
Email: enquiries@shieldhill.co.uk   Web: www.shieldhill.co.uk

Skaill House

Off B9056, 5 miles N of Stromness, Orkney.
Pri/LA   (map ref: 9C)
Standing close by the important Neolithic village of Skara Brae, Skaill House is the most complete 17th-century mansion house in Orkney. It was built for Bishop George Graham in the 1620s and has fine gardens.

The building is reputedly haunted. Manifestations have included the sound of feet from unoccupied areas, and the apparition of an old woman.

Skaill House open Apr-Sep, Mon-Sat 9.30-18.30, Sun 11.00-18.30; last ticket sold 18.00. (Skara Brae also Oct-Mar Mon-Sat 9.30-16.30, Sun 2.00-4.30; last ticket sold 16.00; closed 25/26 Dec &1-3 Jan).
[Skaill House] Guided tours. Explanatory displays. Gift shop. WC. Disabled access. Garden. Car and coach parking. Group concessions. ££. Joint entry ticket for all Orkney monuments (£££).
Tel: 01856 841501   Fax: 01856 841668

Skene House

Off A944, 4 miles NW of Westhill, Aberdeenshire.
Pri/LA   (map ref: 11G)
Skene House, an extensive castellated mansion, incorporates an old castle. It was a property of the Skene family from 1318 until 1827. One of the family, Alexander Skene of Skene, who died in 1724, was said to be a warlock, although his only crime appears to have been to study on the Continent. He is said not to have had a shadow, and to have been responsible for defiling graves and all sorts of wickedness. A phantom carriage, occupied by himself and the devil, is said to ride across the Loch of Skene at midnight on New Year's Eve, only to sink before it reaches the shore. A similar story is told of James Carnegie, Earl of Southesk, whose castle was at Kinnaird.

150

Skibo Castle

Off A9, 4 miles W of Dornoch, Highlands.
Pri/LA   (map ref: 7D)
The present Skibo Castle dates from the 19th-century, but it stands on the site of an ancient castle. This castle was reputedly haunted by the ghost of a young woman.

   The story goes that a local girl visited to Skibo one day, when it was only occupied by the keeper of the castle, but was never seen again. She was assaulted then murdered by the man, and from then on the apparition of a dishevelled, partially dressed girl was witnessed, running through the building, and unexplained cries and screams were heard. Years later during renovations, a woman's skeleton was found hidden behind a wall. When the remains were buried, the hauntings ceased.

   The castle was owned by the Bishops of Caithness until 1565, but later passed to the Grays. The Marquis of Montrose was imprisoned here after being captured at Ardvreck Castle. Jean Seton, wife of Robert Gray of Skibo, hit one of Montrose's guards with a leg of meat, and the family were fined.

   The present house was built for Andrew Carnegie in 1898. Carnegie was born in Dunfermline in 1835 but emigrated to America in 1848, and made a fortune from railways, and iron and steel. He was one of the richest men of his time, but gave away most of his money, Dunfermline in particular benefiting. The castle now houses an exclusive country club, the Carnegie Club.

Skipness House

Off B8001, 7 miles S of Tarbert, Argyll.
Pri/LA   (map ref: 4M)
Skipness House, built to replace nearby Skipness Castle, was a property of the Campbells, but passed to the Grahams. It was allegedly haunted by a 'Green Lady', a brownie. The brownie, which had golden hair and wore a green dress, would reputedly help the servants to tidy and clean the house, but is also said to have beaten up a man sleeping in another's bed. The ghost is believed to have been witnessed in recent times.

House not open. Skipness Castle open Apr-Sep 9.30-18.30 (£).

Spedlins Tower

Off A74, 3 miles NE of Lochmaben, Dumfries & Galloway.
Pri/LA   (map ref: 9P)
Dating from the 15th century, Spedlins Tower was a stronghold of the Jardine family. It was abandoned for nearby Jardine Hall, and became ruinous, but it was restored in the 1970s.

It was reportedly haunted by the ghost of a miller, called Dunty Porteous, who had the misfortune to be imprisoned here after trying to burn down his own mill. The laird, Sir Alexander Jardine, forgetting about his prisoner, was called away to Edinburgh and took the key to the dungeon with him. Porteous gnawed at his feet and hands before eventually dying of hunger.

His ghost is then said to have manifested itself with all sorts of activity, shrieking through the tower, until contained in the dungeon by a bible, held in a niche by the entrance, this only after many exorcisms had failed to lay the bogle. Once, in 1710, when the bible was removed for repair, the ghost is said to have followed the family to nearby Jardine Hall, and caused all sorts of commotion in the laird's bedroom, such as throwing both the laird and his wife out of their beds, until the bible was returned. It is said that the bible is preserved, but there have been no reports of the ghost in recent times.

Spynie Palace
Off A941, 2.5 miles N of Elgin, Moray.
His Scot   (map ref: 9E)
Reflecting the perilous position many medieval bishops found themselves in, Spynie Palace – the palace of the Bishops of Moray – consists of a massive 15th-century tower 'Davy's Tower' at one corner of a large walled courtyard. The palace was probably built by Bishop Innes, just after Elgin Cathedral had been

burnt by Alexander Stewart, the Wolf of Badenoch. Bishop David Stewart, who died in 1475, excommunicated the Gordon Earl of Huntly, and built the great keep, Davy's Tower, to defend himself against any retribution. Famous visitors include James IV, Mary, Queen of Scots, and the Earl of Bothwell, her third husband who fled the country. The palace was abandoned in 1688 and became ruinous.

The phantom of a piper is said to haunt the buildings, as is the ghost of a lion, said to have been a pet of one of the bishops, witnessed in Davy's Tower and the ruinous kitchen range.

Open Apr-Sep, daily 9.30-18.30; wknds only Oct-Mar, Sat 9.30-16.30, Sun 14.00-16.30; last ticket sold 30 mins before closing.
Explanatory panels. Gift shop. WC. Picnic area. Car and coach parking. £. Joint ticket with Elgin Cathedral available (£).
Tel: 01343 546358

St Andrews Castle

Off A91, in St Andrews, Fife.
His Scot   (map ref: 10K)
Standing close to the remains of the cathedral in the historic seaside town, the castle is a ruinous stronghold of the Bishops of St Andrews. It saw action in the Wars of Independence, and was where Cardinal David Beaton was murdered in 1546 and hung naked from the walls. The mines from the subsequent siege are accessible.

The ghost of Archbishop Hamilton, who was hanged at Stirling after supporting Mary Queen of Scots, is said to haunt the castle. An alternative identity is Cardinal Beaton, who is believed to haunt Melgund and Ethie Castle, while his mistress is thought to haunt Claypotts. The apparition of Beaton is also said to been seen in a phantom coach in the streets of the town.

Open all year: Apr-Sep daily 9.30-18.30; Oct-Mar Mon-Sat 9.30-16.30, Sun 14.00-18.30; last ticket sold 30 mins before closing; closed 25/26 Dec & 1-3 Jan.
Visitor centre with exhibition. Explanatory panels. Gift shop. WC. Disabled access and WC. Car parking nearby. Group concessions. £. Combined ticket for cathedral & castle is available (£).
Tel: 01334 477196

St Andrews Cathedral

Off A91, St Andrews, Fife.
His Scot   (map ref: 10K)

Standing by the sea in the historic town of St Andrews, not much remains of what was formerly the largest and most magnificent cathedral in Scotland. The building was destroyed after the Reformation and then quarried for materials – although there is a fine museum of early Christian sculpture in what remains of the cloister.

St Rule founded a monastery here in the 8th century, and the stair in St Rule's Tower is said to be haunted by a ghostly monk, who was murdered in the building. The apparition is thought to be friendly, to appear around the full moon, and to have been witnessed in recent times.

A 'White Lady', the apparition of a veiled woman in a white dress, also reputedly haunts the ruins.

[Museum and St Rule's Tower] Open all year: Apr-Sep daily 9.30-18.30; Oct-Mar Mon-Sat 9.30-16.30, Sun 14.00-16.30; last ticket sold 30 mins before closing; closed 25/26 Dec & 1-3 Jan.
Visitor centre with fine collection of Christian and early medieval sculpture, including cross-slabs, effigies, and other relics. Explanatory boards. Gift shop. Car parking nearby. Group concessions. £. Combined ticket for cathedral & castle is available (£).
Tel: 01334 472563

St Mary's Church, Haddington

Off A6093, Sidegate, Haddington, East Lothian.
Pri/LA   (map ref: 10M)

In a pleasant and peaceful situation beside the River Tyne, St Mary's is a substantial cross-shaped church with an aisled nave and choir. It is the largest parish church in Scotland, although it has St Nicholas in Aberdeen to rival it. The roof is vaulted, apart from the restored nave. There are interesting medieval carvings, including Green Men and scallop shells, the latter the sign of a place of pilgrimage.

The church houses a marble monument to John Maitland, Lord Thirlestane and Chancellor of Scotland, who died in 1595, his wife and son, which is now known as 'The Chapel of the Three Kings'. Beneath is the Lauderdale family vault. The ghost of John Maitland, Duke of Lauderdale, who died in 1682, is said to have been seen by the chapel, as well as at Thirlestane Castle.

Open daily Apr-Sep 11.00-16.30, Sun 14.00-16.00.
Guided tours available. Explanatory displays. Gift and book shop. WC. Picnic area.
Children's activity area. Disabled access. Car and coach access.
Tel: 01620 823109

St Michael's Parish Church, Linlithgow

Off A803, Kirkgate, Linlithgow, West Lothian.
Pri/LA   (map ref: 8L)
Standing near the extensive ruin of the royal palace, St Michael's was founded in 1242 on the site of an earlier church. The present building dates mostly from the 15th century, and was used by many of the Stewart monarchs, particularly James IV and James V. There are interesting 15th-century relief slabs in the vestry.

It was here that a blue-robed apparition warned James IV not to march into England – but the King ignored the warning, invaded England, and was killed at the disastrous Battle of Flodden in 1513. A similar warning at the Mercat Cross in Edinburgh was also ignored.

Open May-Sep daily 10.00-16.30; Oct-Apr Mon-Fri 10.00-15.00.
Guided tours by arrangement. Explanatory displays. Gift shop. Picnic area. Car and coach parking.
Tel: 01506 842188

St Nicholas Church, Aberdeen

Off A956, Back Wynd off Union Street, Aberdeen.
Pri/LA   (map ref: 12G)
The 'Mither Kirk' of Aberdeen, St Nicholas Church dates from the 12th century, and there has been a church here from early times. The church was divided in two after the Reformation, then largely rebuilt. The East Kirk dates from 1752, the West from 1834-7, while the central tower and spire are from 1874, built after a fire destroyed the old belfry. The congregations were united in 1980. St Mary's Chapel, in the crypt, survives from the 15th-century church, and Sir John Gordon, executed after the Battle of Corrichie in 1562, is interred here. There is also fine 17th-century embroidery.

The adjoining graveyard has many table-tombs and memorials, dating from as early as the 17th century. The area has a reputation for being haunted. In 1982 two men witnessed the apparition of a woman, garbed in a long white dress and veil. She was said to have black hair, and disappeared at the corner of the church.

Open May-Sep, Mon-Fri 12.00-16.00, Sat 13.00-15.00, except closed local holidays.
Guided tours. Explanatory displays. WC. Disabled access and hearing induction loop for the deaf. Car parking nearby.
Tel: 01224 643494

Stair Arms, Pathhead

On A68, Ford, Pathhead, Midlothian.
Pri/LA (map ref: 10M)
Lord and Lady Stair had the inn built after the construction of the bridge, designed by Thomas Telford, to cross the gorge at the village of Ford. The hotel was a temperance establishment in the early 20th century, but in 1990 was remodelled and upgraded, and is set in four acres of grounds.

The hotel is said to be haunted by the ghost of a chambermaid. The poor woman is said to have committed suicide while working here, and her apparition has been seen in the restaurant.

Hotel – open all year and to non-residents.
12 bedrooms with ensuite facilities. Restaurant and bar. Private functions, weddings and small conferences. Children's play facilities. $-$$.
Tel: 01875 320277   Fax: 01875 320929

Stirling Castle

Off A872, Upper Castle Hill, in Stirling.
His Scot (map ref: 8L)
Standing on a rock commanding the important route to the north, Stirling Castle is a magnificent fortress, once the most important stronghold in Scotland. It has a long and violent history, from the 11th century until the Jacobite Risings of the 18th, and is associated with many of the monarchs of Scotland.

Only some of its history can be related here. Alexander I died at the castle in 1124, as did William the Lyon in 1214. Edward I of England captured Stirling in 1304, but it was recovered by the Scots in 1314 after the Battle of Bannockburn. James II was born here in 1430, as was James III in 1451. Mary, Queen of Scots, was crowned in the old chapel in 1543, and the future James VI was baptised here in 1566. The Jacobites besieged the castle in 1746, but they soon had to withdraw.

The castle is said to have several ghosts. One is a 'Pink Lady', the apparition of a beautiful woman in a pink silk gown. She has been identified as a phantom

of Mary Queen of Scots or the ghost of a woman searching for her husband, who was killed when the castle was captured by Edward I. Her ghost is said to venture as far as the Church of the Holyrood, but she is thought to be most frequently seen at Ladies Rock, between the castle and the church.

The 'Green Lady' is thought to a harbinger of ill tidings, often associated with fire. She may have been a lady in waiting to Mary Queen of Scots – believed to have saved Mary when her bedclothes caught fire – and has reputedly been seen in present times. Another story is that she was the daughter of a governor of the castle who killed herself by throwing herself from the battlements after her lover had been accidentally killed by her father.

The sounds of ghostly footsteps are said to have been heard in an upstairs chamber of the Governor's Block, which may have been connected with the death of a sentry in the 1820s. In 1946 and 1956 the footsteps are said to have been heard by soldiers occupying the room.

Open all year: Apr-Sep daily 9.30-17.15; Oct-Mar daily 9.30-16.15; castle closes 45 mins after last ticket sold – joint ticket with Argyll's Lodging.
Exhibition of life in the royal palace, introductory display, medieval kitchen display.
Museum of Argyll & Sutherland Highlanders. Gift shop. Restaurant. WC. Disabled access
and WC. Car and coach parking. Group concessions. ££.
Tel: 01786 450000

Sundrum Castle

Off A70, 4.5 miles E of Ayr, Ayrshire.
Pri/LA (map ref: 6N)
Sundrum Castle, a mansion of 1793, incorporates a 14th-century keep of the Wallace family. The property passed to the Cathcarts, then to the Hamiltons by 1750.

The old part of the building, centred in the vaulted dining room, was reputedly haunted by a 'Green Lady', said to have been the wife of one of the Hamilton lairds. The disturbances have apparently ceased since the building was renovated and divided.

Sunipol

Off B8073, 1 mile N of Calgary, Mull.
Pri/LA (map ref: 2J)
The farm here was at one time said to be haunted by poltergeist activity, and objects were seen flying about the house, as well as many other disturbances.

Tarras

Off A7, 2 miles W of Langholm, Dumfries & Galloway.
Pri/LA (map ref: 10O)
Tarras Water is a swift burn which flows down from the hills north of Langholm and joins the River Esk at Auchenrivock. The area around the Tarras is said to be haunted by a 'White Lady'. An account states that a local farmer murdered and robbed a woman, then hid her body somewhere on the moors. The woman is said to have lodged with the farmer, when he discovered that she had much gold and other valuables. Her apparition has reputedly been seen by many people.

Taymouth Castle

Off A827, 5 miles W of Aberfeldy, Perthshire.
Pri/LA (map ref: 8J)
Taymouth Castle, a large castellated mansion built between 1801 and 1842, incorporates part of a 16th-century castle of the Campbells. The family were made Earls of Breadalbane in the 1681, then Marquises in 1831.

The castle is reputedly haunted, and ghostly footsteps have been reported. The ghost is said to manifest as a harbinger of tragedy in the Campbell family. During its use as a school in the 1980s, it is said that some students were so scared by unexplained happenings that they refused to stay in the castle.

Thainstone House

Off A96, S of Inverurie, Aberdeenshire.
Pri/LA   (map ref: 11F)
In 40 acres of lush meadow land, Thainstone House, a classical mansion which dates from the 18th century, was extended in 1840 by the architect Archibald Simpson and again in 1992. An older house here was sacked by Jacobites in 1745, and it was home to James Wilson, who signed the American Declaration of Independence, and Sir Andrew Mitchell, who was ambassador to the Court of Prussia in the time of Frederick the Great.

The building is said to be haunted by a 'Green Lady', daughter of a former owner of the house. She was killed in a riding accident, and sightings of her apparition describe her as wearing a green cloak. Manifestations reported include objects moving by themselves, and pets will not enter one of the bedrooms.

Hotel – open all year.
48 bedrooms. Restaurant and bar. Conferences, meetings and seminars. Country club with swimming pool, jacuzzi, and sports. Parking. $$$-$$$$.
Tel: 01467 621643   Fax: 01467 625084

The Binns

Off A904, 3 miles NE of Linlithgow, West Lothian.
NTS   (map ref: 8L)
Set in picturesque grounds by the banks of the Firth of Forth, The Binns is a fine castellated mansion, dating from the 17th century, and has impressive plaster ceilings. It was a property of the Livingstones of Kilsyth, but was sold to the Dalziels in 1612.

General Tam Dalziel of The Binns was taken prisoner in 1651 at the Battle of Worcester, but escaped from the Tower of London. He went into exile when the Royalist rising of 1654 collapsed, and served with the Tsar's cossacks, when he is reputed to have roasted prisoners over open fires. Dalziel was made commander of forces in Scotland after the Restoration, and led the force that defeated the Covenanters at the Battle of Rullion Green in 1666. He died in 1685. All sorts of interesting quirks were attributed to Dalziel by his Covenanter enemies, including musket balls bouncing off him at Rullion Green.

The house and grounds are reportedly haunted by Tam's ghost, which is sometimes said to be seen on a white horse riding up to the door of the house. One story is that Dalziel often played cards with the devil, and once when Dalziel won the devil was so angered that it threw a massive marble table, on which they had been playing, into the nearby Sergeant's Pond. The cards, goblet, spoon and table said to have been used are preserved in the house. When the water was low after a drought, this table was supposedly found, some 200 years after Dalziel's death.

Another ghost said to haunt the grounds is that of an old man gathering firewood, said by some to be a Pict.

Open May-Sep except Fri 13.30-17.30; last admission 17.00. Parkland open all year: Apr-Oct daily 9.30-19.00; Nov-Mar 9.30-16.00; last admission 30 mins before closing.
Collections of portraits, furniture and china. Guided tours. Explanatory displays. WC.
Parkland. Disabled access to ground floor and grounds & WC. Car parking. ££.
Tel: 01506 834255

Theatre Royal, Edinburgh
Off A1, at corner of South Bridge and Princes Street, Edinburgh.
Pri/LA   (map ref: 9L)
The old Post Office building, built in the 1860s, stands on the site of the Theatre Royal, which dated from 1768. This building was said to be haunted by the sounds of actors performing on an empty stage, but the manifestations are said to have stopped when the theatre was demolished.

Theatre Royal, Glasgow
Off M9, Hope Street, Glasgow.
Pri/LA   (map ref: 7M)
The theatre here, which dates from 1867, has a fine interior with three levels of circles and sumptuous decoration. Theatre Royal is now the home of Scottish Opera.

The theatre is said to be haunted by the ghost of a former cleaner, 'Nora'. She was an aspiring actress but was not taken seriously, and is reported to have thrown herself to her death from the top circle. Her ghost is said to manifest itself with moaning and slamming doors. The apparition of a fireman killed here has reportedly been seen in the orchestra pit.

Theatre.
Tel: 0141 332 3321   Fax: 0141 332 4477

Thirlestane Castle
Off A68, NE of Lauder, Borders.
Pri/LA   (map ref: 10M)
Standing in picturesque countryside, Thirlestane Castle, dating from the 16th-century, is a large splendid mansion with an old castle at its core. Fine 17th-century plasterwork ceilings survive.

It is a property of the Maitlands, and John Maitland, Duke of Lauderdale, had the house remodelled in 1670. Lauderdale was Secretary of State for Scotland from 1661-80, but he was eventually replaced after the Covenanter uprising which ended with their defeat at the Battle of Bothwell Brig. His ghost is said to haunt Thirlestane, as well as St Mary's in Haddington.

Open 21 Apr-31 Oct, daily except Sat 11.00-17.00; last admission 16.15. Collection of portraits, furniture and china. Exhibition of historical toys and Border country life. Giftshop. Tearoom. WC. Picnic tables. Woodland walks.

Car parking. Coaches by arrangement. Group concessions. ££.
Tel: 01578 722430 Fax: 01578 722761 Email: thirlestane@great-houses-scotland.co.uk

Thunderton House, Elgin

Off A96, Thunderton, Elgin, Moray.
Pri/LA (map ref: 9E)
Thunderton House may incorporate part of a 14th-century castle, built to replace the old stronghold on Ladyhill. It was later a property of the Sutherland Lord Duffus, but passed to the Dunbars of Thunderton. It was altered in later years, and is now a public house.

The building is said to be haunted by Bonnie Prince Charlie, who stayed here for 11 days before going on to defeat at the Battle of Culloden in 1746, although an alternative identity has been given as Lady Arradoul, his host on this occasion. Disturbances include the faint sounds of bagpipes and voices coming from the second floor, and the movement of objects.

Public house.
Tel: 01343 554921

Tibbie Shiel's Inn, St Mary's Loch

Off A708, 1.5 miles S of Cappercleuch, St Mary's Loch, Borders.
Pri/LA (map ref: 9N)
Located by the lovely and tranquil St Mary's Loch, Tibbie Shiel's Inn was opened as a drinking house in 1823 by Isabella Shiel – also known as Tibbie – after her husband died and she was left penniless. The inn grew in popularity and was visited by James Hogg, the Ettrick Shepherd, and many other writers and poets, including Sir Walter Scott, Robert Louis Stevenson and Thomas

Carlyle. Tibbie died in 1878 at the age of 96 and was buried in Ettrick kirkyard, but the inn remained open.

The building is said to be haunted by Tibbie's ghost, which reputedly manifests itself with a cold hand on the shoulder, but keeps a watchful eye on the hotel. A report of the ghost was recorded in one of the bedrooms in 1996. The spirit of a dog has also been witnessed, apparently the ghost of an animal belonging to a previous innkeeper who died while away from the inn, and the dog starved to death in his absence.

Hotel – open all summer and Thu-Sun Nov-Good Friday and to non-residents.
Ensuite accommodation available. Refreshments and food. Free fishing for residents.
Parking. $.
Tel: 01750 42231

Tombuie

Off A827, 2 miles NE of Aberfeldy, Perthshire.
Pri/LA   (map ref: 8J)
Tombuie, a farmhouse, is said to be haunted by the apparition of a young girl. She had fallen in love with the son of the house, but it was not reciprocated and he was soon married to another woman. The story goes that the poor girl despaired and drowned herself in the water butt at Tombuie. Her weeping apparition then appeared to the couple in the bedroom of the house, and has reputedly been seen on other occasions

Transport Depot, Aberdeen

Off A92, King Street, Aberdeen.
Pri/LA   (map ref: 12G)
The building here, dating from about 1861, was used as a barracks until World War I. It is said to be haunted by the ghost of a Captain Beaton of the Gordon Highlanders, who hanged himself here. His apparition has reputedly been seen in recent times, and other manifestations include tapping on windows, the

unexplained switching on and off of lights, and areas of offices becoming suddenly very cold.

Traquair House

Off B709, 1 mile S of Innerleithen, Borders.
Pri/LA (map ref: 9N)
With a strong claim to being the oldest continuously inhabited house in Scotland, Traquair House is an altered and extended tower house, which may incorporate work from as early as the 12th century.

Alexander I had a hunting lodge here, but the lands had passed to the Douglases by the 13th century, then through several families until sold to the Stewart Earls of Buchan in 1478. Mary, Queen of Scots, visited with Lord Darnley in 1566. The 4th Laird helped her escape from Lochleven Castle in 1568.

Bonnie Prince Charlie visited in the house in 1745, entering through the Bear Gates. One story is that the 5th Earl closed and locked them after Charlie's departure, swearing they would not be unlocked until a Stewart once more sat on the throne of the country. They are still locked. The house has a collection of Stewart mementoes.

The ghost of Lady Louisa Stewart, sister of the 8th and last Earl of Traquair, is said to haunt the vicinity of the house. She was 100 years old when she died in 1875, and the apparition of an old lady has been reported in the grounds. There is a portrait of Lady Louisa at Traquair.

Open Easter-Sep daily 12.30-17.30, Jun-Aug daily 10.30-17.30; open Fri, Sat & Sun only in Oct 12.30-17.30.
Working 18th-century brewery. Guided tours and explanatory displays. Tea room. WC. Gardens, woodland walks and maze. Craft workshops. Gift and Cashmere shop. Brewery. Car and coach parking. Group concessions. Accommodation. *££.*
Tel: 01896 830323   Fax: 01896 830639
Email: traquair.house@scotborders.co.uk

163

Trumpan Church

Off B886, Trumpan, Skye.
Ruin or site   (map ref: 1E)

Trumpan Church, the ruins of a medieval church formerly with a thatched roof, is the scene of a cruel massacre. A raiding party of MacDonalds came ashore here one Sunday about 1578. The congregation of MacLeods were at worship, and the MacDonalds set fire to the thatch. They then cut down anyone who tried to flee, while the rest of the congregation were burnt alive. Only one woman escaped and the alarm was raised. The MacLeods of Dunvegan, bringing with them the Fairy Flag, quickly arrived and the MacDonalds were exterminated to a man. On the anniversary of the massacre it is said that the singing of a ghostly congregation can be heard.

In the churchyard is the Trial Stone, which has a small hole near the top. The trial was carried out by blindfolding the accused, who would be proved to be telling the truth if they succeeded in putting their finger in the hole at the first attempt.

Open at all reasonable times.
Parking Nearby.

Vayne Castle

Off B57, 7 miles W of Brechin, Angus.
Ruin or site   (map ref: 10I)

Vayne Castle is a ruinous Z-plan tower house, dating from the 16th century, which is said to be haunted. The lands were once a property of the Mowats, but passed to the Lindsay Earls of Crawford in 1450, then the Carnegie Earl of Southesk in 1594, who sold it to the Mills in 1766. The castle was replaced by the nearby mansion of Noranside.

Wellwood House

Off A70, 2 miles W of Muirkirk, Ayrshire.
Ruin or site   (map ref: 7N)

Wellwood House, a mansion of 1878, incorporated an old house or tower of the Campbells, which dated from about 1600. The later house was built by the Bairds, who bought the estate in 1863. The house was demolished in 1926.

The house was reputedly haunted by the apparition of young woman, called 'Beanie'. She appears to have been murdered, perhaps on the stairs of the house, for it was said a blood stain here could not be removed. Her ghost was allegedly seen walking from her room in the older part of the house out to the grounds, where she wept. If her apparition was closely approached, it would slowly vanish.

Wemyss Castle
Off A955, 3 miles NE of Kirkcaldy, Fife.
Pri/LA (map ref: 9L)
Wemyss Castle is the large sprawling stronghold and mansion of the Wemyss family, who have held it from ancient times until the present day.

Sir Michael Wemyss was one of the ambassadors sent to Norway at the end of the 13th century to bring Margaret, Maid of Norway, back to Scotland. The castle was sacked by the English during the Wars of Independence. Royal visitors include Mary, Queen of Scots, who first met Lord Darnley here in 1565, and Charles II, who visited in 1650 and 1657. The Wemyss family were forfeited for their part in the Jacobite Risings, but later regained the property.

A 'Green Lady' – Green Jean – reputedly haunts the castle, and is said to have been seen in all parts of the building.

West Bow, Edinburgh
Off A1, E of Edinburgh Castle, off the Royal Mile, Edinburgh.
Pri/LA (map ref: 9L)
A house in the West Bow, the street between Victoria Street and the Grassmarket, was occupied by a Major Thomas Weir and his sister Grizel. On the face of it,

Weir was an upstanding member of the community: he was commander of the city guard and it was he who led the Marquis of Montrose to the scaffold. In 1670, however, he confessed to many crimes, including witchcraft and meetings with the devil, and implicated his sister. The couple were convicted and both executed: Weir was strangled then burnt

at Gallowlea, beneath Calton Hill, while his sister was hanged in the Grassmarket.

Both their apparitions were then reportedly seen around the West Bow, sometimes on a dark horse. His house was also reputed to be haunted, and although empty, strange lights were seen at the windows and the sounds of partying and screaming were heard. A black coach and horses, sent by the devil, are supposed to have arrived at the house to take Weir and his sister back to Hell after the forays into the corporeal world. In the 1850s, a couple occupied the house but only stayed one night after an apparition of a calf was seen in their bedroom. The house was finally demolished around 1830, although ghostly manifestations are still reported, including the headless ghost of Weir and the apparition of his sister, blackened by fire.

Sightings of an apparition of William Ruthven, Earl of Gowrie, have also been reported here. Gowrie led the 'Ruthven Raid' of 1582, in which the young James VI was imprisoned in Huntingtower Castle. James had him executed in 1584.

Gowrie had a town house here, but it has also been demolished.

Accessible at all times.

Western Infirmary, Glasgow

Off A82, Dumbarton Road, Glasgow.
Pri/LA   (map ref: 7M)
The infirmary, dating from 1871 and first built as a massive castellated building, has been much altered and extended in later years. The buildings are said to be haunted by the ghost of Sir William MacEwen, who died in 1924. His apparition is said to have been witnessed several times, before vanishing outside an operating theatre.

Windgate House

Off A702, 5 miles SW of Biggar, Lanarkshire.
Ruin or site   (map ref: 8N)
Known locally as 'The Vaults', Windgate House is a small ruined tower house of the Baillies of Lamington, dating from the 16th century, with a vaulted basement. An apparition of a couple in Victorian dress has reportedly been witnessed here, and the story goes that they only appear when something significant is going to happen in the lives of the Lamington family.

Windhouse

Off A968, Windhouse, Yell, Shetland.
Ruin or site   (map ref: 11A)
In a desolate and windswept location, the two-storey house dates from 1707 and was remodelled with castellated wings about 1880. It was abandoned in the 1930s and is now ruinous, and stands in a bird sanctuary.

Windhouse was a property of the Swanieson family, but passed to the Nevens in the early 17th century. The house was sold in 1878, and during renovations a large human skeleton was found.

One apparition was reportedly that of a large man, dressed in a black cloak and hat. It appeared out of the ground outside the house, then walked through the wall, and may have been the spirit of a peddler who disappeared and whose skeleton was found as mentioned above.

Another phantom was reputedly a lady dressed in silk. The swishing of her skirts was reported at the top of the stair. She was said to be a housekeeper and mistress, whose neck was broken after she had fallen down the stairs.

A third ghost was thought to be that of a child, witnessed in the kitchen, while yet another was of a black dog. Ghostly footsteps were also recorded as having being heard.

Wrychtishousis, Edinburgh

Off A702, Gillespie Crescent, Edinburgh.
Ruin or site   (map ref: 9L)
Site of old house or castle, part of which may have dated from the 14th century, Wrychtishousis, or Wrightshouses, was described as 'a curious old pile'. It was demolished in 1802 to build James Gillespie's school, on the site of which was the Blind Asylum – Gillespie's was moved to Bruntsfield House.

It was a property of the Napiers, passed to the Clerks in 1664, but by the end of the 18th century was occupied by a Lieutenant General Robertson of

Lawers. During his occupancy, a servant reported seeing the apparition of a headless woman, with an infant in its arms, appearing – on several occasions – emerging from the hearth in his bedroom. The building was demolished a few years later, and the remains of a woman and child were found under the hearth. The woman's head had been removed, possibly to fit the rest of her into the space under the hearth.

The story goes that after 1664 the house was occupied by a James Clerk, his wife and child. Clerk was killed in battle, and his younger brother murdered his widow and child so that he would inherit the property.

Ghost
Tours

Mercat Tours, Edinburgh

Tours leave from the Mercat Cross, Edinburgh, The Shore for Hidden Historic Leith, or Information Office, George Square, Glasgow.
Pri/LA   (map ref: 9L)
EDINBURGH
Ghosts and Ghouls is a journey through the closes and wynds of the city's haunted underworld and features authentic tales of Old Edinburgh and underground vaults.

The Ghost Hunter Trail is a terrifying late-night walk with macabre tales of the supernatural, including a visit to Edinburgh's underground vaulted chambers and concludes in an ancient Edinburgh graveyard.

Hidden Underground Vaults offers a descent into recently uncovered dark vaulted chambers under the South Bridge. Both tours visit them and tales of sinister secrets are recounted – see entry for Niddry Street.
LEITH
Hidden Historic Leith is a new tour offering tales of piracy, plague and witchcraft associated with the harbour town.

Tours are also available for Mary King's Close – see entry.
GLASGOW
Ghosts and Ghouls is a walk around the streets and alleys of Glasgow to discover the tales of horror, ghosts, witches and wickedness associated with the city.

Ghosts & Ghouls 19.00 & 20.00 all year (1.5 hrs.). Refreshments.

Ghost Hunter Trail 21.30 all year (1.5 hrs). Also Midnight Tour Apr-Oct 22.30, Nov-Mar book.

Hidden Underground Vaults 11.00, 12.00, 13.00, 14.00, 15.00 & 16.00 Apr-Sep; 12.00 & 14.00 Oct-Mar.

Hidden Historic Leith daily 14.00 Apr–Sep; Sat & Sun 14.00 Oct–Mar.

GLASGOW

Ghosts and Ghouls daily 21.00 (lasts 90 mins)
££-£££.
Tel: 0131 225 6591   Fax: 0131 225 6591
Email: dbrogan@mercat-tours.co.uk   Web: www.mercat-tours.co.uk

Auld Reekie Tours, Edinburgh

Tours leave from Tron Church, Royal Mile, Edinburgh.
Pri/LA   (map ref: 9L)
The Ultimate Ghosts and Torture Tour features terrifying true stories of Edinburgh's past, and a trip into the city's underground chambers, which are believed to be haunted.

The Underground City Tour is a journey through 200-year-old underground chambers, where over 70 supernatural occurrences have been reported in the last two years.

Ghost and Torture Tours at 19.00, 20.00, 21.00 and 22.00 nightly.

Underground City Tour at 12.30, 13.30, 14.30 and 15.30 (45 mins)
£££ & ££. Telephone for details, bookings, parking and discounts.
Tel: 0131 557 4700/07000 285373   Fax: 0131 557 4700
Email: auldreekietours@cableinet.co.uk

Witchery Tours, Edinburgh
Outside The Witchery Restaurant, Castlehill, Royal Mile, Edinburgh.
Pri/LA   (map ref: 9L)
Ghost tour of Edinburgh, through dark courtyards and eerie closes, conducted by Adam Lyal, Highwayman, executed for his crimes in the Grassmarket on 27 March 1811.

Every evening by appointment. Murder and Mystery Tour all year; Ghosts and Gore Tour May-Sep only.
Times vary, tours last 1.25 hours. Booking in advance is essential. *£££*.
Tel: 0131 225 6745   Fax: 0131 220 2086
Email: lyal@witcherytours.demon.co.uk   Web: www.clan.com/edinburgh/witchery

The Original St Andrews Witches Tour
Tours leave from Tudor Inn, North Street, St Andrews.
Pri/LA   (map ref: 10K)
The Original St Andrews Witches Tour retells the history of the town under the guidance of Mrs W T Linskill (deceased). She was the wife of Dean of Guild Linskill who wrote St *Andrews Ghost Stories*.
The Saints and Sinners tour is another night-time walking tour through the haunted streets and closes of St Andrews.
The Fishwife's Tale, a day-time tour, is also available.

The Original St Andrews Witches Tour and Saints and Sinners Tour – times/days vary, advance booking is essential. (1.25 hrs.)
£££. Telephone for details and bookings.
Tel: 01334 655057   Fax: 01334 655057

These are only a selection of tours available. There are other tours in Aberdeen (Bon Accord Tours Tel: 01224 733 704), Stirling (Heritage Events Company [seasonal] Tel: 01786 447150) and Inverness (Terror Tours Tel: 0777 176852).

Selected
Further
Reading

Selected Further Reading

Ghost story books

Adams, Norman *Haunted Scotland*, Edinburgh, 1998

Alexander, Marc *Haunted Castles*, London, 1974

Campbell, Margaret *Ghosts, Massacres and Horror Stories of Scotland's Castles*, Glasgow (no date of publication)

Love, Dale *Scottish Ghosts*, London, 1995

Mitchell, Robin *Adam Lyal's Witchery Tours*, Edinburgh, 1988

Robertson, James *Scottish Ghost Stories*, London, 1996

Tales from Scottish Lairds, Norwich, 1985

Thompson, Francis *The Supernatural Highlands*, Edinburgh, 1997

Tranter, Nigel *Tales and Traditions of Scottish Castles*, Glasgow, 1993

Underwood, Peter *Gazetteer of Scottish Ghosts*, Glasgow, 1973

Underwood, Peter *Guide to Ghosts and Haunted Places*, London, 1996

Whitaker, Terence *Scotland's Ghosts and Apparitions*, London, 1991

Wilson, Alan J; Brogan, Des & McGrail, Frank *Ghostly Tales & Sinister Stories of Old Edinburgh*, Edinburgh, 1991

Historical *and* general books

Campbell, Johanna *Touring Guide to Scotland*, London, 1998

Connachan-Holmes, JRA *Country Houses of Scotland*, Frome, 1995

Coventry, Martin *The Castles of Scotland* (2nd edition), Edinburgh, 1997

Coventry, Martin & Miller, Joyce *Wee Guide to Old Churches and Abbeys of Scotland*, Edinburgh, 1997

Groome, Francis *Ordinance Gazetteer of Scotland* (5 volumes), Glasgow, c1890(?)

Hudson's Guide to Historic Properties in Scotland, Banbury, 1998

MacGibbon, D & Ross, T *The Castellated and Domestic Architecture of Scotland*, 1887-92

McKean, Charles (series editor) *The Illustrated Architectural Guides to Scotland* (14 volumes by area currently available), Edinburgh, 1985

New, Anthony *A Guide to the Abbeys of Scotland*, London, 1988

Salter, Mike *The Old Parish Churches of Scotland*, Malvern, 1994

Scottish Churches Scheme *Churches to visit in Scotland 1998*, Glasgow, 1998

Tranter, Nigel *The Fortified House in Scotland*, (5 volumes), Edinburgh, 1986

Indexes

Index *by* place

O = open regularly or occasionally to the public
G = garden or park open regularly or occasionally to the public
H = hotel, bed & breakfast or public house
A = accommodation available by appt only (T = ghost tour)

CASTLES
Abergeldie Castle
Ackergill Tower (A)
Airlie Castle
Airth Castle (H)
Aldourie Castle
Ardblair Castle (O)
Ardincaple Castle
Ardrossan Castle (O)
Ardvreck Castle (O)
Ashintully Castle
Auchinvole House
Balcomie Castle
Baldoon Castle
Balgonie Castle (O)
Ballindalloch Castle (O)
Balnagown Castle
Balvenie Castle (O)
Balwearie Castle
Barcaldine Castle (O)
Barnbougle Castle [Dalmeny House] (O)
Bedlay Castle
Benholm Castle
Berwick Castle
Borthwick Castle (H)
Braco Castle
Braemar Castle (O)
Brahan Castle
Brodick Castle (O)
Brodie Castle (O)
Buchanan Castle
Buckholm Tower
Caisteal Camus
Carleton Castle (O)
Castle Cary (H)
Castle Coeffin
Castle Fraser (O)
Castle Grant
Castle Lachlan
Castle Levan
Castle Loch Heylipol
Castle Spioradain
Castle Stuart (O/A)
Castle Tioram (O?)
Castle of Mey (G?)
Castle of Park (A)
Cawdor Castle (O)
Cessnock Castle

Claypotts Castle (O)
Cloncaird Castle
Closeburn Castle
Colquhonnie Castle (H)
Comlongon Castle (H)
Corgarff Castle (O)
Coroghon Castle
Corstorphine Castle
Cortachy Castle
Coull Castle
Craigcrook Castle
Craighouse
Craignethan Castle (O)
Cranshaws Castle
Crathes Castle (O)
Crichton Castle (O)
Cromarty Castle
Culcreuch Castle (H)
Culzean Castle (O)
Dalhousie Castle (H)
Dalkeith House (G)
Dalzell House (G)
Dean Castle (O)
Delgatie Castle (O/A)
Dolphinston Tower
Drumlanrig Castle (O)
Duchal Castle
Dunnottar Castle (O)
Dunphail Castle
Dunrobin Castle (O)
Duns Castle (A)
Dunskey Castle (O?)
Dunstaffnage Castle (O)
Duntrune Castle
Duntulm Castle (O?)
Dunure Castle (O?)
Dunvegan Castle (O)
Earlshall
Edinample Castle
Edinburgh Castle (O)
Edzell Castle (O)
Eilean Donan Castle (O)
Ethie Castle
Fairburn Tower
Falkland Palace (O)
Fedderate Castle
Fernie Castle (H)
Ferniehirst Castle (O)
Fetteresso Castle

Finavon Castle (doocot O)
Fort George (O)
Frendraught Castle
Fulford Tower
Fyvie Castle (O)
Galdenoch Castle
Garleton Castle
Garth Castle
Gight Castle
Glamis Castle (O)
Grandtully Castle
Grange House
Hallgreen Castle
Hermitage Castle (O)
Holyroodhouse (O)
Huntingtower Castle (O)
Inchdrewer Castle
Inverey Castle
Invergarry Castle (Glengarry House Hotel H)
Inverquharity Castle
Jedburgh Castle
Kellie Castle (O)
Kindrochit Castle (O)
Kinnaird Castle
Kinnaird Head Castle (O)
Knockderry Castle
Largie Castle
Lauriston Castle (O)
Leith Hall (O)
Linlithgow Palace (O)
Littledean Tower
Loch of Leys
Lochleven Castle (O)
Lordscairnie Castle
Loudon Castle (O?)
Luffness House
Macduff's Castle (O?)
Mains Castle
Meggernie Castle
Megginch Castle (G)
Meldrum House (H)
Melgund Castle
Monymusk Castle
Moy Castle
Muchalls Castle
Neidpath Castle (O)
Newark Castle [Bowhill] (O)
Newton Castle

Noltland Castle (O)
Old Woodhouselee Castle
Penkaet Castle
Pitcaple Castle
Pittodrie House (H)
Rait Castle
Rockhall
Rosslyn Castle
Rothesay Castle (O)
Roxburgh Castle (O)
Ruthven Castle (O)
Saddell Castle
Sanquhar Castle (O?)
Scone Palace (O)
Shieldhill (H)
Spedlins Tower
Spynie Palace (O)
St Andrews Castle (O)
Stirling Castle (O)
Sundrum Castle
Thirlestane Castle (O)
Traquair House (O)
Vayne Castle
Wemyss Castle

CHURCHES & ABBEYS
Ardchattan Priory (O)
Banchory (O)
Blantyre Priory
Carmelite Street, Aberdeen (O)
Clydesdale Hotel, Lanark (H)
Culross Abbey (O)
Deer Abbey (O)
Dryburgh Abbey (O)
Fortingall (O)
Iona Abbey (O)
Maryculter House (H)
Melrose Abbey (O)
Newbattle Abbey
Rathen Church (O)
Rosslyn Chapel (O)
Royal Hotel, Cupar
Spynie Palace (O)
St Andrews Castle (O)
St Andrews Cathedral (O)
St Mary's, Haddington (O)
St Michael's, Linlithgow (O)
St Nicholas Church, Aberdeen (O)
Trumpan Church (O)

HOSPITALS & MUNICIPAL BUILDINGS
County Buildings, Ayr
Gartloch Hospital
Glasgow Infirmary
Hawkhead Hospital, Paisley
Jedburgh Castle Jail (O)

Newbattle Abbey (adult education college)
Transport Depot, Aberdeen
Western Infirmary, Glasgow

HOTELS, B&B & PUBLIC HOUSES
Airth Castle (H)
Amatola Hotel, Aberdeen (H)
Ardoe House Hotel (H)
Atholl Palace Hotel (H)
Aultsigh (Youth Hostel)
Borthwick Castle (H)
Broadford Hotel (H)
Busta House (H)
Cameron House (H)
Cameron's Inn, Aberdeen (H)
Cartland Bridge Hotel (H)
Castle Cary (H)
Cathedral House, Glasgow (H)
Clydesdale Hotel, Lanark (H)
Cobbler Hotel, Arrochar (H)
Colquhonnie Castle (H)
Comlongon Castle (H)
County Hotel, Dumfries (demolished)
County Hotel, Peebles (H)
Coylet Inn (H)
Cross Keys Hotel, Peebles (H)
Culcreuch Castle (H)
Dalhousie Castle (H)
Dalmahoy (H)
Dryburgh Abbey Hotel (H)
Fernie Castle (H)
Gairnshiel Lodge (H)
Gight House Hotel, Methlick (H)
Hunter's Tryst, Edinburgh (H)
King's Arms Hotel, Dumfries (demolished)
Kylesku Hotel (H)
Learmonth Hotel, Edinburgh (H)
Lochailort Inn (H)
Maryculter House (H)
Meldrum House (H)
Nivingston House Hotel (H)
Norwood Hall, Aberdeen (H)
Old Post Horn Inn, Crawford (closed)
Pannanich Wells, Ballater (H)
Pittodrie House (H)
Ravenswood Hotel, Ballater (H)
Roxburghe House (H)
Royal Hotel, Cupar (old folks' flats)
Salutation Hotel, Perth (H)

Shieldhill (H)
Stair Arms, Pathhead (H)
Thainstone House (H)
Thunderton House, Elgin (H)
Tibbie Shiel's Inn, St Mary's Loch (H)

HOUSES & FARMS
Ann Street, Edinburgh
Ardgay
Ardnadam
Auchnarrow
Avoch
Charlotte Square, Edinburgh
Chessel's Court, Edinburgh
Clumly Farm
Devanha House, Aberdeen
Fordell
Fountainhall, Aberdeen
Glenluce
Glenmallan
Howlet's House
India Street, Edinburgh
Johnstone Lodge, Anstruther
Mary King's Close, Edinburgh (T)
Melville Grange
Moncrieffe Arms, Bridge of Earn (H)
New Lanark (O)
Niddry Street, Edinburgh (T)
Old Manse, Lairg
Princes Street, Edinburgh
Ring Croft of Stocking, Auchencairn
Sunipol
Tombuie
West Bow, Edinburgh
Windgate House

MANSIONS AND GREAT HOUSES
Abbotsford (O)
Achindown
Allanbank House
Arbigland House (O)
Ardachy
Ardchattan Priory (G)
Auchlochan House
Aultsigh (H)
Ballachulish House
Ballechin
Barbreck House
Barnbougle Castle [Dalmeny House] (O)
Biel
Big House
Broomhill

Busta House (H)
Cameron House (H)
Caroline Park House
Cartland Bridge Hotel (H)
Cobbler Hotel, Arrochar (H)
Cullen House
Culzean Castle (O)
Dalkeith House (G)
Dalmahoy (H)
Dalry House, Edinburgh
Dalzell House (G)
Doune
Drumlanrig Castle (O)
Dunrobin Castle (O)
Duns Castle (A)
Dunvegan Castle (O)
Durris House
Earlshall
Falkland Palace (O)
Fasque (O)
Floors Castle (O)
Fyvie Castle (O)
Glamis Castle (O)
Glenlee
Grange House
Greenlaw House
Haddo House (O)
Holyroodhouse (O)
Hopetoun House (O)
Houndwood House
Inverawe House
Kingcausie
Kinneil House (G)
Laudale House
Lauriston Castle (O)
Leith Hall (O)
Liberton House
Linlithgow Palace (O)
Lochnell House
Logie House, Dundee (O)
Luffness House
Marlfield House
Maryculter House (H)
Medwyn House
Meldrum House (H)
Menie House
Newbattle Abbey
Pinkie House
Place of Bonhill
Rammerscales House (O)
Ravenswood Hotel, Ballater (H)
Saltoun Hall
Scone Palace (O)
Skaill House (O)
Skene House
Skibo Castle (A)

Skipness House
Taymouth Castle
Thainstone House (H)
The Binns (O)
Thirlestane Castle (O)
Traquair House (O)
Wellwood House (O)
Wemyss Castle
Windhouse
Wrychtishousis

MISCELLANEOUS
Discovery Point, Dundee (O)
Scotland's Lighthouse Museum (O)
Montrose Air Station Museum (O)

OUTDOORS
Arnish Moor, Lewis
Banchory (O)
Ben Macdui (O)
Charlotte Square, Edinburgh (O)
Culloden Moor (O)
Dalpeddar
Fortingall (O)
Glencoe (O)
Kilchrenan (O?)
Killiecrankie (O)
Mercat Cross, Edinburgh (O)
Princes Street, Edinburgh (O)
Sandwood Bay (O)
Tarras

THEATRES
Byre Theatre, St Andrews
Citizens's Theatre, Glasgow
Eden Court Theatre, Inverness
Edinburgh Festival Theatre
His Majesty's Theatre, Aberdeen
New Century Theatre, Motherwell
Perth Theatre
Playhouse Theatre, Edinburgh
Royal Lyceum Theatre, Edinburgh
Theatre Royal, Edinburgh
Theatre Royal, Glasgow

Index *by* haunting

Macduff's Castle (Mary Sibbald)
Monymusk Castle (lady)
Pannanich Wells Hotel, Ballater (lady)
Perth Theatre (lady)
Saltoun Hall (lady)
Shieldhill (daughter of Chancellor laird)

GREEN LADY
Ackergill Tower (Helen Gunn)
Ardblair Castle (Lady Jean Drummond)
Ashintully Castle (Jean Spalding)
Atholl Palace Hotel (lady)
Balgonie Castle (Jean Lundie)
Ballindalloch Castle (lady)
Big House (lady)
Borthwick Castle (Anne Grant)
Caisteal Camus (gruagach)
Caroline Park (Lady Royston)
Castle Loch Heylipol (gruagach)
Castle of Mey (Sinclair daughter)
Castle of Park (servant)
Citizens's Theatre, Glasgow (front of house manager)
Cobbler Hotel, Arrochar (wife of Colquhoun laird)
Comlongon Castle (Marion Carruthers)
Craighouse (Elizabeth Pittendale)
Crathes Castle (lady)
Dalzell House (lady)
Dunstaffnage Castle (lady)
Durris House (wife of Fraser lord)
Eden Court Theatre, Inverness (wife of bishop)
Ethie Castle (lady)
Fernie Castle (lady)
Ferniehirst Castle (lady)
Fetteresso Castle (lady)
Fyvie Castle (Lilias Drummond)
Glasgow Infirmary (nurse?)
Huntingtower Castle (lady)
Inverawe House (Mary Cameron)
Menie House (lady)
Muchalls Castle (lady)
Newton Castle (Lady Jean Drummond)
Pinkie House (Lilias Drummond)
Roxburghe House (lady)
Skipness House (brownie)
Stirling Castle (lady)
Sundrum Castle (wife of Hamilton laird?)
Thainstone House (lady)
Wemyss Castle (lady)

WHITE LADY
Ardoe House Hotel (Katherine Ogston or lady)
Balvenie Castle (lady)
Biel (Anne Bruce of Earlshall)
Castle Levan (Lady Montgomery)
Claypotts Castle (Marion Ogilvie)
Corstorphine Castle (Christian Nimmo)
Dalmahoy (Lady Mary Douglas)
Dalpeddar (Lady Hebron)
Dalzell House (servant)
Drumlanrig House (Lady Anne Douglas)
Edzell Castle (Catherine Campbell)
Falkland Palace (lady)
Frendraught Castle (Lady Elizabeth Gordon)
Fulford Tower (Lady Hamilton)
Hunter's Tryst, Edinburgh (lady)
Meldrum House (lady)
Melville Grange (lady)
Old Woodhouselee (Lady Hamilton)
Saddell Castle (lady)
Sanquhar Castle (Marion of Dalpeddar)
St Andrews Cathedral (lady)
St Nicholas Church (Aberdeen)
Tarras (lady)

GREY LADY
Balnagown Castle (lady)
Brodick Castle (lady or servant)
Dalhousie Castle (Lady Catherine, mistress of Ramsay laird)
Dalzell House (nurse?)
Dryburgh Abbey Hotel (daughter of house)
Fyvie Castle (lady)
Glamis Castle (Janet Douglas, Lady Glamis)
Glenlee (Lady Ashburton)
Hawkhead Hospital (nurse?)
His Majesty's Theatre, Aberdeen (lady)
Holyroodhouse (lady)
King's Arms Hotel, Dumfries (lady)
Loudon Castle (lady)

BLACK LADY
Auchlochan House (lady)
Broomhill (lady)
Gartloch Hospital (matron?)
Johnstone Lodge, Anstruther (Princess Tetuane Marama)
Logie House, Dundee (Indian princess)
Mary King's Close, Edinburgh (lady)

BLUE LADY
Barcaldine Castle (Harriet Campbell)
Cawdor Castle (lady)
Linlithgow Palace (lady)
Lochailort Inn (lady)
Royal Lyceum Theatre, Edinburgh (lady)

PINK LADY
Ballindalloch Castle (lady)
Stirling Castle (lady)

OTHER FEMALE APPARITIONS
Abergeldie Castle (Kitty Rankie)
Achindown (Elspeth Munroe)
Airth Castle (housekeeper)
Aldourie Castle (lady)
Allanbank (Pearlin Jean)
Amatola Hotel (old lady)
Arbigland House (Craik daughter)
Ardachy (Mrs Brewin)
Ardgay (servant)
Ardvreck (MacLeod daughter)
Auchinvole House (lady)
Aultsigh (Annie Fraser)
Baldoon Castle (Janet Dalrymple)
Ballindalloch Castle (lady)
Barbreck House (lady)
Braemar Castle (lady)
Broadford Hotel (housekeeper)
Brodie Castle (lady)
Busta House (Barbara Pitcairn)
Busta House (lady)
Castle Cary (Lizzie Baillie)
Castle Coeffin (Beothail)
Castle Fraser (lady)
Castle Fraser (Lady Blanche Drummond)
Castle Grant (Lady Barbara Grant)

Cessnock Castle (lady)

Charlotte Square, Edinburgh (lady)

Chessel's Court, Edinburgh (lady)

Coroghon Castle (lady)

County Hotel, Peebles (lady)

Craignethan Castle (lady)

Cross Keys Hotel, Peebles (Marion Ritchie)

Culzean Castle (lady)

Delgatie Castle (Rohaise)

Devanha House, Aberdeen (lady)

Drumlanrig Castle (lady)

Dunrobin Castle (Margaret, daughter of 14th Earl)

Dunskey Castle (nursemaid)

Duntulm Castle (Margaret MacLeod)

Duntulm Castle (nursemaid)

Earlshall (old woman)

Eilean Donan Castle (Lady Mary)

Fasque (Helen Gladstone)

Gairnshiel Lodge (old woman)

Garth Castle (Mariota, wife of Nigel Stewart)

Glenmallan (lady)

Greenlaw House (lady)

Hallgreen Castle (ladies)

Howlet' House (wife of farmer)

Inchdrewer Castle (lady)

Kellie Castle (Anne Erskine)

Kinneil House (wife of Cromwellian officer)

Linlithgow Palace (Margaret Tudor??? or Mary of Guise?)

Mains Castle (sister of William the Lyon?)

Meggernie Castle (wife of Menzies laird)

Megginch Castle (two women?)

Neidpath Castle (Jean Douglas)

New Lanark (lady)

Newark Castle (many women?)

Niddry Street, Edinburgh (lady)

Nivingston House Hotel (old lady)

Norwood Hall (wife of James Ogston?)

Princes Street, Edinburgh (Moira Blair)

Rait Castle (daughter of Cumming laird)

Ravenswood Hotel, Ballater (woman's voice)

Rothesay Castle (Lady Isabella)

Skaill House (old woman)

Skibo Castle (lady)

Stair Arms, Pathhead (chambermaid)

Theatre Royal, Glasgow (cleaner called 'Nora')

Thunderton House, Elgin (Lady Arradoul?)

Tibbie Shiel's Inn (Tibbie Shiels)

Tombuie (lady)

Traquair House (Lady Louisa Stewart)

Wellwood House ('Beanie')

West Bow, Edinburgh (Grizel Weir)

Windhouse (lady)

Wrychtishousis (wife of James Clerk?)

CHILDREN

Avoch (young lad)

Balcomie (young lad)

Broomhill (lad fishing)

Cartland Bridge Hotel (Annie Farie)

Castle of Park (child)

Cathedral House, Glasgow (children)

Clydesdale Hotel, Lanark (child)

Coylet Inn (Blue Boy, lad)

Dalpeddar (lad)

Dunnottar Castle (young girl)

Ethie Castle (child)

Glamis Castle (lad)

Kingcausie (James Turner Christie, lad)

Mary King's Close (young girl)

Niddry Street, Edinburgh (small lad)

Old Post Horn Inn, Crawford (young girl)

Old Post Horn Inn, Crawford (5-year-old girl)

Windhouse (child)

DARK MEN

Balnagown Castle (Andrew Munro)

Buckholm Tower (Pringle laird)

Glamis Castle (4th Earl of Crawford)

Hermitage Castle (William de Soulis)

Kinnaird Castle (James Carnegie)

Littledean Tower (Kerr laird)

Lordscairnie Castle (4th Earl of Crawford)

Ruthven Castle (Wolf of Badenoch)

Skene House (Alexander Skene)

The Binns (Tam Dalziel)

West Bow, Edinburgh (Thomas Weir)

OTHER MALE APPARITIONS

Ann Street, Edinburgh (Mr Swan)

Arbigland House (groom called Dunn)

Ardnadam (old soldier)

Ardvreck Castle (grey-clad man)

Arnish Moor (lad)

Ashintully House (Crooked Davy)

Ashintully House (tinker)

Balgonie Castle (17th-century soldier)

Balgonie Castle (hooded figure)

Ballachulish House (Stewart of Appin)

Ballachulish House (tinker)

Ballechin (Major Robert Stewart)

Ballindalloch Castle (General James Grant)

Balvenie Castle (groom and horses)

Balwearie Castle (Thomas Scott)

Ben Macdui (large man)

Braemar Castle (Colonel John Farquharson of Inverey)

Brodick Castle (man)

Brodie Castle (Hugh 23rd Brodie of Brodie)

Byre Theatre, St Andrews ('Charlie')

Carleton Castle (Sir John Cathcart)

Castle Cary (General Baillie)

Castle Loch Heylipol (MacLaren the factor)

Castle Spioradain (lots!)

Cawdor Castle (John Campbell, 1st Lord Cawdor)

Charlotte Square, Edinburgh (old man)

Cloncaird Castle (man)

Clumly Farm (son of house)

County Buildings, Ayr (man)

Crichton Castle (Sir William Crichton)

Crichton Castle (rider)

Cullen House (3rd Earl of Findlater)

Culloden Moor (many)

Dalry House, Edinburgh (Johnnie Chiesly)

Dean Castle (4th Earl of Kilmarnock)

Discovery (Charles Bonner)

Doune (son of Grant laird)

Dunnottar Castle (Nordic man)

Dunphail Castle (Comyns)

Duns Castle (Alexander Hay)

Duntulm (Hugh MacDonald)

Duntulm (Donald Gorm MacDonald)

Earlshall (Sir Andrew Bruce)

Edinample Castle (male)

Eilean Donan (Spanish soldier from 1719)

Fairburn Tower (Mackenzie laird)

Fasque (butler called MacBean)

Finavon Castle (Jock Barefoot)

Floors Castle (gardener)

Fordel (assistant miller)

Garleton Castle (man)

Index by haunting

Glencoe (many)
Grange House, Edinburgh (miser)
Haddo House (Lord Archibald
Gordon)
Hallgreen Castle (man)
Hermitage Castle (Sir Alexander
Ramsay)
His Majesty's Theatre, Aberdeen
(stagehand 'Jake')
Houndwood House ('Chappie')
Howlet' House (farm worker)
Inverawe House (Duncan Campbell)
Inverey Castle (Colonel John
Farquharson of Inverey)
Inverquharity Castle (Sir John Ogilvie)
Kellie Castle (James Lorimer)
Killiecrankie (many)
Killiecrankie (Brown of Priesthill)
Kylesku Hotel (old man)
Leith Hall (John Leith?)
Liberton House (man?)
Parliament Square, Edinburgh (town
guard)
Montrose Air Station Museum
(airman)
Monymusk Castle (men)
Moy Castle (headless horseman, Ewen
MacLaine)
New Century Theatre, Motherwell
('Oscar')
Niddry Street, Edinburgh (men)
Norwood Hall (James Ogston)
Old Post Horn Inn, Crawford
(coachman)
Old Post Horn Inn, Crawford
(Romans)
Penkaet Castle (Alexander Hamilton)
Penkaet Castle (John Cockburn)
Playhouse Theatre, Edinburgh
('Albert')
Rammerscales (Dr James Mounsey)
Ravenswood Hotel, Ballater (old man)
Rosslyn Castle (knight in black
armour)
Rosslyn Chapel (ghost of apprentice)
Roxburgh Castle (horseman)
Roxburghe House (soldier)
Sandwood Bay (sailor)
Sanquhar Castle (John Wilson)
Spedlins Tower (Dunty Porteous)
St Mary's Church, Haddington (Duke
of Lauderdale)
Stirling Castle (sentry)

The Binns (Pict?)
Theatre Royal, Glasgow (fireman)
Thirlestane Castle, Haddington (Duke
of Lauderdale)
Transport Depot, Aberdeen (Captain
Beaton)
West Bow, Edinburgh (Earl of
Gowrie)
Western Infirmary, Glasgow (Sir
William MacEwen)
Windhouse (peddler)

FAMOUS PEOPLE
Abbotsford (Walter Scott)
Ardrossan Castle (William Wallace)
Balgonie Castle (Alexander Leslie)
Berwick Castle (Edward I of England)
Cessnock Castle (John Knox)
County Hotel, Dumfries (Bonnie
Prince Charlie)
Craigcrook Castle (Lord Francis
Jeffrey)
Craignethan Castle (Mary, Queen of
Scots?)
Culloden House (Bonnie Prince
Charlie)
Discovery (Ernest Shackleton)
Edinburgh Festival Theatre (Great
Lafayette)
Ethie Castle (Cardinal David Beaton)
Hermitage Castle (Mary, Queen of
Scots)
Killiecrankie (Bonnie Dundee)
Lochleven Castle (Mary, Queen of
Scots)
Melgund Castle (Cardinal David
Beaton)
Salutation Hotel, Perth (Bonnie Prince
Charlie)
St Andrews (Cardinal David Beaton)
Stirling Castle (Mary, Queen of Scots?)
Thunderton House, Elgin (Bonnie
Prince Charlie?)

ECCLESIASTIC
Ardchattan Priory (nun)
Ballechin (nun)
Banchory (monk)
Bedlay Castle (Bishop Cameron)
Carmelite Street, Aberdeen (friar)
Castle of Park (monk)
Charlotte Square, Edinburgh (monk)
Clydesdale Hotel, Lanark (friar)
Deer Abbey (monk)
Dryburgh Abbey (monks)

Duchal Castle (monk)
Ethie Castle (Cardinal David Beaton)
Fortingall (nuns)
Gight House Hotel, Methlick (Rev
John Mennie)
Iona Abbey (monks)
Kilchrenan (monk)
Melrose Abbey (monk)
Old Manse, Lairg (Rev Thomas
MacKay)
Rosslyn Chapel (monks?)
Royal Hotel, Cupar (friar)
Saddell Castle (monk)
St Andrews (Cardinal David Beaton)
St Andrews Castle (Archbishop
Hamilton)
St Andrews Cathedral (monk)

PIPERS, DRUMMERS & MUSI-
CIANS
Colquhonnie Castle (Forbes male
piper)
Cortachy Castle (male drummer)
Culcreuch Castle (female harper,
clarsach)
Culross Abbey (male piper)
Culzean Castle (male piper)
Duntrune Castle (male MacDonald
piper)
Edinburgh Castle (male drummer)
Edinburgh Castle (male piper)
Fort George (male piper)
Fyvie Castle (male drummer)
Fyvie Castle (Andrew Lammie,
trumpeter)
Gight Castle (male piper)
Lochailort Inn (pipes)
Place of Bonhill (male piper)
Spynie Palace (piper)

BROWNIES, FAIRIES & KELPIES
Ardincaple Castle (brownie)
Auchnarrow (Maggie Moloch)
Brahan Castle [Conon River] (kelpie)
Caisteal Camus (gruagach)
Caisteal Camus (glaistig)
Castle Lachlan (brownie)
Castle Loch Heylipol (Green Lady,
gruagach)
Castle Tioram (frog)
Claypotts Castle (brownie)
Cranshaws (brownie)
Dolphinston Tower (brownie)
Dunskey Castle (brownie)
Dunstaffnage Castle (Green Lady,

gruagach)
Dunvegan Castle (fairy wife of
   MacLeods)
Invergarry Castle (brownie)
Largie Castle (brownie)
Lochnell House (brownie)
Noltland Castle (brownie)
Skipness House (Green Lady,
   brownie)

HARBINGERS OF DOOM &
   PORTENTS OF GOOD FORTUNE
Abergeldie Castle (bell)
Airlie Castle (ram)
Barnbougle Castle (hound)
Brodick Castle (white deer)
Closeburn Castle (red-breasted swan)
Cobbler Hotel, Arrochar (Green Lady,
   wife of Colquhoun laird)
Cortachy Castle (drummer)
Coull Castle (bell of church)
Culzean Castle (male piper)
Dunstaffnage Castle (green lady)
Fyvie Castle (Andrew Lammie,
   trumpeter)
Hopetoun House (dark figure)
Huntingtower Castle (green lady)
Jedburgh Castle (apparition)
Mercat Cross, Edinburgh (ghostly
   herald)
Moy Castle (headless horseman, Ewen
   MacLaine)
Noltland Castle (boky hound)
Noltland Castle (spectral lights)
Pitcaple Castle (robin)
Rosslyn Chapel (flames)
Sanquhar Castle (White Lady, Marion
   of Dalpeddar)
St Michael's Church, Linlithgow (blue-
   robed apparition)
Stirling Castle (lady)
Taymouth Castle (harbinger)
Windgate House (couple)

ANIMALS
Balgonie Castle (dog)
Barnbougle Castle (hound)
Culcreuch Castle (animal head)
Drumlanrig Castle (monkey?)
Dunnottar Castle (deer hound)
Edinburgh Castle (dog)
Inchdrewer Castle (lady? as white
   dog)
Loudon Castle (dog)
Mary King's Close (dog)

Noltland Castle (boky hound)
Rockhall (monkey)
Rosslyn Castle (mauthe dog)
Spynie Palace (lion?)
Tibbie Shiel's Inn (dog)
Windhouse (dog)

OTHER PHENOMENA
Caroline Park (cannon ball)
Kindrochit Castle (ghostly company)
Maryculter House (bolt of lightning)
Montrose Air Station Museum
   (biplane)
Noltland Castle (spectral lights)
Penkaet Castle (disturbed bed)
Rathen Church (singing ghostly
   congregation)
Theatre Royal, Edinburgh (actors)
Trumpan Church (singing ghostly
   congregation)

POLTERGEIST AND NON-
   SPECIFIC ACTIVITY
Benholm Castle
Blantyre Priory
Braco Castle
Buchanan Castle
Cameron House
Cameron's Inn, Aberdeen
Castle Stuart
Cromarty Castle
Dalkeith House
Fedderate Castle
Galdenoch Castle
Glenluce
Grandtully Castle
Knockderry Castle
Lauriston Castle
Learmonth Hotel
Luffness House
Marlfield House
Medwyn House
Moncrieffe Arms, Bridge of Earn
Newbattle Abbey
Pittodrie House
Ring Croft of Stocking
Scone Palace
Sunipol
Taymouth Castle
Vayne Castle

Index *by* area

ABERDEEN & ABERDEENSHIRE
Amatola Hotel, Aberdeen [12G]
Cameron's Inn, Aberdeen [12G]
Carmelite Street, Aberdeen [12G]
Castle Fraser [11G]
Colquhonnie Castle [9G]
Corgarff Castle [9G]
Devanha House, Aberdeen [12G]
Fountainhall, Aberdeen [12G]
Frendraught Castle [10F]
Gight Castle [11F]
Gight House Hotel, Methlick [11F]
Haddo House [11F]
His Majesty's Theatre, Aberdeen [12G]
Leith Hall [10F]
Meldrum House [11F]
Menie House [12F]
Monymusk Castle [11G]
Norwood Hall, Aberdeen [12G]
Pitcaple Castle [11F]
Pittodrie House [11F]
Skene House [11G]
St Nicholas Church, Aberdeen [12G]
Thainstone House [11F]
Transport Depot, Aberdeen [12G]

ARGYLL & BUTE
Ardchattan Priory [4J]
Ardnadam [5L]
Barbreck House [4K]
Barcaldine Castle [4J]
Castle Coeffin [4J]
Castle Lachlan [4L]
Castle Loch Heylipol [1J]
Coylet Inn [5L]
Dunstaffnage Castle [4J]
Duntrune Castle [4L]
Glenmallan [5L]
Inverawe House [5K]
Iona Abbey [2K]
Kilchrenan [5K]
Largie Castle [4M]

Lochnell House [4J]
Moy Castle [3K]
Rothesay Castle [5M]
Saddell Castle [4N]
Skipness House [M4]
Sunipol [2J]

AYRSHIRE, RENFREW & DUNBARTON
Ardincaple Castle [6L]
Ardrossan Castle [5M]
Brodick Castle [5N]
Cameron House [6L]
Carleton Castle [3O]
Castle Levan [5L]
Cessnock Castle [7N]
Cloncaird Castle [6O]
Cobbler Hotel, Arrochar [6K]
County Buildings, Ayr [6N]
Culzean Castle [7O]
Dean Castle [6N]
Duchal Castle [6M]
Dunbarton
Dunure Castle [5N]
Hawkhead Hospital [7M]
Knockderry Castle [5L]
Loudon Castle [7N]
Place of Bonhill [6L]
Sundrum Castle [6N]
Wellwood House [7N]

BORDERS
Abbotsford [10N]
Allanbank House [11M]
Berwick Castle [12M]
Buckholm Tower [10N]
County Hotel, Peebles [8M]
Cranshaws Castle [11M]
Cross Keys Hotel, Peebles [8M]
Dolphinston Tower [11N]
Dryburgh Abbey Hotel [10N]
Dryburgh Abbey [10N]
Duns Castle [11M]
Ferniehirst Castle [11N]
Floors Castle [11N]

Hermitage Castle [10O]
Houndwood House [11M]
Jedburgh Castle [11N]
Littledean Tower [11N]
Marlfield House [11N]
Melrose Abbey [10N]
Neidpath Castle [9N]
Newark Castle [10N]
Roxburgh Castle [11N]
Roxburghe House [11N]
Thirlestane Castle [10M]
Tibbie Shiel's Inn, St Mary's Loch [9N]
Traquair House [9N]

DUMFRIES & GALLOWAY
Arbigland House [8P]
Baldoon Castle [7Q]
Closeburn Castle [7O]
Comlongon Castle [8P]
County Hotel, Dumfries [8P]
Dalpeddar [8O]
Drumlanrig Castle [7O]
Dunskey Castle [5P]
Galdenoch Castle [5P]
Glenlee [7P]
Glenluce [5P]
King's Arms Hotel, Dumfries [8P]
Old Post Horn Inn, Crawford [8N]
Rammerscales House [9P]
Ring Croft of Stocking, Auchencairn [8Q]
Rockhall [9P]
Sanquhar Castle [8O]
Spedlins Tower [9P]
Tarras [10P]

DUNDEE & ANGUS
Airlie Castle [9J]
Claypotts Castle [10J]
Cortachy Castle [9I]
Discovery Point, Dundee [10K]
Edzell Castle [10H]
Ethie Castle [10J]
Finavon Castle [10I]

Glamis Castle [10J]
Inverquharity Castle [9I]
Kinnaird Castle [10I]
Logie House, Dundee [10K]
Melgund Castle [10I]
Montrose Air Station Museum [11I]
Vayne Castle [10I]

**EDINBURGH, MIDLOTHIAN &
    EAST LOTHIAN**
Ann Street, Edinburgh [9L]
Barnbougle Castle [9L]
Biel [10L]
Borthwick Castle [10M]
Caroline Park House, Edinburgh
    [9L]
Charlotte Square, Edinburgh [9L]
Chessel's Court, Edinburgh [9L]
Corstorphine Castle, Edinburgh
    [9L]
Craigcrook Castle, Edinburgh [9L]
Craighouse, Edinburgh [9L]
Crichton Castle [10M]
Dalhousie Castle [9M]
Dalkeith House [9M]
Dalmahoy [9L]
Dalry House, Edinburgh [9L]
Edinburgh Castle [9L]
Edinburgh Festival Theatre,
    Edinburgh [9L]
Fulford Tower [9M]
Garleton Castle [10L]
Grange House, Edinburgh [9L]
Greenlaw House [9M]
Holyroodhouse, Edinburgh [9L]
Howlet's House [9M]
Hunter's Tryst, Edinburgh [9L]
India Street, Edinburgh [9L]
Lauriston Castle, Edinburgh [9L]
Learmonth Hotel, Edinburgh [9L]
Liberton House, Edinburgh [9L]
Luffness House [10L]
Mary King's Close, Edinburgh [9L]
Melville Grange [9M]
Mercat Cross, Edinburgh [9L]
Newbattle Abbey [9M]
Niddry Street, Edinburgh [9L]
Old Woodhouselee Castle [9M]
Penkaet Castle [10M]
Pinkie House [10M]
Playhouse Theatre, Edinburgh [9L]

Princes Street, Edinburgh [9L]
Rosslyn Castle, Roslin [9M]
Rosslyn Chapel, Roslin [9M]
Royal Lyceum, Edinburgh [9L]
Saltoun Hall [10M]
St Mary's Church, Haddington
    [10M]
Stair Arms, Pathhead [10M]
Theatre Royal, Edinburgh [9L]
West Bow, Edinburgh [9L]
Wrychtishousis, Edinburgh [9L]

FIFE
Balcomie Castle [10K]
Balgonie Castle [9L]
Balwearie Castle [9L]
Byre Theatre, St Andrews [10K]
Culross Abbey [8L]
Earlshall [10K]
Falkland Palace [9K]
Fernie Castle [9K]
Fordell [9L]
Johnstone Lodge, Anstruther [10K]
Kellie Castle [10K]
Lordscairnie Castle [10K]
Macduff's Castle [9L]
Nivingston House Hotel [9L]
Royal Hotel, Cupar [10K]
St Andrews Castle [10K]
St Andrews Cathedral [10K]
Wemyss Castle [9L]

GLASGOW & LANARKSHIRE
Auchinvole House [7L]
Auchlochan House [8N]
Bedlay Castle [7L]
Blantyre Priory [7M]
Broomhill [8M]
Cartland Bridge Hotel [8M]
Cathedral House, Glasgow [7M]
Citizens' Theatre, Glasgow [7M]
Clydesdale Hotel, Lanark [8N]
Craignethan Castle [8M]
Dalzell House [7M]
Gartloch Hospital [7M]
Glasgow Infirmary [7M]
Mains Castle [7M]
New Century Theatre, Motherwell
    [7M]
New Lanark [8N]
Shieldhill [8N]
Theatre Royal, Glasgow [7M]

Western Infirmary, Glasgow [7M]
Windgate House [8N]

HIGHLANDS & ISLANDS
Achindown [8E]
Ackergill Tower [9B]
Aldourie Castle [7F]
Ardachy [6G]
Ardgay [7D]
Ardvreck Castle [5C]
Arnish Moor, Lewis [2C]
Aultsigh [6G]
Avoch [7E]
Ballachulish House [4I]
Balnagown Castle [7D]
Ben Macdui [8G]
Big House [8A]
Brahan Castle [6F]
Broadford Hotel [3F]
Caisteal Camus [3G]
Castle Grant [8F]
Castle of Mey [9A]
Castle Spioradain [7F]
Castle Stuart [7E]
Castle Tioram [3H]
Cawdor Castle [8E]
Coroghon Castle [1G]
Cromarty Castle [7E]
Culloden Moor [7F]
Doune [8G]
Dunrobin Castle [8D]
Duntulm Castle [2E]
Dunvegan Castle [1E]
Eden Court Theatre, Inverness [7F]
Eilean Donan Castle [4F]
Fairburn Tower [6F]
Fort George [7E]
Glencoe [5I]
Invergarry Castle [5H]
Kylesku Hotel [5B]
Laudale House [3I]
Lochailort Inn [4H]
Old Manse, Lairg [7D]
Rait Castle [8E]
Ruthven Castle [7G]
Sandwood Bay [5A]
Skibo Castle [7D]
Trumpan Church [1E]
Kincardine & Deeside
Abergeldie Castle [9G]
Ardoe House Hotel [11G]

185

Index by area

Banchory [11G]
Denholm Castle [11I]
Braemar Castle [8G]
Coull Castle [10G]
Crathes Castle [11G]
Dunnottar Castle [11H]
Durris House [11G]
Fasque [10H]
Fetteresso Castle [11H]
Gairnshiel Lodge [9G]
Hallgreen Castle [11H]
Inverey Castle [8G]
Kindrochit Castle, Braemar [8G]
Kingcausie [11G]
Loch of Leys [11G]
Maryculter House [11G]
Muchalls Castle [11H]
Pannanich Wells Hotel, Ballater [9G]
Ravenswood Hotel, Ballater [9G]

MORAY, BANFF & BUCHAN
Auchnarrow [9F]
Ballindalloch Castle [F9]
Balvenie Castle [10F]
Brodie Castle [8E]
Castle of Park [10E]
Cullen House [10E]
Deer Abbey [11E]
Delgatie Castle [11E]
Dunphail Castle [8E]
Fedderate Castle [11E]
Fyvie Castle [11F]
Inchdrewer Castle [10E]
Kinnaird Head Castle, Fraserburgh [11E]
Rathen Church [12E]
Spynie Palace [9E]
Thunderton House, Elgin [9E]

ORKNEY & SHETLAND
Busta House [11B]
Clumly Farm [9D]
Noltland Castle [10C]
Skaill House [9C]
Windhouse [11A]

Perth & Kinross
Ardblair Castle [9J]
Ashintully Castle [8I]
Atholl Palace Hotel, Pitlochry [8I]
Ballechin [8J]

Braco Castle [8K]
Fortingall [8J]
Garth Castle [8J]
Grandtully Castle [8J]
Huntingtower Castle [9K]
Killiecrankie [8H]
Lochleven Castle [9L]
Meggernie Castle [7K]
Megginch Castle [9K]
Moncrieffe Arms, Bridge of Earn [9K]
Newton Castle [9J]
Perth Theatre [9K]
Salutation Hotel, Perth [9K]
Scone Palace [9K]
Taymouth Castle [8J]
Tombuie [8J]

STIRLING, FALKIRK & WEST LOTHIAN
Buchanan Castle [7L]
Culcreuch Castle [7L]
Edinample Castle [7K]
Stirling Castle [8L]
Hopetoun House [9L]
Linlithgow Palace [8L]
Medwyn House [9M]
St Michael's Parish Church, Linlithgow [8L]
The Binns [8L]
Airth Castle [8L]
Castle Cary [8L]
Kinneil House [8L]

General index

A

Abbotsford, 9
Aberdeen Friary, 38
Abergeldie Castle, 9, 32
Abernethy Lords Saltoun, 147
Achindown, 10
Ackergill Tower, 10-11
Adair family, 75
Adam, John, 89, 101
Adam, Robert, 46, 63, 101
Adam, William, 65, 88, 89, 98, 101, 121
Adamnan, St, 89
Adamson family, 55
Agnew, Alexander, 97
Agnew, Gilbert, 92
Aikwood, 25
Airlie Castle, 11
Airlie, Earls of see Ogilvie family
Airth Castle, 12
Albany, Robert Duke of, 85, 143
Aldourie Castle, 12
Alexander I, 156, 163
Alexander II, 90, 124, 131
Alexander III, 107
Allanbank House, 12
Amatola Hotel, Aberdeen, 13
Angus Mor, 113
Ann Street, Edinburgh, 13
Applebank Inn, 35
Apprentice Pillar, 143
Arbigland House, 13-14
Arbroath, Battle of, 87
Ardachy, 14
Ardblair Castle, 14-15, 132
Ardchattan Priory, 15
Ardgay, 16
Ardincaple Castle, 16
Ardnadam, 16
Ardoe House Hotel, 16-17
Ardrossan Castle, 17
Ardvreck Castle, 17-18
Argyll, Earls and Dukes of see
  Campbell family
Arnish Moor, Lewis, 18
Arradoul, Lady, 161
Ashburton, Lady, 96
Ashintully Castle, 18-19
Atholl Palace Hotel, 19
Auchencairn, 141
Auchinvole House, 19
Auchlochan House, 20
Auchnarrow, 20
Auld Reekie Tours, 170

Aultsigh, 20
Avoch, 20

B

Baillie family, 39,166
Baillie, General, 40
Baillie, Lady Grizel, 71
Baillie, Lizzie, 40
Baird family, 164
Balblair, 139
Balcarres, Lord, 109
Balcomie Castle, 21
Baldoon Castle, 21
Balfour, Gilbert, 134
Balgonie Castle, 21-22
Ballachulish House, 22
Ballechin, 23
Ballindalloch Castle, 23-24
Balnagown Castle, 24
Balvenie Castle, 25
Balwearie Castle, 25-26
Banchory, 26
Banff, Lord, 104
Barbie's Tower, 41
Barbreck House, 26
Barcaldine Castle, 26-27
Barclay family, 17
Barnbougle Castle, 27
Baronald House, 39
Bear Gates, Traquair, 163
Beaton family, 83
Beaton, Captain, 162
Beaton, Cardinal David Archbishop of
  Scotland, 48, 83, 124, 134, 153
Beauty of Braemore see Gunn, Helen
Bedlay Castle, 28
Bell Macdonald family, 140
Ben Macdui, 28
Benholm Castle, 29
Beothail, 40
Bertha of Loch of Leys, 117
Berwick Castle, 29
Biel, 29
Big House, 30
Binns, The see The Binns
Black Dinner, 58, 81
Black Lady, 20, 35, 40, 46, 47, 118
Blackett family, 13
Blair family, 14
Blair of Ardblair, Patrick, 14
Blair, Moira, 139
Blantyre Priory, 30
Blind Asylum, Edinburgh, 167
Blue Boy, 54

Blue Lady, 27, 116, 117, 146
Boky House, 134
Bon Accord Tours, 171
Bonner, Charles, 69
Bonnie Dundee see Graham of
  Claverhouse
Bonnie Prince Charlie, 33, 43, 54, 61,
  62, 64, 70, 76, 78, 97, 101, 105, 137,
  144, 147, 161, 163
Borthwick Castle, 30, 51
Borthwick Church, 30
Borthwick, Sir William, 30
Bothwell, Francis 5th Earl of, 24, 86,
  100
Boyd family, 28, 67
Boyd, Robert, 67
Braco Castle, 31
Braemar Castle, 31-32, 105
Brahan Castle, 32
Brahan Seer, 10, 32, 59, 84
Breadalbane, Earls of, see Campbell
  family
Brewin, Mrs, 14
Bride of Lammermuir, 21
Bridge of Avon, 24
Broadford Hotel, 33
Brodick Castle, 33-34
Brodie Castle, 34
Brodie family, 34
Brodie, Hugh 23rd Brodie of, 34
Broomhill, 35
Brown family, 20
Brown of Priesthill, 109
brownie, 16, 20, 42, 48, 57, 69, 75, 105,
  113, 118, 134, 151
Bruce family, 12, 79
Bruce of Earlshall, Anne, 29
Bruce, Mary, 144
Bruce, Sir Andrew, 79
Bruce, Sir William, 79
Bruce, William, 101
Buccleuch, Earls and Dukes of, see
  Scott family
Buchanan Castle, 35, 68
Buckholm Tower, 35-36
Bullock, Sir George, 9
Burnett family, 57, 116, 128
Burnett, Alexander, 116, 117
Busta House, 36
Byre Theatre, St Andrews, 36
Byron, Lord, 93

C

Caifen, 40
Cairnburg Castle, 128
Caisteal Camus, 37
Caithness, Bishops of, 44
Caithness, Earls of, see Sinclair family
Calda House, 18
Calder, Muriel, 45
Caledonian Canal, 43
Cameron family, 43
Cameron House, 37

General index

Cameron of Callart, Mary, 104
Cameron's Inn, Aberdeen, 37
Cameron, Bishop, 28
Cameron, Richard, 79
Campbell 1st Lord Cawdor, John, 46
Campbell family, 15, 16, 26, 28, 38, 45,
   46, 76, 104, 105, 118, 151, 158, 164
Campbell of Barcaldine, John, 27
Campbell of Glenlyon, Colin, 122
Campbell of Glenorchy, Duncan, 80
Campbell of Glenure, Colin, 15, 27
Campbell of Inverawe, Diarmid, 104
Campbell of Inverawe, Duncan, 105
Campbell, Catherine, 82
Campbell, Gilbert, 96, 97
Campbell, Harriet, 27
Campbell, John Earl of Loudon, 119
Campbell, Margaret, 51
Carleton Castle, 38
Carlyle, Thomas, 161
Carmelite Street, Aberdeen, 38
Carnegie family, 13, 111, 164
Carnegie, Andrew, 151
Carnegie, James Earl of Southesk, 111,
   150
Carnforth, Earls of, see Dalziel family,
   66
Caroline Park House, 38
Carruthers of Mouswald, Marion, 50
Cartland Bridge Hotel, 39
Cassillis, Earls of, see Kennedy family
Castle Cary, 39
Castle Coeffin, 40
Castle Fraser, 40-41
Castle Grant, 41-42
Castle Jail, Jedburgh, 107
Castle Lachlan, 42
Castle Levan, 42
Castle Loch Heylipol, 42
Castle of Mey, 44
Castle of Park, 45
Castle Spioradain, 43
Castle Stuart, 43
Castle Tioram, 44
Cathcart family, 38, 158
Cathcart, Sir John, 38
Cathedral House, Glasgow, 45
Catherine, Lady, 64
Cawdor Castle, 45-46
Cessnock Castle, 46
Chancellor family, 149
Chanonry Point, 32
Chapel of the Three Kings, 155
Charles I, 64, 85, 116, 136, 137
Charles II, 53, 72, 85, 138, 149, 165
Charles, Prince, 144
Charlotte Square, Edinburgh, 46
Chessel's Court, Edinburgh, 47
Cheyne family, 10
Chiesly, John, 65
Christian Nimmo, 52
Citizens's Theatre, Glasgow, 47

City Chambers, Edinburgh, 121
Clan Ranald, 44, 52, 105
Claypotts Castle, 47-48, 83
Clerk family, 167
Clerk, James, 168
Cloncaird Castle, 48
Closeburn Castle, 48
Clumly Farm, 48-49
Clydesdale Hotel, Lanark, 49
Cobbler Hotel, Arrochar, 49-50
Cockburn family, 75
Cockburn, John, 136
Colquhonnie Castle, 50
Colquhonnie Hotel, 50
Colquhoun family, 16, 49
Columba, St, 106, 127
Comlongon Castle, 50-51
Comyn family, 25, 73, 139
Comyn of Dunphail, Sir Alexander, 73
Comyn, William Earl of Buchan, 67
Conon Ferry, 84
Conon River, 32
Constable, Archibald, 55
Copland, Dr Patrick, 89
Corgarff Castle, 51-52
Coroghon Castle, 52
Corstorphine Castle, 52-53
Corstorphine Old Parish Church, 53
Cortachy Castle, 53
Coull Castle, 53
Coull Church, 53
County Buildings, Ayr, 54
County Hotel, Dumfries, 54
County Hotel, Peebles, 54
Covenanter's Oak, 66
Coylet Inn, 54-55
Craigcrook Castle, 55
Craighouse, 55-56
Craignethan Castle, 56-57
Craik, William, 13, 140
Cranshaws Castle, 57
Crathes Castle, 57-58, 117
Crawford family, 85
Crawford, Earls of, see Lindsay family
Crichton Castle, 58
Crichton family, 89-90, 148
Crichton, Robert 6th Lord Sanquhar,
   148
Crichton, Sir James, 90
Crichton, Sir William, 58
Cromarty Castle, 59
Crooked Davie, 19
Cross Keys Hotel, Peebles, 60
Culcreuch Castle, 60-61
Cullen House, 61
Culloden House, 62
Culloden Moor, 10, 42, 61-62, 67, 88
Culross Abbey, 62
Culzean Castle, 62-63
Cupar Friary, 145

D

Dairsie, George, 107
Dale, David, 130
Dalhousie Castle, 63-64
Dalhousie, Earls of, see Ramsay family
Dalkeith House, 64
Dalmahoy, 65
Dalmeny House, 27
Dalpeddar, 65, 149
Dalry House, Edinburgh, 65-66
Dalrymple family, 65
Dalrymple of Carscreugh, Janet, 21
Dalzell House, 66
Dalziel family, 66
Dalziel, Tam, 110, 159
Darnaway Castle, 73
David I, 71, 81, 101, 124, 131
De Soulis, William, 99
Dean Castle, 67
Deer Abbey, 67-68
Deil of Littledean, 116
Delgatie Castle, 68
Devanha House, Aberdeen, 69
devil, the, 18, 93, 95, 111, 119, 141,
   146, 150, 159, 165
Discovery Point, Dundee, 69
Discovery, 69
Dods, Meg, 60
Dolphinston Tower, 69
Doom of Airlie, 11
Douglas family, 25, 57, 64, 65, 70, 99,
   100, 124, 129, 163
Douglas of Drumlanrig, Sir James, 50
Douglas, Janet, 95
Douglas, Jean, 129
Douglas, Lady Anne, 70
Douglas, Lady Mary, 65
Douglas, Sir William, 63, 99, 100
Doune, 69-70
Drambuie, 33
Drumlanrig Castle, 70-71
Drummond family, 14, 110, 123, 132
Drummond, George, 14
Drummond, Lady Blanche, 41
Drummond, Lady Jean, 14, 132, 137
Drummond, Lilias, 90-91
Dryburgh Abbey Hotel, 71
Dryburgh Abbey, 71
Duchal Castle, 72
Duff Countess of Buchan, Isabella, 29
Duff family, 25
Dumbarton Castle, 99
Dunbar family, 21
Dunbar of Baldoon, Sir David, 21
Dunbar, Patrick Earl of, 30
Duncan, 45
Duncan, Earl of Fife, 145
Dunfermline, Earls of, see Seton family
Dunkeld Cathedral, 147
Dunn, 14
Dunnet family, 99
Dunnottar Castle, 72-73, 87

Dunphail Castle, 73
Dunrobin Castle, 73-74
Duns Castle, 74-75
Dunskey Castle, 75
Dunstaffnage Castle, 75-76
Duntrune Castle, 76
Duntulm Castle, 76-77
Dunure Castle, 77
Dunvegan Castle, 78
Durris House, 78-79
Durward family, 53

E

Earl Beardie see Lindsay, Alexander, 4th Earl of Crawford
Earlshall, 79
Eden Court Theatre, Inverness, 79
Edinample Castle, 80
Edinburgh Castle, 58, 80-81, 149
Edinburgh Festival Theatre, 81-82
Edward I of England, 29, 90, 116, 149, 156
Edzell Castle, 82
Eglinton, Earls of see Montgomery family
Eilean Donan Castle, 83
Ell-Maid of Dunstaffnage, 76
Elliot of Park, Wee Jock, 100
Elphinstone, John, 55
Elphinstone, Sir Thomas, 55
Empire Palace Theatre, 81
Errol, Earls of, see Hay family
Erskine Earls of Mar, 31
Erskine family, 31, 108, 138
Erskine, Anne, 108
Ethie Castle, 83-84
Ettrick kirkyard, 162
Ewen of the Little Head, 128

F

Fair Ellen's Tree, 11
Fairburn Tower, 84
Fairy Flag, 78, 164
Falkland Palace, 84-85, 144
Farie of Farme, Captain James, 39
Farie, Annie, 39
Farquharson family, 32
Farquharson of Inverey, Colonel John, 32, 105
Fasque, 85
Fedderate Castle, 85
Fernie Castle, 86
Ferniehirst Castle, 86-87
Fetteresso Castle, 87
Finavon Castle, 87-88, 106
Findlater, 3rd Earl of, 61
Findlater, Earls of see Ogilvie family
Fletcher, Sir Andrew, 147
Flodden, Battle of, 79, 126, 155
Floors Castle, 88
Forbes family, 9, 126, 127
Forbes of Culloden, Duncan, 62
Forbes, 50, 51

Fordell, 88
Forrester of Corstorphine, 52
Fort George, 88-89
Fortingall, 89
Fountainhall see Penkaet Castle
Fountainhall, Aberdeen, 89
Frankie, Catherine, 10, 32
Fraser family, 12, 14, 41, 78, 79, 111, 129
Fraser of Philorth, Sir Alexander, 111, 112
Fraser, Annie, 20
Fraser, Isabella, 112
Frendraught Castle, 89-90
Fulford Tower, 90, 135
Fyvie Castle, 90-92

G

Gairnshiel Lodge, 92
Galbraith family, 60
Galdenoch Castle, 92
Gallowlea, 139, 166
Garleton Castle, 93
Garth Castle, 93
Gartloch Hospital, 93
Ghost of the Three Crossroads, 14
Gifford, Gideon, 36
Gifford, Thomas, 36
Gight Castle, 93-94
Gight House Hotel, Methlick, 94
Gillespie Graham, James, 33, 75
Gladstone, Helen, 85
Gladstone, William Ewart, 85
Glamis Castle, 87, 94-95, 119
Glasgow Castle, 95
Glasgow Infirmary, 95
Glen Fruin, 49
Glencoe, Massacre of, 22, 26, 95-96
Glengarry Castle Hotel, 105
Glenlee, 96
Glenluce Abbey, 25
Glenluce, 96-97
Glenmallan, 97
Glenshiel, Battle of, 83
Gordon family, 9, 45, 51, 73, 85, 90, 91, 93
Gordon of Auchindoun, Adam, 51
Gordon of Haddo, Sir John, 98
Gordon, Lady Elizabeth, 90
Gordon, Lord Archibald, 98
Gordon, Sir John, 155
Gowrie Conspiracy, 103
Gowrie House, Perth, 103
Gowrie, Earls of, see Ruthven family
Graham family, 31, 35, 99, 151
Graham of Claverhouse Viscount Dundee, John, 47, 109
Graham, Bishop of Orkney, George, 150
Grandtully Castle, 97
Grange House, 97
Grange, Lady, 44
Grant family, 12, 24, 42, 69, 127

Grant, Ann, 31
Grant, Barbara, 41
Grant, Elizabeth, 69
Grant, General James, 24
Gray family, 151
Gray of Skibo, Robert, 151
Great Lafayette, 81
Green Lady, 11, 15, 19, 22, 24, 30, 37, 39, 42, 44, 45, 47, 49, 50, 52, 56, 57, 66, 76, 79, 84, 86, 87, 90, 91, 95, 104, 126, 129, 137, 145, 151, 157, 158, 159, 165
Green Men, 142, 154
Greenlaw House, 98
Grey Friar, 49
Grey Lady, 12, 23, 24, 34, 64, 66, 71, 91, 95, 96, 99, 100, 101, 110, 119, 120, 127, 135, 137, 147, 149
Grey Man of Ben Macdui, 28
Grierson, Sir Robert, 141
Gunn family, 10
Gunn, Helen, 10
Gunn, Jamie, 74

H

Haddo House, 98
Hair, Earl, 71
Hairy Meg, 20
Hallgreen Castle, 98-99
Hamilton 2nd Lord Belhaven, John, 29
Hamilton family, 29, 33, 35, 56, 66, 112, 135, 158
Hamilton of Bothwellheugh, James, 135
Hamilton of Finnart, Sir James, 57
Hamilton, Alexander, 136
Hamilton, Archbishop of St Andrews, 153
Hamilton, Janet, 117
Hamilton, Lady, 90, 135
Hawkhead Castle, 99
Hawkhead Hospital, Paisley, 99
Hawley, General, 116
Hay family, 68, 75, 129
Hay of Delgatie, Sir William, 68
Hay, Alexander, 75
Henderson family, 88
Hepburn 4th Earl of Bothwell, James, 31, 59, 100, 153
Hepburn family, 119
Hepburn, 1st Earl of Bothwell, Patrick, 100
Hermitage Castle, 51, 63, 99-100
His Majesty's Theatre, Aberdeen, 100
Historic Scotland, 15, 25, 47, 51, 56, 58, 62, 67, 71, 75, 80, 82, 88, 99, 103, 111, 112, 115, 117, 124, 133, 143, 146, 152, 153, 154, 156
Hogg, James, 161
Holyroodhouse, 81, 100-101
Home family, 74, 102
Honeyman family, 23
Hope family, 101, 102, 119

Hope, Sir Charles, 101
Hopetoun House, 101-102
Hopetoun, Earls of, see Hope family
Horn of Leys, 57
Hound Point, 27
Houndwood House, 102
Howlet's House, 102
Hunter's Tryst, Edinburgh, 103
Huntingtower Castle, 103-104, 166

I

Iain the Toothless, 128
Inchdrewer Castle, 104
India Street, Edinburgh, 104
Innes family, 25
Innes, Bishop of Moray, 152
Inverawe House, 104-105
Inverey Castle, 105
Invergarry Castle, 105
Inverkeithing, Battle of, 88
Inverquharity Castle, 106
Iona Abbey, 106-107
Irvine family, 110
Island House, 42

J

Jacobite Risings, 10, 11, 15, 25, 32, 33,
  42, 44, 45, 54, 61-62, 67, 70, 81, 83,
  85, 87, 88, 92, 101, 105, 109, 110,
  116, 128, 147, 156, 159, 161, 165
James Gillespie's School, 167
James I, 116
James II, 88, 144, 156
James III, 12, 85, 116, 156
James IV, 12, 21, 64, 76, 85, 116, 126,
  137, 153, 155
James V, 26, 85, 95, 116, 155
James VI, 24, 64, 81, 85, 86, 103, 129,
  156
James VII, 116
James VIII, Old Pretender, 87, 128
Jardine family, 151
Jardine Hall, 151-152
Jardine, Sir Alexander, 152
Jean of Allanbank, Pearlin', 12
Jedburgh Castle, 107
Jeffrey, Lord Francis, 55
Jock Barefoot, 87
Johnnie One Arm, 65
Johnstone Lodge, Anstruther, 107-108
Jones, John Paul, 13

K

Keith family, 10, 28, 72, 87
Keith, Dugald, 10
Keith, Robert Lord Altrie, 67
Kellie Castle, 108
Kennedy family, 62, 77
Kennedy of Culzean, May, 38
Kerr family, 86, 88, 116, 131, 144
Kilchrenan, 108
Killiecrankie, 42, 97, 105, 109-110
Kilmarnock, Boyd 4th Earl of, 67
Kilmarnock, Earls of, see Boyd family
Kindrochit Castle, 110

King's Arms Hotel, Dumfries, 110
Kingcausie, 110
Kinnaird Castle, 111, 130
Kinnaird Head Castle, 111, 112
Kinneil House, 112
Kirkbean, 14
Kirkpatrick family, 48
Kitty Rankine, 10, 32
Knights Templars, 122
Knockderry Castle, 113
Knox, John, 46
Kylesku Hotel, 113

L

Ladies Rock, 157
Lady Hebron, 65
Lambhill, 28
Lammie, Andrew, 91
Lanark Friary, 49
Langside, Battle of, 46, 49, 57
Largie Castle, 113
Laudale House, 113
Lauder family, 136
Lauriston Castle, 114
Lawson, Richard, 126
Learmonth family, 21
Learmonth Hotel, Edinburgh, 114
Leith family, 90, 114
Leith Hall, 114-115
Leith, John, 115
Lennox family, 37, 138
Lennoxlove, 30
Leslie family, 137
Leslie of Pitcaple, Sir John, 138
Leslie, Alexander, 21
Leslie, Grizel, 91
Liberton House, 115
Lindsay family, 82, 87, 90, 93, 118, 120,
  138, 164
Lindsay of the Mount, Sir David, 93
Lindsay, Alexander, 4th Earl of
  Crawford, 87, 95, 118, 119
Linlithgow Palace, 26, 115-116
Lismore, 40
Little, William, 115
Littledean Tower, 116
Loch Ness Youth Hostel, 20
Loch of Leys, 57, 116-117
Loch of Skene, 150
Lochailort Inn, 117
Lochleven Castle, 117-118, 163
Lochnell House, 118
Lockhart of Carnwath, Sir George, 65
Logan, Alexander, 38
Logie House, Dundee, 118
Lordscairnie Castle, 87, 95, 118-119
Lorimer, James, 108
Lorimer, Sir Robert, 108
Lothian, Earls of, see Kerr family
Loudon Castle, 119
Loudon, Earls of see Campbell family
Lover's Leap, 98
Luffness House, 119-120

Lundie family, 21, 28
Lyle family, 72
Lyon family, 94

M

MacAulays, 16
Macbeth, 45, 94, 95
MacCulloch family, 13
MacDonald family, 26, 37, 44, 52, 76,
  77, 95, 96, 113, 164
MacDonald, Alasdair Colkitto, 15
MacDonald, Angus Og, 147
MacDonald, Donald Gorm, 77
MacDonald, Flora, 33, 76, 78
MacDonald, Hugh, 77
Macdonnell, Alasdair, 20
Macdonnell, Malcolm, 20
MacDougall family, 40, 76
MacDougall, Duncan, 15
Macduff's Castle, 120
MacEwen family, 14
MacEwen, Sir William, 166
MacFarlane family, 49
MacGregor, Rob Roy, 21
MacIain, chief of MacDonalds of
  Glencoe, 26
MacKay family, 30
MacKay, Reverend Thomas, 134
Mackenzie Earl of Seaforth, William, 83
Mackenzie family, 10, 32, 38, 83, 84
Mackenzie, Isabella Countess of, 32
Mackenzie, Kenneth see Brahan Seer
Mackenzie, Sir James, 39
Mackie, Andrew, 141
Mackinnon, chief of, 33
Mackintosh family, 12, 43, 139
MacLachlan family, 42
MacLaine family, 128
MacLaren, factor, 42
MacLean family, 43, 128
MacLeod family, 17, 37, 78, 164
MacLeod, Margaret, 77
MacMath, John, 50
Macpherson family, 133
MacRae family, 83
MacRuari, Amy, 44
Maggie Moloch, 20
Maid of Neidpath, 129
Mains Castle, 120-121
Maitland family, 154, 160
Maitland, John, Duke of Lauderdale,
  155, 160, 161
Maitland, John, Lord Thirlestane, 154
Malcolm Earl of Fife, 62
Malcolm family, 76
Malcolm II, 94
Malcolm the Maiden, 107
Mansfield, Earls of see Murray family
Mantle House, 71
Margaret Tudor, 64, 116
Margaret, daughter of 14th Earl of
  Sutherland, 74
Margaret, Saint, 81, 106

Marie de Coucy, 131
Marie of Baden, Prince, 33
Marion of Dalpeddar, 148
Mariota, wife of Nigel Stewart of Garth, 93
Marischal, Earls see Keith family
Marlfield House, 121
Mary King's Close, Edinburgh, 121
Mary of Guise, 21, 116
Mary, Lady of Eilean Donan, 83
Mary, Queen of Scots, 21, 25, 31, 46, 57, 59, 68, 72, 81, 82, 85, 100, 101, 103, 104, 116, 117, 118, 119, 129, 134, 137, 153, 156, 157, 163, 165
Maryculter House, 121-122
Mauthe Dog, 142
McNeil-Hamilton, Captain Henry, 35
Medwyn House, 122
Meggernie Castle, 122-123
Megginch Castle, 123
Meldrum family, 90, 123
Meldrum House, 123-124
Melgund Castle, 124
Melrose Abbey, 25, 124-125
Melville Grange, 125
Menie House, 126
Mennie, Rev John, 94
Menzies family, 121, 122, 123, 134
Mercat Cross, Edinburgh, 126, 155
Mercat Tours, 170
Mill family, 164
Miller family, 96
Mitchell, Sir Andrew, 159
Moncrieffe Arms, Bridge of Earn, 126
Monkstadt, 76
Montgomery family, 17
Montgomery, Lady, 42
Montgomery, Sir John, 17
Montrose Air Station Museum, 127
Montrose, Marquis of, 18, 24, 39, 68, 79, 87, 90, 97, 98, 131, 133, 137, 138, 140, 151, 165
Monymusk Castle, 127
Monymusk Reliquary, 127
Moot Hill, 149
Moray, Regent, 135
Moray, Sir Andrew, 73
Moray, Stewart Earls of, 43
Morison family, 90
Morton family, 42
Morton, Earls of, see Douglas family
Mounsey, Dr James, 140
Mowat family, 164
Mowbray family, 27
Mowbray, Sir Roger, 27
Moy Castle, 128
Muchalls Castle, 128-129
Munro, Black Andrew, 24
Munroe, Elspeth, 10
Munroe, Hamish, 10
Murdoch the Stunted, 128
Mure family, 48

Murray family, 13, 50, 59, 149
Murray, Sir William, 50
My Lady Greensleeves, 104

N

Napier family, 114, 167
Napier University, 55
National Trust for Scotland, 33, 34, 40, 52, 57, 61, 62, 84, 90, 95, 98, 108, 109, 114, 159
Neidpath Castle, 129-130
Neven family, 167
New Century Theatre, Motherwell, 130
New Lanark, 130
Newark Castle, 131
Newbattle Abbey, 125, 131-132
Newton Castle, 132-133
Niddry Street, Edinburgh, 133
Nine Stane Rig, 99
Nivingston House Hotel, 133
Noltland Castle, 133-134
Norwood Hall, Aberdeen, 134

O

Ogilvie 1st Earl of Airlie, James, 11
Ogilvie 4th Earl of, 11
Ogilvie family, 11, 28, 53, 61, 104, 106
Ogilvie of Inverquharity, 87, 106
Ogilvie, Alexander, 106
Ogilvie, Marion, 48, 83
Ogilvie, Sir John, 106
Ogston family, 134
Ogston, Alexander Milne, 16
Ogston, James, 134
Ogston, Katherine, 16
Old Manse, Lairg, 134
Old Post Horn Inn, Crawford, 135
Old Woodhouselee Castle, 90, 135
Oliphant family, 15, 108
Oliphant, Caroline, 15
Oliphant, Laurence, 15
Original St Andrews Witches Tour, 171
Owen, Robert, 130

P

Pannanich Wells, Ballater, 135-136
Pearlin' Jean, 12
Penkaet Castle, 136
Perth Theatre, 137
Philiphaugh, Battle of, 11, 106, 131
Pink Lady, 24, 156
Pinkie House, 137
Pitcairn, Barbara, 36
Pitcaple Castle, 137
Pitfodels Castle, 134
Pittendale, Elizabeth, 55
Pittodrie House, 138
Place of Bonhill, 138
Playhouse Theatre, Edinburgh, 138-139
Pontius Pilate, 89
Porteous, Dunty, 152
Preston family, 90
Primrose Earl of Rosebery, Archibald Philip, 27

Primrose family, 27
Princes Street, Edinburgh, 139
Pringle family, 35, 36

Q

Queen Mother, 44, 94
Queen Victoria, 10, 92
Queensberry, Earls and Dukes of, see Douglas family

R

Ragman Roll, 29
Raid of Ruthven, 103, 166
Rait Castle, 139
Rait family, 99
Rammerscales House, 140
Ramsay family, 63
Ramsay of Dalhousie, Sir Alexander, 63, 99, 100
Randolph, Thomas, 74, 81, 83
Rathen Church, 140
Ravenswood Hotel, Ballater, 140-141
Read family, 118
Reginald, son of Somerled, 106, 147
Reid family, 114, 134
Reilig Odhrain (Street of the Dead), 107
Rerrick, 141
Rex Cinema, Motherwell, 130
Ring Croft of Stocking, Auchencairn, 141
Ritchie, Marion, 60
Rizzio, David, 101
Robert I see Robert the Bruce
Robert II, 143
Robert III, 143
Robert the Bruce, 15, 25, 76, 83, 90, 124, 140, 142, 147
Robertson of Lawers, Lieutenant General, 167, 168
Rockhall, 141
Rohaise, 68
Rory Mor's Horn, 78
Ross family, 24, 59, 99
Ross of Balnagown, Alexander, 24
Ross of Balnagown, George, 24
Ross, Katherine, 24
Rosslyn Castle, 141-142
Rosslyn Chapel, 142-143
Rothesay Castle, 143-144
Rothesay, David Duke of, 85, 143
Rothiemurchus, 69-70
Roxburgh Castle, 88, 144
Roxburghe House, 144
Roxburghe, Dukes of, see Kerr family
Royal Hotel, Cupar, 145
Royal Lyceum Theatre, Edinburgh, 146
Royston, 38
Royston, Lady, 39
Rule, St, 154
Rullion Green, Battle of, 159
Rutherford family, 19
Rutherford, Archibald, 21
Ruthven Castle, 146-147

Ruthven family, 103, 104
Ruthven, Raid, 103
Ruthven, William 1st Earl of Gowrie, 103
Ruthven, William 3rd Earl of Gowrie, 103, 166

S

Saddell Castle, 147
Saint Margaret, 81, 106
Saltoun Hall, 147
Salutation Hotel, Perth, 147-148
Sandwood Bay, 148
Sanquhar Castle, 148-149
Scone Palace, 149
Scotland's Lighthouse Museum see Kinnaird Head Castle
Scott family, 25, 28, 38, 70, 100
Scott of Balwearie, Thomas, 26
Scott, Sir Michael, 25, 124
Scott, Sir Walter, 9, 71, 161
Scottish regalia, 76, 81
Seaforth, Earls of, see Mackenzie family
Selkirk, 131
Seton family, 90, 123, 136
Seton, Alexander Earl of Dunfermline, 90-91, 137
Seton, Jean, 151
Shackleton, Ernest, 69
Sheriffmuir, Battle of, 44
Shiel, Isabella or Tibbie, 161
Shieldhill, 149-150
Sibbald family, 21
Sibbald, Mary, 120
Sinclair Earls of Orkney, 141
Sinclair family, 44, 141, 142
Sinclair, daughter of 5th Earl, 44
Sinclair, Sir William Earl of Caithness and Orkney, 142
Sinclair, Sir William, 142
Skaill House, 150
Skara Brae, 150
Skene family, 150
Skene House, 150
Skene, Alexander, 150
Skibo Castle, 151
Skinner, William, 88
Skipness Castle, 151
Skipness House, 151
Smith family, 96
Smollett family, 37, 138
Southesk, Earls of see Carnegie family
Spalding family, 18
Spalding, Jean, 19
Spedlins Tower, 151-152
Spynie Palace, 152-153
St Adamnan, 89
St Andrews Castle, 153
St Andrews Cathedral, 154
St Columba, 106, 127
St Giles Cathedral, 98
St Mary's Church, Hawick, 63

St Mary's, Haddington, 154-155, 161
St Michael's Parish Church Linlithgow, 116, 155
St Nicholas Church, Aberdeen, 155
St Rule's Tower, 154
St Ternan, 26
Stair Arms, Pathhead, 156
Stevenson, Robert Louis, 15, 27, 161
Stewart Duchess of Richmond and Lennox, Frances, 30
Stewart family, 12, 22, 23, 25, 43, 97, 122, 143, 163
Stewart of Allanbank, Robert, 12
Stewart of Garth, Nigel, 93
Stewart of Minto, Walter, 30
Stewart, Alexander Wolf of Badenoch, 93, 146, 152
Stewart, Allan, Commendator of Crossraguel, 77
Stewart, David Bishop of Moray, 153
Stewart, Henry Lord Darnley, 101, 134, 165
Stewart, James, 27
Stewart, Lady Louisa, 163
Stewart, Major Robert, 23
Stirling Castle, 156-157
Stone of Destiny, 75, 81, 149
Stone of Scone see Stone of Destiny
Sundrum Castle, 158
Sunipol, 158
Sunlaws see Roxburghe House
Sutherland, Countess of, 120
Sutherland family, 73
Sutherland, Robert Sutherland 6th Earl of, 73
Swan, Mr, 13
Swanieson family, 167

T

Tarras, 158
Taymouth Castle, 158
Telford, Thomas, 156
Ternan, St, 26
Tetuane Marama, Princess, 107-108
Thainstone House, 159
The Binns, 159-160
Theatre Royal, Edinburgh, 160
Theatre Royal, Glasgow, 160
Thirlestane Castle, 155, 160-161
Thomas the Rhymer, 70, 91
Thunder Hole, 122
Thunderton House, Elgin, 161
Tibbie Shiel's Inn, St Mary's Loch, 161-162
Tiger Earl see Lindsay, Alexander, 4th Earl of Crawford
Tombuie, 162
Towie Castle, 52
Transport Depot, Aberdeen, 162-163
Traquair House, 163
Trentham family, 73
Trial Stone, Trumpan, 164
Trumpan Church, 78, 164

Turner Christie, James, 110

U

Urquhart family, 59, 123

V

Vaults, The see Windgate House
Vayne Castle, 164

W

Wallace family, 158
Wallace's Larder, 17
Wallace, William, 12, 17, 72, 117
Wars of Independence, 17, 29, 53, 81, 116, 117, 141, 153, 165
Weeping Stones of Fyvie, 91-92
Weir, Grizel
Weir, Major Thomas, 139, 165
Wellwood House, 164-165
Wemyss Castle, 165
Wemyss Caves, 120
Wemyss family, 120, 165
Wemyss, Sir Michael, 165
West Bow, Edinburgh, 139, 165-166
Western Infirmary, Glasgow, 166
White Lady, 16, 29, 42, 48, 52, 65, 66, 82, 85, 103, 124, 147, 148, 154, 155, 158
Whiteadder River, 57
William the Lyon, 90, 156
Williamson family, 60
Wilson, James, 159
Wilson, John, 148
Windgate House, 166
Windhouse, 167
Witchery Tours, 171
Wolf of Badenoch see Stewart, Alexander
Woodhouselee see Old Woodhouselee and Fulford Tower
Wrychtishousis, 167-168

Y

youth hostel, 20, 87